This book is dedicated to my mother
Elsie Roderick

# Contents

# Preface

My initial inspiration for writing this book stems from my experiences as a young professional and then semi-professional footballer from the early 1980s to mid-1990s. As an eager young apprentice-professional I was told that I had an opportunity that I should not waste; most boys of my age would not be offered the chance to make it in the professional game. What could be better than to play football for a living; to do something you love? If I played well there was the chance to earn good money; to be outside in the fresh air every day; to be the envy of schoolmates. I heard all these clichés regularly at the training ground, before and after matches, in the treatment room and whilst cleaning boots or undertaking other non-playing work tasks throughout my apprenticeship. In truth there were few hiding places: within the confines of the football club the realities of work for young players were addressed on a regular basis by first, reserve and youth team coaches.

Daily life as a young player can at times be an intensely physical and emotional experience. Physically tough fitness sessions (mostly without a ball) were something each player could adjust to in my view; I don't look back and recall the pain of interval running. I do however recollect the highs of playing well and receiving praise from teammates. There isn't a better feeling than executing a piece of skill or, ultimately, scoring a goal in front of a crowd, however small in number. By contrast, the emotional pain of watching friends depart the club having been released, or of being ridiculed or undermined by a senior professional in training, or of returning to work on Monday morning following a poor performance on Saturday, are all moments which reside strongly in my memory. A football club is a positive, self-enhancing workplace for a player who is performing well; by contrast, a club environment for one who has lost form can be unsupportive and marginalizing.

I played left midfield most often, but I was not known for an aggressive, committed style of play. The local evening newspaper in Portsmouth regularly described me as 'talented but lightweight', a description that repeatedly underpinned the banter of teammates expressed at my expense. The first team manager would often say that he would 'rent a crowd' to stand on the side opposite the team dugout, because I seemed to lack self-motivation. In fact, the idea that I lacked motivation for this profession was something that he and other coaches would draw to my attention on a pretty consistent basis, often in the company of colleagues. The first team manager (formerly the youth coach) would also ask: did I want to drive a Mini or a Ferrari? The implication of his question was that if I 'wanted' career success enough, material gain and, possibly, celebrity status could follow.

On many occasions – on match days and in training sessions – the coaches would say to me that I didn't look like I *wanted it* badly enough, that I didn't look like I *fancied it*. I remember the manager asking me on one occasion whether I had read my horoscope that day: did the stars indicate whether I would play well or badly? My inconsistent form was, for all the coaches involved at the club, a question of my 'attitude' to making it as a professional footballer. During such times that coaches questioned my approach to the game, I would often speculate mentally about how I would need to 'look' for them to be convinced of my commitment to the sport and my work. Playing football meant everything to me at the time – I wanted to show them that I was dedicated to, and desperate to make it in, the professional game. At times I would try to appear 'focused', to be more overtly aggressive in the changing room in order to convey to the coach that I was ready and prepared for the forthcoming game. Yet, such surface acting was never sustainable and close teammates would often remark on my odd behaviour. While the importance of displaying a good attitude to work permeates every encounter with senior club staff, the consequences of adhering to such workplace prescriptions may be serious and unforeseen.

Some years following my departure from the professional game, I played for a Conference club as a part-time semi-professional footballer. At 26 years old I began the 1993–4 season strongly and attracted some attention from lower Football League clubs. By Christmas of that season however my fitness levels had reduced significantly. I was experiencing pain in my groin area and the club manager was struggling to justify my inclusion in the starting line-up. Having kept faith in me initially, in January 1994 he started to question my attitude, accusing me of being a 'big-time Charlie' and disregarding my claims of fatigue. The harder I trained – to counter his assertion that I possessed a bad attitude – the more I experienced feelings of exhaustion. The club doctor responded to my ill-defined bouts of pain by suggesting two Ibuprofen tablets before matches and training sessions. By the end of March 1994, the manager informed me that my performances and levels of fitness were so poor that he no longer required my services: I was confused and unable to explain my cata-strophic drop in fitness and form. In June 1994 I was diagnosed with Hodgkin's lymphoma – a cancer of the lymphatic system – and, at 27 years old, my 'career' was over. My hard work to display a good attitude allied with my struggle to prove my commitment to the Conference manager were merely a prelude to a far greater battle which lay ahead.

Ultimately, a player may possess a fantastic 'attitude' to training, levels of fitness, diet and pre-match preparation, but all that really concerns club staff are levels of performance and results in games. All that matters is what happens at three o'clock on Saturday afternoon: the results achieved by players. For club coaches however there is a direct and important correlation between a young player's self-presentation and approach to the game and the likelihood of his making the grade. This connection infiltrates interaction between club staff and players. Constant reminders to players to be 'good professionals' and to display an appropriate 'attitude' subtly establish this correlation in their minds. In this book I attempt in part to examine notions of *attitude*, the way a player's sense of self may be colonized by such workplace prescriptions, and the human costs of such processes of colonization.

My experiences in (semi-) professional football in part fuelled my desire to undertake this research, although there were other motivating factors. Colleagues formerly at Leicester and currently at Durham University denigrate professional footballers regularly and use as proof the relentless stream of negative references in the print media to the ill-disciplined behaviour of 'overpaid' and 'irresponsible' players. Over the past few years the media have certainly expended much time and space to illicit behaviour on and off the pitch and to 'greedy' millionaire professionals who waste vast sums gambling, drinking to excess, taking drugs and, latterly, (sexually) abusing women. I do not deny the veracity of these accusations or argue that footballers somehow seem immune from the everyday laws which apply to the rest of us; I do however want to make clear that these characteristics and patterns of behaviour are not representative of the vast majority of players whom I know personally or who I interviewed for this study. It is my belief that most players are bound up with rather more normal concerns than people would imagine and that, far from being awash with money, most are attempting to make a living and provide as best they can for partners and children in order to create a stable family environment.

I drive a Ford Fiesta.

# Acknowledgements

I would like to thank sincerely all the people who contributed to the completion of this book. This manuscript is based on a doctoral thesis completed in 2003. I would like to thank everyone who assisted me during the period of my research. Undoubtedly, my deepest dept is owed to Ivan Waddington. His wealth of sociological knowledge has been invaluable for me whilst undertaking the research. While Ivan has been my principle influence, it would be improper to isolate him from our friends from the University of Leicester's former Centre for Research into Sport and Society. Of these, Dominic Malcolm, Lisa Heggs and Eric Dunning provided support ceaselessly throughout the research by reading early drafts of chapters and, most importantly of all perhaps, through their encouragement. I am particularly grateful also to Ian Bates, John Taplin and Sharon Colwell, who read, assessed and criticized the manuscript in its final stages so meticulously and honestly. And I would like to thank my wife, Lucy, for the patience and generosity she has shown in the course of this long project. I am indebted to her in so many ways.

Finally, I would like to thank all the players who gave up their time and agreed to be interviewed. Any achievements that accrue from this study are due, in large measure, to their candour during our encounters.

# Football League descriptors

One of the problems I experienced whilst writing this book was attempting to make clear when quoting from the player transcripts exactly which football leagues and divisions were being referred to. For example, a number of interviewees had commenced their careers prior to the formation of the FA Premier League and had played, therefore, through two alterations to division titles. Since the formation of the FA Premier League in 1992, there have been a number of different sponsors: currently, the top division in English football is entitled the Barclays Premiership. The table below, from which sponsors are omitted, attempts to provide easily understandable descriptors for readers to follow in the book. The descriptors employed relate to the division in which each interviewee was playing at the time of the incident to which he is referring, or to the highest status position achieved by him by division.

| 1963–92 | 1992–2004 | 2004–5 |
|---|---|---|
| Football League Division One | The FA Premier League The Premiership | The FA Premier League The Premiership |
| Football League Division Two | Football League Division One (i) | Football League The Championship |
| Football League Division Three | Football League Division Two (i) | Football League League One |
| Football League Division Four | Football League Division Three (i) | Football League League Two |

# Introduction

Since the development of the professional game in the nineteenth century, professional footballers have been heroes for people worldwide. In newspapers and magazines globally there is a vast amount written each week of each football season about professional football and the players, most of which emphasizes the glamour of the game and dramatic and decisive moments on the pitch (Gearing 1997). It would be difficult to argue against the notion that professional football is a relatively prestigious occupation. Many supporters of the game would not hesitate to describe the work of professional footballers as a 'labour of love'. Gearing (1999: 47) suggests that they are 'immersed in an occupational world of intense emotionality and drama', and goes on to remark that 'the sheer excitement and intensity can lift players out of the everyday world into a kind of high octane, intoxicating existence'. For many people worldwide too, supporting their team is a very important aspect of their lives. Despite the enormous amount of attention paid to players, most of which debates levels of performance, there has been relatively little scrutiny of their working lives and how they cope with the 'authoritarianism, ruthlessness and hyper-masculine workplace practice(s)' (Parker 1996a: 1) of the football world. Over the last twenty-five years, academic analysis of football has focused overwhelmingly on the issue of hooliganism (see Giulianotti 1999). The study of players and their work by sociologists has been marginal at best. Some academics, for example King (1999), have written about *the sociology of football* and neglected totally to mention players. This marginalization is, perhaps, unusual, since *work* and how it is organized and experienced is central among the traditional concerns of sociologists. The careers of professional footballers will be examined in this book in an attempt to add to knowledge in this relatively neglected area.

Williams *et al.* (2001: 1) indicate that there has been an 'astounding growth' of interest in professional football over the past twenty-five years: books and studies are widely available covering diverse subjects including 'local histories, fan remembrances, life biographies and statistical accounts'. Indeed, research on football at all levels of the game extends over several areas and themes. It would be impossible to review all these bodies of work here, although a substantial number of sociological studies which feature professional players as part of their focus are included throughout this book. Frustratingly, a considerable number of these studies do not employ the testimony of players collected as part of a systematic research project. Most rely heavily on newspaper articles, (auto)biographies and other journalistic sources and tend to focus on aspects of players' careers away from the football club and 'deviant' behaviour during games. A number of these studies, for example Cashmore's (2002) social biography of David Beckham and Giulianotti and Gerrard's (2001) study of the (im)moral football and public career of Paul Gascoigne are packed full of insight, examining primarily the media representations of these 'sports stars' as cultural icons. The focus of much of this work is different from mine; even so, these studies neither deal with the realities of work for the players in question, nor have the authors interviewed their research subjects face-to-face.

A small number of academics and journalists have managed either to gain access to a substantial number of players for the purpose of depth interviews (Back et al. 2001; Magee 1998) or to undertake non-participant observation among the inner sanctums of individual football clubs (Davies 1996 [1972]; Parker 1996a). These studies have been central among the secondary sources upon which I have built my research. These analyses elucidate to some extent the culture of work in professional football and the fragile and uncertain nature of playing careers. The first and, indisputably, most outstanding journalistic investigation of this kind was undertaken by Hunter Davies (1996 [1972]). Thus, in the introduction to his classic study, *The Glory Game*, Davies suggests that players find it difficult to comprehend the unexpected events which, in part, change the course of their careers, such as a loss of form and confidence and the accidents and bad luck which befall them. If their playing careers can be conceptualized as a status passage (Strauss 1962) involving a series of formal and informal positions (e.g. apprentice, young professional, senior professional, retired professional), then such events can be considered fateful moments (Giddens 1991) which may change the trajectory of their career paths. In terms of understanding their working lives sociologically, it is important to examine the occasions which significantly alter the course of a career and how players retrospectively consider such turning points. Two examples taken from the player interviews conducted for this study may help to explain the significance of these kinds of occasions.

A former senior professional with a Division One (i) club, for example, recounted how in the 1998–9 season he had turned down a renewed and improved offer from his club situated in the north of England in favour of a move south to a lower division club. He said his decision to move south was motivated by the death of his mother; simply put, he wanted his family to move so they could be nearer to his father. In the subsequent two seasons as a player for this Division Two (i) club, the club directors appointed five new managers. The fifth manager, in the view of this player, did not consider him crucial to his future plans for the team and he eventually left to play for a semi-professional team in the Southern League; he was pushed out, unjustifiably he thought, at a time when he was still able to do a good job for the team. However, the northern team for which he had originally turned down an improved contract had won promotion to the Premier League. So, while his career had in his view plummeted, he had witnessed (somewhat enviously) many of his former colleagues at the northern club develop national and international reputations. For this player, his career decision to transfer to the southern club was significant. Even though he knew he had moved, as he put it, 'for the right reasons', his reputation as an established Division One (i) player had nevertheless been wiped out in a relatively short period and, at his age (33 years), it was unlikely that he would be able to return to the professional game.

Other incidents that also mark the beginning of a passage of vulnerability and change for players are injuries. A young Division Three (i) player, for example, who had been watched regularly by a number of scouts from clubs in higher divisions, broke his collarbone at a time when he was expecting a firm offer to be placed. In his interview, which took place eight years later, this player said that, since this time, he did not think that an opportunity to make such a step up in playing standard had ever presented itself. For this player, the injury that he suffered was a turning point of some significance. His injury marked the beginning of a passage of time in which he was forced to sit and watch his colleagues playing. While he was looking on and reflecting on what might have been, other players took his place in the team and attempted to take this opportunity to establish themselves as first team regulars.

The point of drawing attention to such events in the careers of these two players is to highlight the significance of key occurrences that set in motion unexpected changes in their career trajectories. There are, I will argue, consequences for the decisions made by players to which, at the time, they are blind. Momentous occasions (Giddens 1991) are features of the careers and working lives of all people; they are not solely the preserve of professional footballers. Even so, while no one can be sure of their career paths in advance, the career decisions and trajectories of most employees do not get discussed and evaluated publicly. One crucial characteristic of the occupational situation for professional footballers therefore is the highly public nature of their 'performances at work'. Like other public figures – such as actors and musicians – footballers are subject to close scrutiny by an audience who claim a degree of expertise (or who have a perception that they have knowledge) of the field. What is more, this audience pays for the privilege of voicing an opinion. In professional football, 'mistakes at work' (Hughes 1958) are closely watched by fans, judged by outsiders, broadcast on, and published regularly in the mass media. Professional footballers struggle constantly – on both an individual and collective basis – to retain a degree of control over the setting of the standards by which they are judged; and this, perhaps, is why professional football clubs remain so 'closed' to outsiders. Other

conflictual situations may arise in the context of the professional game from differences between players who strive for economic success (or stability) and those
who seek personal fulfilment, club owners who are concerned with team success
and club profits and managers who strive, among other tasks, to blend players
into a winning combination while maintaining the loyalty of all members of the
squad.

When players start out they may think that, as young professionals, their destinies are in their own hands. Even so, as they mature, they find themselves
increasingly caught up in ties of interdependence which they cannot comprehend very easily, if at all (Elias 1978). Players attribute injuries, particularly those
which lead them to miss matches, and poor performances by themselves or by
their team collectively, to a constellation of depersonalized forces, particularly
'bad luck' (Gowling 1974). Only slowly do they come to understand that people
– that is, other people as well as themselves – exert the constraints within which
they labour. The very same players who may feel compelled to perform, perhaps
carrying an injury or (having been dropped from the first team) in the reserves,
are at the same time actively exerting pressure on those around them with whom
they are enmeshed. However, it must not be forgotten that players have also to
be understood as exercising pressure on themselves as much as on other people.
While the focus for players during interviews may have been, in part, on individual – albeit fateful and momentous – events such as a bad injury or rejection by a
manager, such occasions must be understood as inseparable from the development of their working lives as professional footballers just as these are inseparable
from the development of professional football overall. Players continually
attempt to orientate themselves within the social networks in which they are
bound up in the hope of dealing or coping better with the problems that continually arise. The focus of this book will be on career contingencies such as those
discussed thus far, examining the processes by which interaction unfolds, the
meaning which particular experiences have for players, the problematic and
negotiable dimensions of a working life in a professional team sport and how
players work out these activities with each other.

## The approach of this book

Professional football is among the most popular and universally recognized sports.
A great deal has been written about footballers by biographers, journalists and the
players themselves. A small number of the elite players, for instance, Ronaldo and
David Beckham, can rightfully claim to be among the most well known 'sports
stars' on earth. Even so, it is hard to think of a professional sporting practice that
has been so mythologized and so little researched by social scientists. With precious
few exceptions, existing serious studies of the professional game are dominated by
'quasi-insiders' (Wacquant 1992: 222) such as journalists who tend to concentrate
on the *public* (and commercial) side of the sport at the top echelons (Bowers 2003;

McGill 2001). Therefore, in a manner similar in kind to the study of boxers undertaken by Wacquant (1992: 223), I try to 'break with the spectators' point of view' and instead attempt to approach the occupation of professional football through its least known and least spectacular sides.

To orient their way through life, people look to a variety of what are termed reference groups (Shibutani 1962), and as they move through a range of situations which bestow identity on them they are said to follow a career. By employing 'career' as a sensitizing concept (Becker 1998), symbolic interactionists have made a key contribution to the sociology of work. Examining 'work' in (moral) career terms enables an investigation of the opportunities, dangers, sanctions and rewards that characterize the living world of the occupational setting (Atkinson and Housley 2003). Interactionists analyse the social drama of work – the interaction and 'focused encounters' (Goffman 1961) that take place at work – noting the problems and tensions that are socially constructed in this context. Sociological concern, therefore, turns to how individuals cope with and adapt to these problems and relates them to the problem of maintaining their identity, a proposition which is central to the interactionist strand of the sociology of work.

Hence, *interaction* is the critical link between 'individual' and 'society' (Fine 1993) and becomes a focus of concern in relation to the study of the careers of professional footballers. The focus of symbolic interactionism is mainly on small group situations and face-to-face encounters: this perspective represents the dominant 'micro' version of sociology (Fine 1993). Interactionism constitutes an appealing approach in relation to a study of people whose daily work is situated among a relatively small, tight-knit group that is all but 'closed' to non-group members.[1] Examining the points of view of individual footballers thus necessitates a consideration of both *micro* and *macro* social contexts in which they, as players, reflect on their experiences and consider appropriate future action. An approach of this kind enables questions to be addressed which focus on, for example, how players ascribe meaning to the behaviour of others, such as club physiotherapists or managers, when attempting to make a decision about, for instance, whether or not to have a painkilling injection; or how managerial succession or changes to the personal life of the player such as the birth of a child or the death of a parent may precipitate transformations in their long-term behaviour and outlook. Hence, this study has the hallmarks of a traditional interactionist study of career.

By adopting an interactionist framework, I was keen to examine the developing careers of players from their viewpoints but with a particular focus on the fateful moments (Giddens 1991) or 'catalytic' (Swain 1991) situations which may, in part, lead them to adjust their sights with regard to career 'goals' and outlooks. The concept of *contingency* refers to the way in which careers are beset by particular turning points, chance happenings and episodes that mark the decisive passage in the life history of an individual. Catalytic events emphasize the contingent character and also the processual nature of the careers of professional athletes (Prus 1984). In interview however, the players did not compartmentalize their responses into neat and convenient patterns for the purposes of analysis. Many of the players discussed the way their outlooks changed towards certain contingencies and their careers in general as they became more experienced or in the light of developing personal circumstances, and all talked of a number of contingencies concurrently when recounting the details of certain periods in their work histories. Thus, it was not unusual for a player to mention his age and the prospect of a future contract or transfer as a consequence of a disabling injury. In short, any circumstances that led the player to be 'inactive' generated a number of uncertainties all of which were relevant to his experiences at any one particular period in time. In the next section of this introduction I detail an overview of the research process and the study sample.

## The research

This study involved interviews with forty-seven male professional footballers.[2] Of these players, thirty-seven were, at the time of interview, contracted to clubs in one of the four professional football divisions in England. Ten (recently) retired professional footballers were also interviewed. The ages of the thirty-seven current players ranged from eighteen to thirty-five years. All ten former players were over thirty-five years. All the players interviewed played for English professional football clubs after 1963 and all had careers in English professional football: that is, after the abolition of the maximum wage and the initial changes to the 'retain and transfer' system. Two of the players interviewed were of black Afro-Caribbean descent, although social class and minority group effects could not be explored with the interviewees satisfactorily. Five foreign (that is, non-United Kingdom) players are included in the sample; all players however were from European Union countries. Certain demographic information was offered by the players during the course of their interview, in particular their ages. It was not the intention of the interviewer to 'force' the players to discuss issues of ethnicity, gender and social class, but to let them raise such matters in the course of retelling their stories. Twelve club doctors and ten club physiotherapists[3] were interviewed as part of a related research project, the object of which was to investigate the role of football club medical staff and the way in which injuries are managed in the professional game.[4] Finally, three agents were interviewed, one of whom worked for the Professional Footballers' Association (PFA) and two who were FIFA (International Federation of Association Football) accredited.

The players who comprised the sample were not selected in accordance with a carefully considered research design. Contact with some players had been made using information obtained from the former deputy chief executive of the Professional Footballers' Association who acted as gatekeeper. A very small number of players responded to speculative letters; most did not reply. The majority of interviewees came via personal contacts. The sample therefore was constructed on a 'snowball' basis. The players who were interviewed first were asked to recommend others whom they thought may also have been prepared to discuss their career experiences. *All* the players who responded positively to the request were interviewed as there are considerable problems attempting to contact professional footballers in order to organize face-to-face encounters. Footballers, on a local or national level, are public figures who acquire varying degrees of celebrity. They do not willingly grant permission for unknown academics to interview them for extended periods. Attempting to be selective with a group who do not give extended interviews readily would have been a mistake. At the outset of each interview the players were given an assurance of confidentiality. Part of the 'access' problem involves a residual fear for players that they may be viewed either as openly criticizing their teammates or team management or identified, more simply, as 'complainers' (Roderick *et al.* 2000). The players were asked questions to which their replies would almost certainly involve descriptions of interaction among former and present playing colleagues. It was important to reassure them that their comments, whether positive or negative, would not be traceable to them. If they had not received this type of assurance they may not have responded to questions so unguardedly.

A great deal of information is available about professional footballers, including information relating to playing statistics and career histories. Also, there are many biographies and autobiographies of footballers in which the thoughts and feelings of players are expressed openly. However, between the extremes of outstanding success and miserable failure lie many middle courses. The majority of players who write up their (often overly sentimental) memoirs, with only a small number of notable exceptions,[5] tend to be those who, on balance, would be positioned closer to the outstanding success extreme. It was considered important to interview players who experienced a variety of career trajectories. For example, some of the players were well known international players; others had played for one club solely and had never experienced the process of transferring, although all had experienced managerial succession; the bulk of players however could be described best as 'journeymen'. A number of these players had played their careers to date in Divisions Two and Three, some had only played for Premiership and Division One clubs, while others had experienced first team football in all four professional divisions. The interviews generated a large amount of data that could be sociologically analysed. The sample of players interviewed was not randomly selected, so cannot be considered, in the positivist sense of the word, to constitute a group that is statistically representative of a broader population of footballers. While this sample may, therefore, fall foul of specific methodological standards, it is important to note that, while footballers are often interviewed by journalists about their views on team performances, it is rare for players, like actors and other people who achieve celebrity (Rojek 2001), to grant interviews in which they respond to questions so frankly and for such an extended period.

I knew something of the players, including aspects of their career trajectories, prior to our encounter. In all cases, judgements could be formed about whether they had been 'successful' thus far in 'objective' career terms (Hughes 1958). The most noteworthy factor influencing the overall research process and my experiences of it relates to the fact that I have formerly been employed as a *player* by a football club, first as an apprentice-player and second as a young professional. For the duration of my professional career I was, in Merton's (1972) terms, an 'insider'. This point is particularly important to stress, for there are innumerable ways in which my former position of 'insider' and *my* perceptions and 'knowledge' of the culture of the professional game could affect the research process. For example, such 'insider knowledge' would inevitably influence the questions formulated for the interview schedule prior to the interviews, my instant reactions to their responses throughout our 'encounter' (Goffman 1961), the patterns of behaviour that I expected to identify, the 'meanings' players attributed to occurrences in their daily working lives, and the manner in which players interpreted turning points in their careers. This list is not exhaustive; even so, it is important sociologically to acknowledge the frames of reference that were brought to bear upon most aspects of the research process.

My former 'insider' status was important in terms of initially attempting to build a rapport with the players, a point noted by Magee (1998). While admitting to interviewees that I had been a professional footballer clearly did not make me 'one of them' (Finch 1983), I thought this information might lend greater legitimacy to my line of questioning (Cannon 1992). I attempted to build a trusting relationship with people who were to some extent 'famous' either locally or nationally and had achieved a degree of celebrity. It was difficult to gauge in advance whether or not *any* of the players would openly express their thoughts, but particularly those who were better known. Many players are *interviewed* regularly by journalists mainly about their views on previous and forthcoming matches through the course of their careers. During these media orchestrated encounters the players are reluctant to publicly criticize their teammates or their managers. I was aware that they might view me as someone who could betray their trust. I did not want to recreate an interview similar in kind to those conducted by journalists. I wanted to understand their thoughts on their daily activities within the clubs and, in particular, about momentous and fateful moments during their careers so far. In relation to these occasions, I wanted to understand whether, and how, their relationships with significant others might be transformed.

During interview, players were asked questions that encouraged them to talk about turning points (Strauss 1962) in their careers to date, and were prompted to discuss the wider networks of people who may also have been inescapably involved during these indeterminate periods: vulnerable periods were associated mostly with injury and the process of labour mobility, but also with other contingencies such as managerial succession. Any circumstances that led players to be 'inactive' generated feelings of uncertainty and were relevant in terms of gaining an understanding of players' self-conceptions of their status at work, and the relationships that reproduce and 'furnish' (Denzin 1989) those conceptions. The interviewees were urged to talk about workplace interaction such that a clear comprehension of the players' meanings and interpretations of events could be obtained. Enduring themes were identified in the data, which were analysed using elements of narrative analysis (Silverman 2001) and an interpretive interactionist approach (Denzin 1989). This approach employed the 'players-as-workers' accounts of their jobs and feelings of security to explore the relationship between broader social structures and subjective experiences (Eakin and MacEachen 1998; Ezzy 1997). The analysis therefore emphasizes, for example, the issue of uncertainty as socially produced through the meanings associated with certain conditions of work and workplace relations.

Undertaking depth interviews was, for me, the only viable option. The opportunity to engage in fieldwork – a method that would have been an alternative source of rich data – was all but non-existent for the following reasons. First, a central barrier to initiating fieldwork in this specific occupational world concerns the issue of access. Football clubs are 'closed' to people who are perceived as 'outsiders' with very few exceptions (see, for example, Parker (1996a) and the classic investigative study undertaken by Hunter Davies (1996 [1972])), and it would have proved very difficult, if not impossible, to gain access. I would have liked to have been able to observe interaction within the changing room on a daily basis and before and after matches; encounters between managers and players on both a team and individual basis, for instance when players are left out for forthcoming matches; and negotiations among managers, physiotherapists and players about whether an 'unfit' player should start a game. It would be highly unlikely that a sociologist could gain such access and it is even more unlikely that such rich and meaningful data would be obtained from observing training sessions and training ground interaction. Second, 'covert' fieldwork was not a viable option because to have joined in seamlessly as a player – even as a trialist – among a squad would have been *physically* impossible in terms of age and fitness levels. As an 'overt' fieldworker it would have been difficult, although not impossible, to gain the trust of players. The process of developing trust, such that I was not identified as, for example, the 'manager's spy', would have taken time that was not available.

The main difference between the depth interviews conducted for this study and those directed by journalists relates to time. The sociological interviews requested by me were considerably longer than 'normal' interviews with journalists, which are generally swift affairs. I accepted immediately the offers from players who were prepared to be interviewed, for it is unusual – perhaps lucky – to be in a position to find out intimate details about the *private* lives and thoughts of *public* figures about whom a great deal is written and speculated by fans and media alike. Interactionism highlights a very important aspect of interviewing as a method of generating research data: namely, the interplay between the meanings imparted orally to questions by the respondent and the interpretations of those meanings received by the interviewer. However, the question of tacit understanding raises the spectre of interviewees responding in a manner in which they present their 'self' in more credible ways, a point emphasized in Chapter 6. In other words, in what sense could I be sure that interviewees were not selectively distorting, masking or lying about their thoughts and feelings on any given question? A number of sociologists have noted the problems of the question of the way respondents may selectively (or conveniently) distort information (Finch 1993; Lee 1992; Parker 1998; Ramsey 1996). Finch (1993) argues, for example, that *trust* is an issue of paramount importance in an interview context in which respondents may feel exploitable. Ramsey (1996) states that people are likely to reveal more of themselves when they are allowed to identify issues that are relevant to them, and notes that interviewees will be more open when talking to interviewers who seem to share some of their beliefs and assumptions.

I found it difficult to be neutral towards the interviewees (see Goodwin and O'Conner 2002) and was humbled by the degree to which most seemed prepared to discuss 'black days' in their careers in which they felt isolated from their colleagues, were separated from their families or considered themselves to be a burden to others. I found real interest in what they had to say because I could, in part, compare and contrast their experiences to my own (Cannon 1992; Finch 1993). In the light of my experiences as a player, I was conscious when writing about the career contingencies that I did not portray the interviewees as victims. It was clear to me that I developed sympathy for a number of them, particularly those journeyman players who seemed to be so candid when questioned about their feelings. At times, the responses of players concerned matters that were relatively *new* to me, and at other times they recounted moments and events about which I had experience and possessed a value stance.

I considered continuously the balance of power between the players and myself. Players are used to people in general, but particularly football supporters, treating them as though they are, in some ill-defined sense, 'special'. When I first began to interview players I, too, thought it necessary to consider them in this manner: that is, with due deference – not least because they do not generally agree to lengthy interviews with unknown 'outsiders'. Thus, I was aware that in the context of the interview the power differentials were skewed in *their* favour. I thought it was necessary at least to appear to be on their side when they explained, as they viewed it, moments of injustice for them. However, as someone who has experienced to some extent passages of vulnerability in relation to fateful moments in my own career, I came to wonder whether it was the case that my capacity for clear sociological thinking may have been clouded by my own feelings of relief at not having *instrumentally* pursued a career as a footballer and establishing an alternative profession. In short, did my feelings of a relatively high degree of personal security affect my reactions to their stories – many of which focused on their insecurities – or my subsequent questioning? Readers of this study will judge whether I achieve an adequate understanding of the culture of work in professional football, the fragile and uncertain nature of playing careers, the ways in which the orientations of players to their work change over the course of their careers and the transformation of their workplace identities, and the subjective meanings players impute to their experiences.

There are a number of aspects of the careers of players that are not discussed in detail in this study. Thus, it may appear as though I have omitted to consider what, for some, are anticipated and central aspects of sociological analyses. In other studies of professional football (Back et al. 2001; King 2004; Magee 1998), notions of race and nationality are clearly part of the contingent social relations of 'players-as-employees'. For me the most important of these structural dimensions was 'race'. However, I did not interview enough black or Asian players to be able to explore patterns of behaviour along racial lines in any substantial way. In fact, the black players interviewed rarely mentioned the way in which their 'race' impacted on their careers, and offered negative responses to the question of whether it affected daily social interaction within the club. This became problematic for me. In the light of the work of Back et al. (2001), whose book is indisputably the leader in this field, there is an issue here for, as they highlight, cultural practices (including racial practices) inside clubs have come to be institutionalized to some extent. The issue of 'race' however is not something I thought I could write about in depth in this study because I could not give it sufficient coverage; moreover, I did not want simply to reproduce the work and conclusions of Back et al. (2001). It would have been inappropriate to emphasize this dimension of the social life of players given the limited data on this issue that my research generated.

Similar thoughts emerged in terms of the issue of nationality. There exists a great deal of work on football and nationality already and I wanted the focus of my study to be different. Again, a number of authors have examined issues of nationalism, particularly as they impact on labour migration (Lanfranchi and Taylor 2001; Magee 1998; Maguire and Stead 1998; McGovern 2002; Stead and Maguire 2000). My interviewees (particularly those who were not from the UK) did not refer to issues of nationality when discussing the ways in which they coped when they had been dropped from the first team or at times when they were out of action because of injury. Some players did mention the expanding labour market in football – resulting from the 1995 Bosman ruling – and, because of the availability of European and other non-European Union players, the increasingly limited chances of Premier League managers 'taking a chance' on a lower league footballer. For many players outside the Premier League however, this is still not a major feature of their working week. It was my conclusion that players outside the Premier League displayed a lack of reflexivity in relation to their employment circumstances – that is, beyond the central and pressing problems of team selection and their next contract – and the daily constraints within which they are embedded.

Finally, I discuss the role of agents in Chapter 7. In the press there are many celebrated stories about their presence in the professional game, emanating specifically from managers who talk about the ways in which they are ruining the football industry. It is my contention that, as it stands, most players have only limited contact with agents. I pushed many of my interviewees to discuss the nature and frequency of their contact with them and at what times they proved useful in their careers. Most however rarely have contact with their agents from one week to the next, for many players are not the cash cows the agents had hoped for. I was left in a bit of a quandary. The hype surrounding agents is for me out of proportion to the degree to which they shape the daily lives of the over-whelming majority of players. The number of transfers to 'big' clubs is minimal as a proportion of all labour mobility within each football season, so most agents would be receiving only a small remuneration from deals that are struck. Also, while many of the younger players I interviewed did make a point of mentioning agents – although no agents contacted me to see what I was up to – it is clear that, at present, many agents figure more prominently in the early career stages of players. That said however, I do not think the position of agents is clear to any-one in the contemporary game in any concrete fashion; rather, their role and function is a site for future investigation.

## Book structure

This book will take the following structure. In Chapter 1 I examine the variety of definitions of career as used by sociologists, particularly symbolic interactionists, and make some preliminary comments about the careers of professional footballers. One of the central themes of this study concerns the orientations of players to their work. In Chapter 2, I describe, and offer some initial thoughts concerning, what constitutes a *good attitude* in professional football.[6] I examine also a number of cir-cumstances and contexts in which the display of a good attitude is meaningful; for example, I focus on the tension between individual progress versus team success and the management of injury. A number of the ideas examined in this chapter are emphasized throughout later chapters in this book, but particularly Chapter 8.

Accidents and injuries are permanent features of professional football and they constantly threaten to terminate careers early. While football injuries are potentially fatal to a player's career, they are accepted as an inevitable feature of the professional game. In Chapter 3 and Chapter 4 I examine the ways in which players deal with and experience the consequences of 'being' injured. A point that is central to both these chapters is that accidents and injuries at work occur within, and are products of, networks of social relationships. Hence, injuries in the professional game are socially constructed, because a footballer will be expected to play tolerating a certain level of pain. Perhaps more than any other chapters that comprise this book, Chapters 3 and 4 demonstrate the fragile and uncertain nature of professional footballers' careers.

Labour market migration is a relatively rare event. In the context of professional football however simultaneous job and geographical relocation is becoming increasingly commonplace for players and, maybe, the members of their families. Chapter 5 is the first of three chapters which focus on the process of transferring in which I attempt to relate the process of transferring from one club to another, a clear punctuation mark in the onward-moving career of a player, to transformations of self-identity. These socially patterned transformations relate to what in other occupations might be understood as *promotion* and *demotion*. A sense of rejection which is experienced subjectively and transformations of identity more generally are always the outcome of interaction with others. Thus, in Chapter 6 I look more closely at the mechanics of the process of transferring in terms of who speaks to whom and where and when, and I explain how players develop informal friendship networks that may facilitate their movement between clubs. In Chapter 7 I address the problem of the relative power of players – as employees – in relation to the process of transferring. Thus, I set out, first, to understand who possesses greater or lesser ability to control the process of transferring. Second, I examine the nature and forms of this control. I argue in this chapter that if one is to understand adequately the movement of players from one club to another, it is necessary to examine the dynamic balances of power among the network of interdependent relations which characterize professional football, including managers, club directors, club doctors, physiotherapists, agents and the partners of players.

In Chapter 8 I examine the way in which players develop more realistic orientations to their 'work' *over time*. I examine how players come to realize that being a professional footballer is not, to quote one interviewee, all about 'appearances at Wembley'. While players rarely lose their ideals with regard to the 'playing side' of the game, most with whom I spoke argued *cynically* that for them professional football has become, first and foremost, a way of making a living. I argue that the development of an increasing 'cynicism' is related to changing circumstances. In the short Conclusion, I draw together a number of the key sociological ideas and themes raised throughout each of the chapters in this book.

# Chapter 1

# Professional football in context

## Introduction: work and self

In industrialized societies most people spend their adult lives at work and that commitment to work can be a central feature of a person's life (Grint 2005). There may be an intricate relationship between work and self such that the work in which people engage comes to be closely bound up with their conception of self – that is, who they have been, who they are and who they would like to be. Research on work (Grint 2005; Watson 1995) has revealed the profound influence of distinctive occupational cultures in terms of how people perceive, define and evaluate themselves and interact with their peers. As such, waged work can be a principal source of an individual's self-confidence and self-fulfilment (Bain 2005). As Thomas (1999: v) notes,

> work is a virtually inescapable part of the human condition. Many of us spend most of our working hours engaged in it. It absorbs our energies and preoccupies our thoughts. It involves us in close relations with other people and gives us our sense of identity.

In more elaborate terms, Glaeser (2000) argues that the ways in which the self derives meaning from work are associated with the activities of the process of work, the end products of work, the prestige associated with the work of a particular occupation, the prestige of the social contexts within which work occurs, and the position that work is allocated relative to other pastimes. In football, these dimensions feature strongly, for individuals in the professional game derive a sense of self not only from the work in which they are engaged but also from a shared workplace culture – as such, the culture of work in professional football features centrally in this book. For many followers of the game also, there is a high degree of prestige attached to football, for players are idealized as members of a 'sacred profession' (Simpson 1981) and this idealization is rooted in part in a romanticization of their creative abilities. Such romanticized attachments are not solely confined to the thoughts of spectators. There is a strong sense of 'special-ness' imbued in the identities of players who are often told that, as an activity, football holds the prospect of being a source of satisfaction, gratification and pleasure. It is assumed by many bound up in the football industry that, in some ill-defined sense, players are 'out of the ordinary' and that, if offered an opportunity, 'you should be playing football because you love it'.

Themes of this kind are central to a study undertaken by McGillivray *et al.* (2005: 102) who suggest from a Bourdieusian perspective that players become 'caught up in and by the beautiful game'. Although they examine Scottish professional footballers, they make three points (among others) which have direct relevance for the contemporary English players examined in this book. First, employing the work of Wacquant (1995a) on the careers of boxers as their primary point of departure, McGillivray *et al.* (2005: 107) argue that:

> The relatively autonomous footballing field ... represents a self-contained territory with its own inner logic, rules, and way of being in the field. In essence, the professional footballer is 'inhabited by the game he inhabits' (Wacquant 1995a: 88) and finds it difficult to see without its logic, language, and aspirations.

For McGillivray *et al.* (2005: 108) this 'life-world colonization' is total and complete since, for many players, football is the only thing they have ever done and the only thing they know how to do. Second, they develop the relationship between professional football and 'the body' with respect to the labour which players-as-workers 'do' on and for their bodies (Shilling 2005), in order to earn a living in this physical occupation: hence, a professional footballer's identity is rooted in his body. They focus in particular on the ways in which the culture of the game comes to be ingrained into the very *bodily capital* of its participants 'so that it comes to possess them' (McGillivray *et al.* 2005: 103): following Wacquant (1995a), they argue correctly that football is an embodied practice. Thirdly, McGillivray *et al.* (2005) make the important point that, even if players were offered alternative career choices, most would still select the life of a footballer as the game holds out the possibility of a way of escape (Rojek 1993) from an insecurity and *ontological obscurity* they would otherwise have faced. For the working-class players who, they posit, continue to populate the game, professional football may still enable them to transcend the objective conditions in which they grew up (McGillivray *et al.* 2005).

So, McGillivray *et al.* (2005) imply that the structures of football engulf players to such an all-encompassing extent that they unwittingly collude in fashioning for themselves blindness to alternative sources of self-identity and self-enhancement: Merton (1957) refers to this process as 'trained incapacity'. The chief executive of the Professional Footballers' Association and former player, Gordon Taylor, similarly hints at a form of colonization of self in the foreword to a study of the history of professional footballers entitled *Living to Play* (Harding 2003). Focusing on the way in which the culture of the professional game may come to be part of the very essence of a player, Taylor argues the following point:

> It can safely be said of heroes past and present, as well as of the many thousands of paid players who have graced our football pitches down the years, that not one of them would have swapped their football career for any other and that nothing in their lives since football has ever quite lived up to the thrill of being a player.

Taylor goes on to quote Robert Louis Stevenson by way of summarizing his point: 'If a man loves the labour of his trade, then regardless of any question of success or fame, the gods have called him' (Harding 2003).

A theme of numerous football-related studies (Bower 2003; Conn 1997; McGill 2001) and a strong one among followers of the game is that the work of a professional footballer is *a labour of love* and that players have *a calling* to play. Professional football is such an all-consuming and physically demanding career that it is inevitable that self-identity is, essentially, determined by it. From a sociological point of view, one might well argue that professional football is a vocation or, perhaps, *a calling*. In the terminology of Max Weber (2002: 312), whereas a job is simply a means of making a living, a calling is an end in itself that requires no further justification. Hall and Chandler (2005) define a calling as work that a person perceives as his or her purpose in life. Therefore, as Dobrow (2004: 20) notes, people approach their work with a 'subjective, self-relevant view of [the] meaning' of career activities. Somebody with a religious vocation for example has been called out of the everyday world to undertake a special task or duty, a task that they experience as a compulsion. A calling is not exactly a personal choice, rather it is an obligation. Professional football as a vocation often assumes this compulsory character and therefore one can describe players as driven, single-minded and obsessed. This calling to play however involves more than the acquisition of exemplary technical ability. Obviously, football is something that a player's 'body' can do, but being a professional footballer is also embodied (McGillivray *et al.* 2005). In other words, being a player is not just something that they *do*, it is something that they *are*.

Much of what has been said so far presupposes a degree of ability and talent possessed by players. In a manner similar to Becker (1982) who examined the work of artists, both players and spectators acknowledge that to 'make it' in the professional game requires a level of ability and athleticism which few individuals possess. Talent in football is accorded special value among certain groups in society and retains, for some, an aura of mystery: some players possess talent which is hard for others to fathom. The danger of romanticizing such ability however lies in that it can be situated outside of the realm of the everyday. Cashmore and Parker (2003: 219) make the point that in spite of his manufactured image(s), England international David Beckham is revered in the first instance because of 'his work, his labor, his productivity and his value'. Thus, without his ability to (re)produce his talent as a performer, Beckham's value as a 'consumable item' would cease to exist. His 'value', in other words, is grounded in the waged labour he fulfils (Cashmore and Parker 2003). David Beckham is someone who has made full use of his abilities and he has earned 'respect' (Sennett 2003) through self-development. While displaying his talents may take only a moment, onlookers understand that the mastery of skills he exhibits is a slow, step by step process requiring dedication.

Someone who does not realise his ability, who does not fulfil his potential or who is considered to have wasted his talent does not command 'respect' (Sennett 2003). The football industry as an institution has developed mechanisms for rewarding the endowment of ability, for giving talent its due. For instance, 'talent scouts' who work for clubs search for young players with 'potential'. Professional football has developed historically such that it is able to make playing careers in this industry 'open to talent' (Sennett 2003)[1]. Role models from working-class social backgrounds such as Wayne Rooney, David Beckham and Rio Ferdinand are there to remind young promising players that 'careers open to talent' (Sennett 2003) are possible. Sennett (2003) makes the point however that 'nature' distributes (football) talent unequally: even so, careers open to talent are a way to honour that inequality. On the face of things, the football industry 'appears' as a meritocracy, for the sole criterion for reward is one's own personal ability.

The prestige associated with professional status in the 'beautiful game' (McGillivray et al. 2005) is a well understood aspect of a rhetoric in which young footballers aspire to emanate local and national heroes and are won over, as McGill (2001) asserts, by 'the chance to earn millions of pounds playing a game [they] love'. Adam Smith (1993: 104) asserted that: 'The chance of gain is by every man more or less overvalued, and the chance of loss is by most men undervalued.' Smith's statement rings true for many young aspirants who are seduced by the possibility of a career in professional football, even though they have little chance of success: Taylor indicates that three out of four players who join the game at the age of sixteen have departed from professional football by the time they are twenty-one years of age (Harding 2003: foreword). Even so, players understand that talent alone will not guarantee professional contracts in the long term. All players come in time to recognize, pace Becker (1982), that, as players, they are embedded in the social relations of the production and consumption of performances on the football pitch and that assessment of talent is socially determined by, in part, the behaviour of club managers and 'coaches-as-employers'.

Yet, what sociologists might understand as a structured characteristic of social relationships may be understood in quite different terms by players entangled in those relationships. The former Newcastle United player Alan Gowling (1973) provides an interesting example in his consideration of the place of 'luck' in a professional footballer's life. He suggests that if one listens to conversations between footballers off the field, a surprising amount of emphasis is placed on luck to assist explanations for those things that happen in games for which no explanation can be found in terms of players' movements, skill or fitness. He quotes the following as typical of regular comments made by players: 'we didn't get the breaks ... we didn't get the run of the ball ... you have to earn your luck'. Gowling suggests that players often explain their careers in similar terms and that it is widely believed that 'getting to the top' necessitates a considerable degree of good fortune. The following example illustrates this point:

> To a certain degree, to be 'spotted' by a scout requires a train of events the causal explanation of which would be put down to luck by the footballer. For example, not only does one have to play reasonably well, showing skill and application, but the scout has to be there to see it, and usually more than once!
>
> Similarly, to keep free of serious injury would require luck in the terminology of the pro. In reverse, they say that to receive a serious injury is 'just bad luck'.
>
> (Gowling 1973: 140)

Gowling's references to 'luck' in the life history of a professional footballer would, in sociological realms, be understood in relation to the social organization of contingencies. In this connection it might be suggested that (employing a phrase from Goffman's (1968) work on mental patients) if those who desire to become professional footballers numerically surpass those who actually make it, as might be expected, one could say that aspiring footballers distinctively suffer, not from a lack of skill or endeavour, but from *contingencies*.

Sociologically it would be inappropriate to suggest that, over the life history of an individual, one 'suffers' from contingencies. A more adequate explanation is one that understands the enabling and constraining features of the network of relationships in which one is bound up over time. So, a schoolboy becomes a professional footballer on the basis of contingently, but not at all randomly, ordered sequences of interaction with other people. From the perspective of players, their route to professional football may seem as though they were on many occasions in the right place at the right time, a series of chance happenings. For the sociologist, it is possible to identify connections between all players who become professionals, for example, in relation to the types of people with whom they mix, the formation of their self-identities and the ways in which they learn to become committed to the role of footballer. The individual biography of every footballer can be read and examined separately, but can only be understood sociologically in accordance with the changing configuration of relationships formed by players and other people embedded in the industry. Prior to an analysis of the work of professional footballers, definitions of the concept 'career' are considered.

## Career: definitions and usages

Sociological interest in careers and career patterns is longstanding, although there are a range of meanings of the concept 'career'. One way that the term has been used traditionally is to refer to an organized sequence of movements made by a person in an upward direction or from one position to another in an occupational system. A number of early papers traced careers in particular occupations (Hall 1948; Becker 1952), while others considered patterns of careers traversing occupational sectors (Form and Miller 1949). The 1950s and 1960s brought continued attention to individual occupations, often emphasizing the relatively orderly, hierarchical career progressions among professionals (Abbott and Hrycak 1990). Thus, looking at individuals' working life in an 'objective' fashion, we see them moving through various structural 'statuses' which may be viewed as making up occupational and organizational careers. The 'objective' career patterns and career lines identified however are generally dissociated in any direct way from the personal views of individual people. Yet for Hughes (1958) and subsequently Goffman (1961), the concept 'career' can refer to more than objective pathways or movements, for it can involve self-identity and reflect an individual's sense of who they are, who they wish to be, their hopes, dreams, fears and frustrations (Young and Collin 2000). Thus, sociologists who attempt to understand the perspectives of the people involved, that is, their personal experiences and feelings, often refer to the concept career as having both 'objective' and 'subjective' components. On this point, one of the central figures in developing this approach, Everett C. Hughes (1958: 295), makes the following remark:

> The career includes not only the processes and sequences of learning the techniques of the occupation but also the progressive perception of the whole system and of possible places in it and the accompanying changes in conceptions of work and of one's self in relation to it.

Most of the work of interactionists has focused on the idea that a person's self – or self-image – is 'actually embedded in a set of social relationships that give it stability and continuity' (Faunce 1968: 93). Transformations of identity can then result from changes in a person's position in society, from their social location, their progress – or lack of it – from one status to another. The moves which individuals make in and out of various social positions during the course of a career can be said to detail the process of a 'status passage' (Strauss 1962). The idea of career, which ties together social structure and an individual identity or self, can be applied usefully outside the occupational field to refer to any development through identity-bestowing structural locations (Deutscher 1962). Of great importance to an understanding of *subjective* careers (Stebbins 1970) are the turning points, contingencies and situations which mark for individuals a change in the network of relationships with others and, therefore, signal a re-evaluation of self and 'identity transformation' (Strauss 1962). That is, as relations with other people start to change for whatever reasons, a person will start to reflect on the impressions received by others of themselves and of their own sense of self (Blumer 1969).

Throughout the 1970s, much of what was written about careers was interwoven into studies of social mobility. Mobility as a concept is of great significance for an understanding of the careers of professional footballers (McGillivray *et al.* 2005), for there have come to be very few 'one club' players in the contemporary game. Unlike the early studies mentioned which emphasized orderly movements, sociological inquiries undertaken in the 1970s indicated that individual careers involved frequent job changes and shifts in occupation, employers and workplaces, and these 'objective' movements often brought about changes in status for individuals (Wilensky 1961). In an analysis of subjective careers, there is no prior assumption of promotion or progress, nor do job changes need to be regular or systematic, which has particular relevance for the careers of professional footballers. Thus, importantly, what might appear somewhat random from an outsider's perspective – a spectator – may in fact be logically structured from the point of view of the incumbent – a player (Wilensky 1961). It is clear, then, that one cannot separate out 'objective' and 'subjective' views of careers, but that these two approaches must be thought of as distinct, yet inseparable levels of occupational life.

Hierarchical careers have traditionally been associated with strong internal labour markets and long-term employment with individual employers, although as human resource policies have become increasingly 'flexible', the understanding of what constitutes a 'career' has shifted (Gold and Fraser 2002). Sennett (1998: 9) argues convincingly that: 'Flexible capitalism has blocked the straight roadway of career, diverting employees suddenly from one kind of work into another' and that in this 'new' post-industrial social world, not only are the careers of employees becoming fragmented, but so too are individuals' experiences of 'the self'. To summarize, the demise of the traditional hierarchical career is widely acknowledged by many sociologists (Watson 1995). It has been 'replaced', according to sociologists such as Sennett (1998), by a proliferation of more fluid and individual career choices. Since the 1980s therefore the emerging literature on occupational careers has been dominated by discussions of 'boundaryless careers' (Arthur and Rousseau 1996), portfolio careers (Handy 1990), and 'new careers' (Arnold and Jackson 1997). These all mark a significant shift away from the traditional focus on organizational careers, concentrating instead on, first, the subjectivities of workers – that is, how workers think and feel about their work – and, second, issues of 'control' and 'power' in the workplace (Ezzy 2001). Both approaches are pertinent for understanding the careers of professional footballers and are employed later in this book.

Ezzy (2001) suggests that in the second half of the twentieth century there has been a noticeable shift from authoritarian to normative forms of control. He argues that authoritarian forms of control rely on financial rewards and threats, whereas normative forms of control attempt to 'shape' work culture and workers' subjectivity in order to ensure compliance. Casey (1995) also indicates a trend in managerial practices which purposefully attempt to 'colonize' the identities of workers such that they become more the kind of person 'the company' would like them to be. Kunda (1992: 10) argues similarly that: 'The ideal employees are those who have internalized the organization's goals and values – its culture – into their cognitive and affective make-up, and therefore no longer require strict and rigid external control.' Managers have 'engineered' workplace culture by utilizing the rhetoric of 'family' and 'team' to engender compliance on the part of employees and to reproduce asymmetrical power relationships (Casey 1995). The trend to organize workers in teams is engineered explicitly to encourage the development of a sense of responsibility among team members (Ezzy 2001). Ideally, co-workers experience peer rather than managerial pressure which leads to the maintenance of organizational commitment among employees.

One important feature of non-traditional (post-Fordist) careers concerns the way in which employees are constrained to cultivate *social networks* in order to enhance their career interests. The research evidence suggests that 'new' types of careers require employees to take responsibility for their own career futures (Giddens 1991; Grey 1994). With respect to getting a job therefore, people in careers without boundaries are more frequently involved in job searches than are individuals bound up in traditional, organizational careers, such that they will more frequently have occasion to call upon their contacts for information regarding opportunities and potential employers. Developing such networks of social contacts is a paramount concern for those who want to 'build' a career. Gaining access to other people's knowledge and resources is a fundamental career step. Social networks are 'constructed' and fostered instrumentally in order to maximize the chances of career success. So, against this background understanding of the sociology of careers, the object of this next section is to provide an initial examination of the careers of male professional footballers in England.

## The careers of professional footballers

As noted, there is a great deal written about footballers, the football industry in general and the careers of professional players, most of which focuses overwhelmingly on the 'heroes' of the game and often exhibits a nostalgic and sentimental attachment to past eras. Before examining the careers of players in relation to the explanatory models discussed in the previous section, it is worth detailing initially a number of salient properties and conditions of the *work* of professional footballers.

## Conditions of work

The first characteristic to note is that professional footballers engage in highly skilled manual labour, although as a form of employment it can be said to differ from industrial working-class occupations in a number of important respects. Unlike workers in industrial jobs – about whom a great deal has been written in the sociology of work (see Braverman 1974; Goldthorpe *et al.* 1968; Gouldner 1964) – the devotion exhibited by professional footballers to their careers is performed willingly, at least initially, because self-fulfilment is anticipated and sometimes found in this career. In short, the idea that a player can 'build' a career as a professional becomes integral to his sense of 'self'. It is perhaps more accurate to call professional football, in Max Weber's (2002: 182) sense, a 'calling' rather than an occupation. Professional football is a vocation or 'technology of the self' (Foucault 1997: 238) that requires kinesthetic intelligence (Gardner 1993) and has much in common with body-centred performance trades such as ballet dancing. The career of a professional footballer is a comparatively short-term affair. Gearing (1997) suggests that the average playing career lasts no longer than eight and a half years.[2] During this time, players are exposed to relatively high levels of risk that for some may result in career termination. For example, although the figure may vary, there are approximately fifty players each season whose careers as professional players are terminated because of injury (see Drawer (2000) for a fuller discussion of the risks of injury in professional football). A professional player spends much of his youth preparing for his football career, and injury spells disaster with the prospect of early retirement. Professional footballers begin their 'careers' from an early age (some promising young players can be linked to football academies from as young as eight years old), but very few players continue beyond thirty-five years of age, the point at which players can draw on their personal pension funds. Their training involves intense and prolonged periods of physical exercise both with and without a football. Many of the players interviewed for this book commented on the dedication and discipline that is required to *make it*.

The work organizations in the football industry are characterized by highly skilled, highly mobile workers who move from one employer to the next, perhaps several times in the course of a career history, while accumulating experience and developing their professional reputation. Since the abolition of the maximum wage in 1960 and the landmark Eastham case in 1963 – a ruling which stipulated that the ability of a player to earn a living was being hindered and, as such, the transfer system could be considered an unreasonable 'restraint of trade' (Dobson and Goddard 2001)[3] – the majority of players have been signed on relatively short fixed-term contracts (mostly lasting from one to five years)[4] with enormous rewards concentrated in the hands of a relatively small number of employees; the majority of entrants into the game fare comparatively poorly in economic terms (Szymanski and Kuypers 1999). The increases to, and current levels of, salaries in professional football are much reported on. It is a common (mostly mythical) understanding that footballers are paid astronomical wages. A small number of individuals do earn very large salaries; even so, in the Football League, salaries do not appear nearly so generous. Since the mid-1990s, salaries for players in all football leagues have increased substantially, promoting critics (Bower 2003; McGill 2001) to speculate about whether their wages reflect the scarcity of the skills they provide. I do not want to become entangled in a discussion of whether player wages are too high as this has been undertaken effectively elsewhere (see Szymanski and Kuypers 1999), although some basic data are worth noting briefly. While the figures compiled on the salaries of individual footballers are not available – published figures include not only playing staff and management but also all the other staff employed by clubs, including accounting and marketing staff and the ground staff – the *Deloitte Annual Review of Football Finance 2005* estimates that Premiership clubs' total wage bill in the 2003–4 season was £583m. For clubs in the Championship, the total player wage bill was £138m; League One was £40m; League Two was £25m (*The Times* 8 June 2005).

Prior to the 1960s, the footballer was traditionally a kind of working-class folk hero (Critcher 1979) who came from the same socio-economic background as the spectators who paid to watch. Following the changes to labour relations in the early 1960s there were dramatic changes in the economic situation of certain players (Wagg 1984). Daily life altered in significant ways and impacted heavily on their cultural identities. The footballer as local hero is, for Critcher (1979), culturally defined by his ability on the field and his role as public figure off it; Critcher argues convincingly that the 'new' deals in labour relations fractured the social and cultural relations by which the identities of players had previously been structured. Thus, Critcher (1979) identifies a sequence of four typologies or styles of player identity in the post-1963 era: the traditional/located player, the transitional/mobile player, the incorporated/embourgeoised player and, finally, the superstar/dislocated player. The changing styles of cultural identity of players were reflected, for Critcher (1979), first on the football pitch, especially in an apparent increase in gamesmanship and petulance and, second, off the pitch, in relation to the influential bearing players possessed. Critcher's study is highly pertinent as it represents the first attempt to examine the economic emancipation of players and understand the subsequent widening gap between the celebrity elite and the 'journeymen'.

Professional footballers rely on their playing skills and athleticism as well as on opportunities, what they may call 'lucky breaks' (Gowling 1973), to achieve positions in clubs with whom they hope to attain 'success'. It is a short career and issues of retirement and ageing present persistent questions for players about their identities and reputations. Because a footballer's sense of self is deeply invested in their 'physical' body, a 'bad' injury is a disruption of the self that is the equivalent to the trauma of a chronic illness (Charmaz 2003). Since players have a *calling* to play football, bad injuries that may potentially end a football career and the wear and tear that accrue from season upon season of physical exertion are accepted as inevitable features of football life. There are few vocations where professional status is so inextricably dependent on the athleticism of the body (see also Turner and Wainwright 2003); in the world of professional football, injury and the threat of injury are routine. Thus, uncertainty is a built-in characteristic of a player's career; career advancement is never secure. Given that the physical capital of players is central to their productive relationship with the club (Giulianotti 1999) and, hence, is a valuable asset, footballers are 'encouraged to follow practices of abstinence and sacrifice, subordinating deleterious lifestyle behaviours to the imperatives of bodily care' (McGillivray et al. 2005: 107). Both Giulianotti (1999) and McGillivray et al. (2005) draw similarities between the way in which players' bodies are trained and regulated – including fitness and diet monitoring – and Foucault's (1977) notion of discipline, which shapes and (re)produces individuals through techniques of surveillance. This focus on rigid governmentality paints a picture of a relatively passive and undifferentiated set of 'working bodies' subject to institutional control (Shilling 2005): a picture that, in a modest way, this book intends to develop.

One of the most striking features of careers in professional football is their temporal dimension. A player's career offers up for scrutiny many examples of what Spilerman (1983: 559) refers to as a 'career-line vulnerability to ageing'. In other words, there are a number of prominent features of this form of physical work that inevitably vary with age. As they get older, players also appear to become increasingly sensitive to job insecurity, to the strain of searching for their next contract or club and to the continual manoeuvering to remain visible in a highly competitive labour market. Contemporary footballers are likely to experience well-patterned sequences of employer changes over the course of their work histories, in ways similar to employees in certain other highly skilled occupations (see, for example, the orchestral musicians examined by Faulkner (1973) and the ballet dancers scrutinized by Wulff (2001)). The chances of upward mobility for players decrease sharply after about the age of thirty, which unavoidably prompts them, earlier or later, to adjust their occupational outlooks and commitments. Football is thus a good example of a form of employment that is highly contingent. In interview, few players spoke of having second jobs, transferable skills or of methods of income risk diversification. McGillivray et al. (2005) argue convincingly that this myopic orientation is, in part, the result of a collective illusion promoted by clubs in which, at the earliest points of contact, players are persuaded to denounce thoughts of the future and the development of alternative interests.

Players possess an external market 'value' based on reputation. Their playing reputations may be thought of as 'capital' which is converted into economic rent.[5] However, the reputations of players are characterized by their high volatility. Sky-rocketing acclaim over the course of a season is likely to lead to sudden shifts in demand towards previously little known players. In terms of understanding their 'value' to significant others, it is possible to distinguish between their 'physical' and 'symbolic' capital (Wacquant 1995a). For instance, certain players have been regarded as exceptionally gifted in terms of their elevated levels of skill and athleticism and thus they enjoy considerable physical capital; that is, prestige flowing from bodily 'investments' (Wacquant 1995a). Ageing inevitably reduces physical capital and so this source of prestige is not renewable and is characterized by its social scarcity. By contrast, ageing can be associated with increases in wisdom, respect and influence. The power that comes with ageing in certain social contexts is associated with symbolic capital (McGillivray *et al.* 2005): that is, honour and social status. The physical and symbolic capital of the body stand in a contradictory relationship. Sporting careers, including professional football careers, can be understood in terms of these contradictory pressures, where retired professional players can retain their symbolic capital by becoming celebrities in related or adjacent fields, for example, television punditry and coaching.[6]

Professional football is a labour intensive industry in which employment is offered by immobile forms of capital to increasingly mobile forms of labour (McGovern 2002). Employers are fixed to specific geographical locations while the employees – the players – can move between cities and countries. There is significant global trade in professional football, which has been the subject of much scrutiny (see Jones and Chappell 1997; Lanfranchi and Taylor 2001; Maguire and Stead 1998; McGovern 2002; Stead and Maguire 2000). Such high levels of mobility indicate that there is a great deal of information available about players. McGovern (2002: 25) suggests that professional football 'is unique' as an industry because the playing contribution of employees 'is unusually transparent'. Potential employers can observe the performances of players and assess at first hand a player's relative strengths and weaknesses. Additionally, employers might seek information about a player's professional reputation informally through personal contacts. The movement of players is enabled and constrained by the *social* capital acquired by managers and players alike through their social ties and contact networks. The central problem facing potential employers is obtaining reliable information on players, for the quality of any future performances cannot be predicted with certainty. McGovern (2002) argues that given this distinctive information problem, managers tend to hire the services of players who most resemble themselves in the belief that they are better able to predict how they will perform in situations of uncertainty.

### Contextualizing careers in football

Football clubs recruit players by transferring them 'in', by employing the services of 'free agents' – that is, players who are 'on a Bosman'[7] as is common parlance among contemporary players – or by developing the talents of gifted young players via the employee-led apprenticeship system. Professional players may move between clubs when their registration is transferred from one club to another, usually subject to the payment of a fee to the club that holds the player's registration. By contrast the primary purpose of the apprenticeship scheme within the football industry is to recruit and develop young players. This hierarchy-based method of recruiting has similarities, according to McGovern (2002), to a *firm internal labour market*, in that it consists of a job ladder with entry at the bottom and upward movement which is associated with the development of skills and knowledge. In contrast to the classical definition of internal labour markets, neither entry at the bottom nor retention at the top are defining features of the job ladder within the football industry (McGovern 2002). Employers view apprenticeship schemes in most cases as a way of 'retaining' trained staff, although this is not necessarily true in professional football where promising young professionals may be sold to finance the recruitment of others (see Monk 2000; Parker 1996a). Within each football club there exists a vertical hierarchy of playing levels (career stages) that represent for each player the possibility of promotion from within. In short, the job ladder in professional football represents the development of teenagers from youth level, through the reserve team and into first team football. A job ladder of the type referred to by McGovern (2002) however is not similar *in kind* to the notion of 'career progression' in relation to traditional careers. There is in professional football no formal understanding of career progression, or in more specific terms, what such *progress* may constitute for individual players: unlike, for instance, workers employed long-term in bureaucratic organizations.

Former professional player Alan Gowling identifies similar *career stages* to those of McGovern (2002): that is, stages which lead from entry level as an apprentice to 'first team regular'. Gowling (1974) uses a traditional career model, similar in kind to those developed by Hall (1948) and Becker (1963), to examine the process of becoming a professional footballer. Initially, such a traditional model can be potentially enlightening. Even so, having reached the position of first team player, Gowling then struggles to conceptualize the manner in which the objective *career trajectories* of players may alter in unplanned ways as they experience, on a subjective level, contingencies such as promotion, demotion, long-term injury, managerial change and ageing. Furthermore, he omits to examine the development of relatively stable patterns of social relations bound up in professional football that enable the establishment, and maybe institutionalization, of particular informal social positions in terms of their authority and prestige; positions of status such as *senior professional* (Gowling 1974). The careers of professional footballers are not similar to careers in traditional bureaucratic organizations as very few players are subject to a unilinear sequence of movements in an upward direction and, in the contemporary game, even fewer encounter long-term attachment to individual employers. The career trajectories of players are best described as unplanned and undirected. The turning points that lead to promotion or demotion are, for the most part, unforeseeable. Few players can aim and work instrumentally for promotion (Grey 1994) and, with the exception of the elite, most footballers focus their energy on securing their next contract at the same or a future club. For many players, their final 'status', unlike professionals in other occupations, may be their least acclaimed.

The career patterns of players may be described from an 'objective' viewpoint as 'disorderly' (Wilensky 1961). The career routes of players involve sequences of vertical and horizontal movements within the four divisions that are difficult to predict. Some players may drop out of the Football League altogether and join 'non-league' clubs in the Conference or below.[8] Still, if traditional career models which focus on orderly progressive stages lack analytical adequacy in terms of understanding the career trajectories of footballers, are the *post-modern* notions of career any more insightful? Is it possible to understand the work histories or careers of professional footballers in relation to 'boundaryless', 'portfolio' or 'new' careers?

In order to understand the development of these models of career, it is necessary to comprehend the onset of 'new' flexible employment arrangements in post-Fordist workplaces. For Sennett (1998: 9), flexibility marks a return to an 'arcane sense of the job' in which people undertake fragments of work over the course of a lifetime. Flexible workplaces are contexts in which workers develop short-term work perspectives that are said to undermine employee trust. With these points in mind it is pertinent to note that professional footballers have always concerned themselves – almost exclusively – with securing their next playing contract. As novice professionals, few are in a position to formulate realistic career goals. The working conditions experienced by employees in 'new' flexible workplaces are similar in kind to the conditions of work under which the bulk of football players have *always* laboured. Historically, all but the most elite of players come in time to be preoccupied with the insecurities and precariousness of their present state of employment. Transformations at work over the past fifteen years have led Doogan (2001: 420) to the conclusion that 'lifetime employment is for most workers a thing of the past'. According to Elliot and Atkinson (1998) we now live in an 'age of uncertainty'. Yet, professional footballers have neither experienced working life which is secure in the sense alluded to by Elliot and Atkinson, nor can they ever consider the prospect of 'lifetime' employment in a manner analogous to Doogan. While some players may consider lifetime employment within the football industry, one might argue that their careers are in-built with a risk of failure.

The focus of attention by managerialist academics on boundaryless careers (Arthur and Rousseau 1996) offers perhaps more purchase in relation to examining the careers of professional footballers. Whilst it is highly competitive, the labour market in professional football has always been relatively flexible and some sociologists have commented on its increasing internationalization (McGovern 2002). Players have always been aware of the uncertainty of the marketplace, the limited duration of average contracts, the excessive supply of potential quality labour and their own vulnerability to ageing. Questions remain however about the degree to which players are able to control or self-manage their careers. If, as Arthur and Rousseau (1996) argue, among the central features of 'new' and 'portfolio' careers is increased 'power' for employees that enables them more and more to determine and take control of their work destinies, is it possible that footballers too enjoy greater measures of control over the organization of their work?

In business worlds it is advisable, according to career guidance counsellors (Richardson 2000), for employees to 'move on' in order to show ambition. Remaining in the same job for too long is perceived negatively. Having the flexibility to accumulate varieties of work experience is one method of 'building' or self-managing one's career. Whilst such career advice is practical and meaningful for employees in flexible enterprises such as, for example, the film industry (Littleton et al. 2000), the merit of such advice for the majority of aspiring footballers is debatable. In order to 'move on' some players may let their contracts expire. At face value this strategy involves a high level of risk for it relies on the accurate self-perception of a player – or perhaps their agent – about their reputation. One might assume that a player who is prepared to risk the prospect of unemployment in order to further their career chances is confident of attracting the attention of other employers. By contrast, other more vulnerable, usually older, players accept willingly most reasonable offers in order to secure future employment, if only in the short term. The strategy adopted by a player will depend on the circumstances experienced by them at the time, although age is an important social factor. In short, some players might feel self-confident of their ability to control the direction of their careers whereas others may not think they have any alternative choices other than to accept what is on offer. Although a much fuller understanding of control is undertaken in this book, it is sufficient at this point to suggest that adopting a 'flexible' approach to managing one's career is a high risk undertaking for most players in an occupation in which it is commonly understood that *you are only as good as your last game*.

In order to conclude these opening notes on players' careers, one final comment will be made. In short, the point is that a professional player's career should not be considered independently of the career of his manager, which develops, so to speak, in parallel. Thus, it is important to bear in mind the interdependent power relationship between players and managers. It is a manager's task to select his starting eleven players (and substitutes) from his playing squad based on his confidence in and knowledge of their ability and, importantly, current form. Managers too attempt to 'build' and self-manage their careers, although like a supervisor in a factory they are not 'active' participants at the point of production, unlike their players.[9] The manager must rely on the team he selects and prepares for matches, for his reputation rests almost exclusively on the results achieved by his players. This is in contrast to players whose reputations can remain intact even though they may be among the members of a losing team. In other words, even though players work as members of a team their performances are often considered in terms of their individual contributions by managers and 'lay' observers. Relations between managers and players therefore are strained by the constant demands of managers for performance returns on player investments. The player-as-worker is put under pressure to 'produce the goods' or else face rejection of some nature. These points are developed in much greater depth in later chapters.

### Football as labour

Any understanding of football as work is intrinsically tied up with public perceptions of what constitutes 'real' work. For most people, work is synonymous with earning a living in the formal labour market. While multiple definitions of work exist (Grint 2005), when interpreted as paid employment, work is understood as those activities involved in the production and distribution of goods, resources and services that are carried out in exchange for wages and fees. In the minds of most people, 'real' work occurs in a place distinct from home, produces surplus value, provides monetary remuneration to produce additional goods and services and conforms to regularized hours in a finite working day (Bain 2005). Professional football is not usually considered in these terms. In one sense, work is the opposite of sport and leisure: it is something we may prefer not to do and for some may even be tremendously arduous. Even so, for employees such as football players, it is not always clear how work and leisure can be separated. Work and non-work cannot be distinguished on the basis of non-work as leisure: for professional footballers, playing sport is an occupation.

There is a more general perspective in which players are portrayed as commodities that can be traded between employers in the same way as machinery or land (McGovern 2002). Unlike employees in other industries, footballers do not have the right to resign from their existing contracts and work their notice in order to take up employment with a different employer within the football industry – although this situation may in time be challenged legally. Given the degree of their bodily colonization and domination, it is surprising that players do not develop a more explicit trade union consciousness and challenge more often their working conditions. Giulianotti (1999: 112) argues convincingly that strikes and collective bargaining have been considered with surprising infrequency in the light of the scarcity of skills players possess and their relatively high level of public popularity.[10] The highly commodified status of players is unlike other commodities that are manufactured, since what is exchanged is *labour power*. Thus, footballers differ from conventional commodities because of their marked variability and plasticity and because the individual 'abilities' that are being purchased – playing talent, athleticism and the *desire* to play well – cannot be separated from their owners (McGovern 2002). Employers must rely on the active participation of the player, since they cannot exclusively control the purchased commodity. McGovern (2002) argues that professional footballers are therefore examples of 'fictive' commodities (Offe 1985).

The early studies examining labour relations in professional football drew heavily on Marxian perspectives (Giulianotti 1999). From such 'objective' (Blyton and Noon 1997) viewpoints, professional football is likened to a capitalist enterprise in which the player becomes a worker alienated from his productive labour, despite the satisfaction he may accrue from his work. Both Rigauer (1981) and Vinnai (1973) examine the strict controls applied to the daily training endured by players such that they come to be programmed to perform patterns of behaviour and movements which have been predetermined. Cashmore and Parker (2003: 219), who focus specifically on England international David Beckham, argue similarly that 'a relentless pursuit of one's dream comes only via a series of predictable, mundane and heavily prescribed workplace behaviours'. Giulianotti (1999) suggests in this vein that the 'corporeal control' established by disciplinarian managers over the football institutions mirrors that of the sergeant within the barracks. For Giulianotti (1999: 109), managers continue to favour 'good professionals' who exhibit concern for their diet and levels of fitness and who can, in short, 'look after themselves'. Such 'pliant' selves, he argues, can be refined more easily from a plastic commodity into *footballing* capital.

It would be a mistake however to characterize the work of professional football, like work undertaken in many industrial settings, as 'routine' in all respects. It is clear that the variety of work which may be undertaken is limited. One may change geographical setting but not the character of work. The proliferation of industrial and mechanical metaphors employed in the review of literature undertaken by Giulianotti (1999), for example, undermines for me the levels of personal autonomy granted players in terms of using their own initiative 'once they have crossed the white line'. There is no denying the fact that training on a daily basis and preparing for matches may involve a relatively high level of routine in terms of mastering a fairly limited range of observable abilities. Weekly training may appear, and be experienced subjectively as, predictable and mundane; even so, the range of less tangible skills developed by competent players – a player's ability to 'read' the game, to be able to create 'space' for oneself and others and to make appropriate decisions when in possession of the ball – are not mental abilities that may be comprehended within the Taylorist approach to workplace organization and job design referred to by Rigauer (1981) and Brohm (1978). Whilst the work of professional footballers entails often 'heavily prescribed' routines, an analysis of the character of their work should be blind neither to the opportunities for creativity and unpredictability in terms of playing styles, nor to the unpredictable course and outcome of matches.

A career as a professional footballer could be considered a good example of a labour of love, for many young players 'labour' quite literally for the *love* they have for playing the game. Usually, 'labour of love' arguments (Freidson 1990) relate to activities to which people are irresistibly committed. A labour of love is an undertaking in which one would participate voluntarily; it is a form of behaviour that people, such as artists, would practise for leisure purposes and from which they may obtain 'self-actualization' and, perhaps, a 'psychic income' (Menger 1999). For Freidson (1990) the only viable criteria for distinguishing leisure from work and various types of work from each other are the social meaning of activities, their value and the context in which they are undertaken. Freidson (1990) argues that the same activity can be leisure or non-work in one context and work in another. Some occupations may be considered *labours of love* as motivations for undertaking such work are not, in the immediate and obvious Marxian sense, self-interested. In other words, as a labour of love, professional football is an activity in which 'income' of an economic variety is not the sole determinant of labour market behaviour; at least, not in the first instance. Young apprentices are often told that they should consider themselves to be lucky and not throw away the opportunity they have been granted. What could be better than to be paid (sometimes a great deal of money) to do something that you love? The bulk of the literature on occupations has been concerned with the fact that when people do have work, it is characteristically unsatisfying (Watson 1995). Professional football in an ideal sense is a form of work which should be the opposite of alienated labour, yet the data obtained for this book, as well as a small number of autobiographies by 'journeymen' players, bear out the financial, physical and emotional insecurities they continue to experience. These points feature centrally in this book.

## Chapter 2

# Attitudes to work in professional football

The idea of footballers being 'good professionals' (Giulianotti 1999) relates centrally to the orientations that players-as-workers conventionally possess about their work. For players, work, in a Marxian sense, is *the* central life interest and they expect to get more from it than most other people. Much discussion of work attitudes and work motivations has centred upon the question of whether people generally are intrinsically or extrinsically orientated to their work (Watson 1995). It is therefore frequently debated whether, on the one hand, people work 'just for the money' or, on the other hand, they work primarily for self-fulfilment. Goldthorpe *et al.* (1968), in their studies of 'affluent workers', pointed to the employees' own 'definition of the situation' as an initial basis for the explanation of their attitudes to work (Watson 1995). More than this however, Goldthorpe *et al.* (1968) argued that the motives, interests and outside-work background of workers had to be taken into account, if not given central emphasis, in debates concerning orientations to work. Given the transient status of employees (including professional footballers), Goldthorpe *et al.* (1968) insist another aspect is critical: attitudes to work are not stable, they change as individuals change their status, their family structure, their age and their interpretation of the discourses intersecting around such categories. Employing Goldthorpe *et al.* as a point of departure, I argue here that in professional football, attitudes to work also influence, and are influenced by, what happens in the workplace. In other words, the orientations to work possessed by players are not independent of the working environment. Footballers do see their work – at least initially – as a source of self-realization and as a site for significant social relations; it is not solely a context for the purpose of earning a living.

The meanings attached to the term *attitude* in the context of professional football are diverse. It is clear that possessing a 'good professional attitude' is important for players, particularly in terms of career progression (Parker 1996a), although what it means to possess a *good* attitude (or for that matter a *bad attitude*) can vary considerably. For example, the meaning may alter according to the stage at which the player has reached in his career, or it may change depending on whether the player is injured, has been dropped from the first team, or is negotiating for his next contract. In the context of many 'professions', for example the academic profession, one is unlikely to hear a colleague regularly suggesting that a lecturer or researcher possesses a 'good professional attitude to their work'. In the context of professional football, references to work attitudes are commonplace, especially for younger players for whom a comment such as this might be interpreted as a benchmark of progress. The patterns of social relationships identifiable in professional football clubs, for example relations among club managers, players and club physiotherapists, relate to structures of power and to patterns of meaning. The ways in which players think and feel about their work will relate to the occupational orientations of coaches and players with whom they have close contact, and also to their wider cultural perspectives which may be of a religious or political nature.

When a young player signs a full-time contract with a football club, he is exposed as part of a process of informal learning to what in professional football are considered appropriate attitudes and values. It is in this context that young players learn what it *means* to possess a good attitude and, of central importance to them, what behaviour elicits the reaction from others that *they* [that is the young players] have a good attitude. In short, players, particularly young players, learn that it is meaningful for them to 'display' and to be praised by significant others for 'showing' a good professional attitude. In the course of their career, each player develops, to a greater or lesser degree, appropriate modes of thought and action which are aspects of their general orientation to their work. These modes of thought and action become ingrained over time and bound up with their conception of 'self'; that is, players build into their self-identities an understanding of what it means to be a 'good professional'. Failure to display an appropriate attitude in the context of the football club may generate unwanted reactions from club personnel and may lead to a diminished sense of 'self' for the player. Consequently, players come to perceive, form judgements and control themselves from the standpoint shared by all the other players – what might be termed an occupational ideology – and thus deliberately, intuitively or unconsciously, 'perform' for the particular people whose judgement of their abilities is deemed important. Once a player has incorporated the culture of his group – the culture of professional football – it becomes a frame of reference he can bring to bear upon all the situations he encounters.

In the light of these opening remarks, the objects of this chapter are first to describe what constitutes a good attitude in English professional football and, second, to examine a number of circumstances in which the 'display' of a good attitude is meaningful. Close attention is given to the social construction and maintenance of a good professional attitude and what it means in the context of the management of injury.

## Attitudes to work

There are some links between a definition of a *good professional attitude* in football and *work ethics* of the kind which are examined in the sociology of work. Sennett (1998) suggests that the 'traditional' work ethic is commonly understood in terms of characteristics such as a self-disciplined use of time, hard work, an understanding of the value of delayed gratification, good grooming and a respect for one's elders. Yet while, for Sennett, a modern work ethic has developed out of the old and concerns teamwork, sensitivity, the ability to listen, co-operation and adaptability, the characteristics of the more traditional work ethic are most identifiable with the occupational attitudes associated with professional football. In short, a work ethic, the type of which may be located in an industrial or manual occupation and which emphasizes the values of 'masculinity, active participation, and victory' (Taylor 1970), seems most closely to resemble the characteristics of a good attitude in professional football.

A good illustration of what, from a manager's point of view, constitutes a 'good attitude', was provided by a former Liverpool manager, Gerard Houllier. Interviewed in the *Sunday Times* (6 December 1998), Houllier said that the kind of players a manager wants are those who will 'fight for you once they are on that grass'. He added: 'I'll name you one – Jamie Carragher. What a professional. He might have a niggly injury, but he'll always be out there giving it some of this' (Houllier smashed a fist into his other palm by way of emphasis). Former Chelsea and Scotland international Pat Nevin further emphasized the aggressive *masculine* dimension of a 'good attitude' in English professional football when considering the initial experiences of overseas players:

> When you arrive in England as a foreign player, the trick is to be able to deal with and adapt to certain cultural changes, not so much in everyday life but more so within football itself. Our attitudes can be very different and rather idiosyncratic ... try explaining to an intelligent foreign player that he really ought to play on with a gaping head-wound à la Terry Butcher, unless he wants to be thought of as a big girl's blouse.
>
> (Nevin and Sik 1998: 48)

Being prepared to play while injured is thus defined as a central characteristic of a good professional attitude. However, this is only one characteristic. Parker (1996a: 48), whose brilliant ethnographic study of the football apprenticeship is shot through with references to professionalism and, in particular, 'attitude', suggests that among the immediate tasks of 'club officials' is to promote attitudes of 'acceptance, obedience and collective loyalty'. He states that at the professional club in which his study took place, an 'explicit institutional logic' existed which incorporated notions of 'personal integrity, conscientiousness, discipline and the development of a healthy "professional attitude"' (Parker 1996a: 200). Parker (1996a: 200) outlines the following as essential characteristics which apprentice-professionals must demonstrate to club coaches as signs of their progress and personal maturity: 'a keen and "hardy" enthusiasm for the game, a forceful "will-to-win", an acceptance of work-place subservience, an ability to conform, and a commitment to social and professional cohesion'. Parker constructs an understanding of the central values of football culture which for him are akin to those of a 'working class shop-floor culture'.

### 'Hard work' and the 'desire to win'

A player who possesses a good attitude is someone who always works hard, both for himself in terms of personal development and for the team. This can be interpreted to mean someone who always tries hard to win in matches *and* in training, who is competitive and who is constantly looking to improve their level of performance. Many of the players who were interviewed made reference to 'hard work' in one context or another by way of explaining what constitutes *a good attitude* in professional football. For example, one experienced player stated succinctly that a young player who possesses a good attitude is:

> someone who is willing to learn. If you are a youngster anyway you've got to be willing to learn, and more importantly willing to train, and also willing to take advice from people who know. And if they do that and they work hard at their game as well then maybe they've got half a chance.

The statement by this player sells short a number of the characteristics of a good attitude in professional football. For example, Parker (1996a: 93) discusses the emphasis placed on winning in *all* competitive situations and states that 'whilst "winning" was encouraged, it was not just a team affair, it was an issue of personal importance structured around the development of an inner drive or motivation and a burning passion to succeed in every competitive situation'. Likewise, former Arsenal and England international player Graham Rix, formerly a youth coach at Chelsea, stresses the need for young players not only to be 'winners', but also to develop an aggressive cutting-edge in their approach to the game. In a television documentary which examines the life of football apprentices, he said of his young players:

> Smile, be happy in your life, but when you cross that line whether it be for training or a match, you've got to become a bastard. You've got to be a hard, tough bastard. Smile, you can have a smile on your face, but in there [points to his head] and in your heart and your stomach, you've got to be as tough as nails.
> (*Channel 4* 7 July 1997)[1]

The problems as far as many young players are concerned are twofold. First, young players are faced with the problem of demonstrating to significant others that they possess a 'burning passion' to win and displaying the attributes of a 'hard, tough bastard'. Many players achieve this by, for example, working hard in matches and in training, by being enthusiastic and always wanting the ball, by injecting a sense of urgency into their play and by being outwardly aggressive when tackling and heading and in other contact situations. The second and related problem concerns the 'informal' nature of the criteria which define a 'good attitude'. From one situation to the next and from one player to another, these criteria are often applied in arbitrary ways by coaches and managers and can lead to the generation of jealousy among teammates and the issue of managerial 'favouritism' (see Parker 1996a): 'attitude' is, to some extent, in the eye of the beholder.

Data collected for this study indicate that younger players (apprentices and young professionals) are made more aware of the need to 'display' a good attitude; this point is born out by a case of negligence brought against Sunderland Association Football Club by a former player. This particular incident was recorded in a court hearing between Keiron Brady, the player in question, and Sunderland Association Football Club (Queens Bench Division, 2 April 1998) who were being sued on the grounds of medical negligence. The precise condition that was discovered during operative treatment was the result of a blockage of the popliteal artery in Brady's right leg. Popliteal entrapment syndrome is a very rare medical condition. Keiron Brady claimed that the club failed to take appropriate action when he reported pain in his right leg. It is alleged by the player that complaints and apparent difficulties in training were attributed to an *attitude* problem – in short, he is accused by a coach of possessing a 'bad' attitude to training. Brady gave a witness statement which reads as follows:

> By this stage Malcolm Crosby [the youth coach] was telling me that I had an attitude problem and in particular in relation to training. I didn't really realise there was something physically wrong. I just wasn't able to keep up all the time. From time to time I would try and explain to him in training sessions why I was unable to keep up but he did not want to listen and told me it was to do with my attitude. Over the following month his opinion about my attitude seemed to harden.
>
> (Queens Bench Division, 2 April 1998)

In this particular case, the player is accused of not liking hard work, particularly stamina running and weights. The coach in his statement said that he did not believe the full extent of the injury to the player and, hence, one might conclude that he thought the player was exaggerating the full extent of the pain in order to excuse himself from hard training. Hypothetically speaking, had the player possessed the 'right attitude', he would have soldiered on without complaint. Thus, the player was stigmatized for possessing a bad attitude. Moreover, his actions might be said to have the unintended consequence of acting as a reminder to his playing colleagues of the types of behaviour that elicit unwanted reactions from significant others.

Many other players spoke similarly of having to (re)prove themselves to new managers, even if they were established professionals, and suggested that one way in which this can be achieved is by demonstrating a good professional attitude to the game. A senior Division Two (i) player recounted a situation in which, despite having been out with an injury for some time, he felt he had contributed to the success of his team that season and had, as he put it, 'earnt the right' to have his contract extended for one year. The management delayed their decision in terms of his request suggesting that they would reconsider an extension to his contract in pre-season. He set himself a number of targets during the close season in addition to the weight targets set by the club physiotherapist. The following extract is an attempt by this player to provide an example of his professionalism:

> I was going to do a lot of work during this summer because I wanted to be better in the second division than I was in the third and obviously to keep my place in the team. I was quite friendly with the assistant manager and at various stages during the summer I was saying to him that I'd been working hard. I really built myself up ... I went back for pre-season and he stuck me on the scales. There were two or three of the other players stood next to me and they said, 'You've put some weight on haven't you? But you must have had a good summer, there's not an ounce of fat on you.' So straight away I got the right response ... [the manager] pulled me aside and he said, 'I can see you've worked your socks off this summer. You look great. You know you mentioned about a contract, we'll give you that contract, we'll give you an extra year.' I thought, I got my rewards for the hard work that I've done.

This player thought the awarding of his 'extra year' by the management was justly deserved and granted on the grounds of his dedication and hard work and, like many of the responses by players to questions concerning their attitude, his comments implicitly address his degree of commitment to professional football. Among the most adequate responses to the question of professionalism was that provided by a Division One (i) player who, when asked to describe what it is to have a good professional attitude, provided details of his early experiences in order to explain his 'professional' approach to the game. Having decided against signing as an apprentice for the Division Three (i) club who had offered him a youth training (YT) contract, he chose instead to study for a sports science degree at a polytechnic. The club, he said, were keen for him to continue playing nevertheless, so whilst studying, he continued to play in their reserve team when it was possible. He said that whilst studying, a psychology of sport lecturer had expressed surprise at the fact that, in general, professional footballers didn't keep training diaries. At this point the player decided to go about his training in a more systematic manner. He said:

> I went and bought this ball and I said to myself, I'm going to go out for an hour every night. I bought a ball and just went out and did drills and all I

did was work on dribbling with my right foot and my left foot. I was just dribbling round cones, dead basic stuff, but my touch and my control and everything improved and I just did it religiously every single day. I think it helped my confidence and everything. I was more comfortable on the ball. I already had the attitude and the competitiveness, I had a bit of pace and it was that next year when I broke into [my club's] first team. I had a bit of luck with injuries to players as well. I was able to take the chance and ... I think it was just the work ethic I think ... but it was something you had been brought up with, an attitude that had been ingrained. There was a point where I realized that I needed to go and do this and this and this to do with work and I was disciplined enough to go and do it.

Having signed as a professional at the Division Three (i) club, the player has subsequently been transferred twice, most recently to a Division One (i) club for over one million pounds. When asked if he continued to train as hard, he replied:

Yes, the thing is now that, when things are going well is to do extra training, do extra crossing. When you go home a couple of times a week, I'd just get the ball out and practise the basic things and it's probably not the same ... some people have different attitudes to me, they are more self-confident and that, but me, I still keep a diary and if I look back on a Friday and if I see I've done all my training right down to an extra weights session, I've done a bit of extra running, been out with the ball a couple of times, if my training diary is full up then I think, 'Right, I've done my work, so there's no reason why I shouldn't have a good game tomorrow. It's all in there, I can go and do it.' I think for me, that is attitude.

This account is informative as the player highlights in detail the *development* of the attitude of perseverance he brings to bear in training and preparation for matches, an attitude that may appear as a very personal mental process. Even so, the diary of training he maintains steadfastly serves not only as a reminder of his training schedule but, perhaps more importantly, to reinforce his sense of self-belief that he is prepared for his next match. Thus the significance of, and the meaning invested in, the diary lies in the fact that his updating of it leads him to think that he has an edge over other players and, hence, to a reinforcement of his sense of self.

All the cases presented so far have confirmed that it is necessary for players to demonstrate and to prove to others that they possess the *right attitude* to the game. For players to think that they have worked hard and performed well in a competitive situation – in short, for them to think they possess the right attitude – is, on its own, by and large meaningless in terms of career progression. Players need to display and make their attitude to the game evident to others in a manner that is acknowledged and approved. A good attitude is not a characteristic that players are born with, unlike potential levels of aerobic fitness, agility or peripheral vision. Rather, it is a quality which is socially constructed and reinforced; the praise received from a significant other to players who display a good attitude serves directly to heighten their self-confidence.

## Individual progress versus team success

Another integral characteristic of a good attitude is the willingness of a player to sacrifice personal achievement and glory for the good of the team. This characteristic is complex sociologically as, whilst players recognize that it is important that they *should be seen to be* team players, many have spoken (both during interviews and in the national newspapers) of the personal conflicts that arise in the context of their daily activities. These 'individual versus club' conflicts surface mostly when players are unable to play, either because of injury or when they are left out of the starting eleven. For some players this will constrain them to engage in a degree of, what Goffman (1959) would term, 'impression management', as they are expected to behave in a manner that contributes, first and foremost, to the morale of the team. Magee (1998: 129), in his study of international labour migration in professional football, examines what he terms 'dressing room culture'. He quotes one of his players as suggesting that English football is characterized in terms of a 'dog-eat-dog' way of life. In short, this player suggests, footballers 'look after themselves'. One inexperienced player from a Division Three (i) club interviewed for this study confirmed these sentiments by expressing the opinion that: 'At the end of the day, you know, everyone is in it for themselves. And quite often players would shit on each other, you know, if it came to it.' When asked how other players reacted to him throughout a period in which he was rehabilitating from a long-term injury, an experienced Premiership player replied by drawing attention to the self-centred, individualistic focus which for him characterizes many players. He said:

> ... players are very selfish people because they know ... At the end of the day, just as long as they're fit ... I mean, they say 'hello' to you and 'how are you doing?' But I know because I'm a player myself, that they will give you so much concern but they're not going to lose any sleep over it. You know what I mean? They're not *that* bothered. Players think exactly what I expect them to think.

The clearest examples of personal conflict occur when players are dropped or unfit for selection and are forced to watch their team play without them. In these respects, the attitudes and behaviour of players reflect the importance attached to playing as a central value in football culture. Active participation in matches seems to be the context through which the identities – the highly masculine identities – of players are given meaning. This is probably what Goffman

(1967: 181) had in mind in his analysis of 'action' and the people who want and need 'a piece of it'. Professional football is arguably a work role that provides a capacity for demonstrating the characteristics of courage and confidence for establishing 'self' through such 'action'. As unemployment in general may lead to a diminished sense of self, particularly among men (Morgan 1992), likewise, having to watch and not participate in matches may foster a loss of sense of importance as well as high levels of anxiety for professional footballers. Unsurprisingly, all players stated that they vehemently disliked missing matches and, typically, one described himself as 'the world's worst spectator'. A number of players, however, distinguished between being *unfit* and *dropped*. An experienced Premiership player, like other more senior players who were interviewed, emphasized not only the differences that may exist, but also the need for players to try to remain positive:

> I think it's the hardest thing ever for a player when they're not fit ... There are times when you have to accept that you're not going to play because you're injured: end of story. I think there's nothing worse than when you're fit and you're not playing because basically the manager is saying that you don't fit into his plans and that is harder to take.

A young Division Two (i) player confirmed the difficulties experienced by players who are unfit and therefore unable to take part in matches. When asked to comment on how he felt having to watch rather than play in games when injured, he said:

> Player: Oh I don't like watching matches. I hate it. You get it stuck in your mind that someone's in your place, doing better than you, and you're not going to get back in the team.
> MR: Does that lead to a conflict of interests?
> Player: It does sometimes, yes. I think it does with every player. I don't think other players would admit it, but it certainly does, yes. I mean, I don't think you blatantly want your team to lose, but you wouldn't mind them scraping a 1–0, and not playing very well and your man having a nightmare.

According to former Scotland international Pat Nevin (Nevin and Sik 1998: 24), by contrast, the 'consummate, "right-thinking" professional' always has the 'good of the team' uppermost in his heart. Likening his approach to this type of model professional, Nevin boasts about his upbringing as a member of the Celtic Boys' Club in Glasgow and their overriding philosophy that laid stress on the 'oneness of the team'. He claims to have been amazed when he signed as a professional to discover that 'not everyone always has the same feelings towards the team' (Nevin and Sik 1998: 25). Parker (1996a) suggests too that an enhancement of team collectivity was something which the trainees in his study had to 'demonstrate' if they were going to succeed but, he claims, for the older, second year boys, 'instances of managerial partiality and selectivity had shown them that the promotion of group cohesion was more often a matter of "official" lip-service than everyday action'. Hence, Parker (1996a: 111) states: 'Experiences of schoolboy football and YT selection had taught trainees that, in reality, being a good "team player" and showing consideration for the welfare of others were relatively unprofitable ventures in terms of occupational success.'

Former Republic of Ireland international Eamon Dunphy (1987) retells perhaps the most revealing account of this type of conflict of interest in his classic diary of a professional footballer's season, *Only a Game*. Dunphy considers himself to be a regular first team player for Millwall Football Club but is left out of the team for a forthcoming match. He finds out about his omission from the first team when he is selected to play for the reserve team in a training match and, filled with a mixture of anger and hurt, claims his first reaction was to 'walk out'. Dunphy agrees finally with the wishes of the manager for him to be thirteenth man[2] for the forthcoming game and, in the following quote, he explains his behaviour and actions among his teammates on the day of the match:

> So we went up to Sheffield. I wasn't on the bench, I went as thirteenth man. You go into the dressing-room before the game, and you smile and say 'All the best, lads.' What does that mean? If they do well you stay out. And when they get beaten, as we did last night, what do you do? You act. Because you can't come in with a big smile all over your face saying 'Great. Now you've been beaten I can get back in.' Everybody else is sick. But you aren't. You are pleased. So you come in and make faces; pretend that you are sick like the rest of them. But everyone knows that you are acting
>
> (Dunphy 1987: 100)

Dunphy (1987: 100–101) goes on to describe his personal conflicts whilst watching his teammates during the game in the following way:

> But while they are out there what am I doing? I'm sitting in the stand, wanting them to lose, but unable to show it. Because there are people around, I've got to pretend to want them to win. I can't jump up in the air when Sheffield score. Which I want to do. And when Millwall score I am sick, but I have to jump up in the air. And there is this terrible conflict the whole time. And it is the same for everyone who is dropped.
>
> You are always pleased when the lads have been beaten, because it means you are a candidate again. You are sick for the lads, of course, but your predominant emotion is delight.

This account is revealing in terms of the way in which Dunphy feels constrained to behave in a manner that is 'appropriate', and which conforms to the cultural norms of a professional footballer who is watching his team compete, rather than being actively involved. Even though he claims that all the other players know that he is 'acting', he still feels that it is appropriate to behave as expected, yet in a manner that contradicts his true feelings. Dunphy is not 'forced' to behave in this way. For him not to conform to the expectations of others however would be tantamount to admitting that he possessed a 'bad attitude' and it is likely that if this pattern of behaviour repeated itself he may become stigmatized, at least in the short term. So, rather than be discredited by his manager and teammates, Dunphy engages in what is commonly understood as 'impression management' (Goffman 1959). This point highlights one of the central properties of the 'good attitude': namely, that it can be thought of as a powerful form of social control in the context of professional football.

There have been only a few studies which have focused on the structures of control within football culture (Tomlinson 1983; Parker 1996a; Giulianotti 1999) and what studies have been undertaken have emphasized the traditional/authoritarian management styles that are closely associated with professional football. Giulianotti (1999: 109) refers to the manager's 'corporeal control over the football institution' and writes of the ways in which the daily lives of players are constrained in terms of, for example, daily training timetables and diet. Tomlinson (1983: 165) examines the internal structures of control, suggesting that the 'professional football club promotes in its players an attitude of general impotence, and structurally delimits any potential that the group of players might have for expansion and growth'. None of the studies examines in any detail the *orientation to work* which players develop as professionals, nor the ways in which this orientation constrains their approach to the game and their daily lives, even if they do not recognize these constraints.

The circumstances which constrain players to behave in a manner that is expected rather than in a way which reflects their actual emotions are structured along a number of lines of which the following might be recognized as central. It might be said that players are more likely to engage in a degree of impression management (Goffman 1959) when they think they can be more easily replaced by other members of their squad, when the squad members are in close and frequent contact with management and coaching staff (and in some cases medical staff), and when the players with whom they have close and often intense relationships share, or need also to conform to, the same culture of football: that is, they too are constrained to display a 'good attitude'. The network of relationships which typify professional football clubs are closed to outsiders with a homogenous culture that tends to be mutually reinforcing.

There has been an examination thus far of what it means to possess a 'good attitude' in professional football. The focus has been on the workplace culture in which the players begin to adopt, deliberately or unconsciously, the mannerisms, attitudes and behaviours that they perceive among the senior professionals at their clubs, or which their managers and coaches reinforce. For example, players are expected to work hard and to manifest characteristics such as a 'positive' frame of mind, a forceful will to win as well as an unquestioning loyalty to the team. In many of these respects, impression management plays a significant role, particularly when a player's position in the starting eleven is threatened. Parker (1996a: 111) suggests that he observed an obvious example of impression management when some of the youth trainees 'denied injury in order to remain eligible for youth team selection, knowing only too well that they would be incapable of performing to their maximum potential'. He goes on to say that it was common for players to deny pain and injuries if it meant preserving their position in the team and that this type of behaviour generated 'increased favour in terms of managerial preference'. This case in point highlights two aspects of the culture of professional football: that this type of behaviour stands in stark contrast to the rhetoric of being a good team player and that it underscores the emphasis placed on aggressive masculine styles of play which 'good professionals', but particularly younger professionals, are required to display.

## Masculinity, pain and injury[3]

There have been a number of studies which have examined men in occupational settings (Cockburn 1983; Collinson 1988, 1992; Collinson and Hearn 1994; Willis 1977). Unlike earlier 'classic' studies of work (Lupton 1963; Walker and Guest 1952; Whyte 1956), these studies have explored specifically the social construction of 'men' and the specific implications for the reproduction of men and masculinity of being, for example, a manager and of working on an assembly line. Collinson and Hearn (1994) argue that a key issue which reinforces and structures 'masculinity'[4] is the deep-rooted nature of economic class inequalities, subcultures and identities that continue to be reproduced in and through routine work practices. Connell (1995: 36) suggests also that 'economic circumstances and organizational relationships enter into the making of masculinity at the most intimate level'. Using the work of Donaldson (1991) as his point of departure, Connell (1995: 36) states that hard labour in all-male working environments (for example in factories and mines) literally 'uses up the workers' bodies' and that this 'destruction, a proof of the toughness of work and of the worker, can be a method of demonstrating masculinity'.[5] According to Connell (1995: 36): 'This happens not because manual work is necessarily destructive, but because it is done in a destructive way under economic pressure and management control.' What is true of workplaces in general, is also true of professional football clubs in England.

Thus, playing with pain or when injured may be viewed as a 'routine work practice' in the context of professional football. All the players interviewed indicated that they had at some time *carried* injuries, denied or masked pain in order to play, or had concealed injuries from significant others. The context within which a player is constrained (i.e. pressured), or may choose to play hurt, can vary from one division to the next and can be dependent upon factors such as the degree to which the player has 'established' himself, the stage of the season and the significance of the match, the number of 'fit' players available to the manager, and the extent of internal competition for places. For all that, the tendency for players to play hurt and to risk further injury cannot be understood simply in terms of these 'external factors' (Messner 1992), for there is a powerful motivating force working in conjunction with these external factors which makes it likely that players will choose to play hurt: namely, the internal structure of masculine identity. In their study of ballet dancers, Turner and Wainwright (2003) propose that their tolerance of pain is a function of the social solidarity of the ballet dancer and the professional discipline that forms the dancing identity. Like footballers, an injury to a ballet dancer can be fatal to his/her career. Turner and Wainwright (2003: 272) argue that, for dancers, pain and injury are masked by a ballet culture that is committed to the notion that 'the show must go on'. They suggest that because ballet dancers have a calling to dance, there is a reluctance to admit to the presence of an injury. Recent writing on pain and injury in sport describes how male sport is an institution through which masculine identities are constructed and reconstructed (Curry 1993; Messner 1992; Young et al. 1994). In this body of research, the tolerance of pain and injury is valued by many athletes as 'masculinizing'. Similarly, in the context of professional football, learning to play with pain or when injured is an important aspect of the construction of masculine identities; it is a means of making an impact on managers and coaches and a convenient way for players to demonstrate their 'attitude' to the game.

It is important, therefore, that players should have, or at least should 'display', an appropriate *attitude* towards playing with pain and carrying injuries; by the same token, those who are not prepared to play through pain and injury are likely to be stigmatized as not having the right attitude or as malingerers. These points were brought out very clearly by one experienced player who summed up what having a 'good attitude' entails in the following way:

> We had a player, I won't mention his name, but he has gone to [another club] now, and he had a fantastic attitude as in, he used to play constantly through injuries and they would get worse and worse. He'd be injured one week and ... two weeks later he'd have the injury again. When you get a dead leg, you know, if you start running on it in the first twenty-four hours, you've got no chance, it can get worse ... he'd play through to show the management that he had a fantastic attitude. But he was constantly injured. Constantly injured.

When asked how managers react to this kind of behaviour on the part of their players he replied:

> They think it's fantastic. Brilliant. He's out there dying for the club; dying for the club. Now, we have another player here who's from [another country] and his attitude is any little niggle, 'That's it, I'm not playing.' Even in

warm-ups before games he walks off. Everyone's attitude towards him is, 'He's a poofter, he doesn't want to play, no heart.' You know, the manager says in front of the players, 'Look at him over there; he's pulled out of the game again. There's a big game coming up ... so he's pulled out.' It might be because he has genuinely got an injury. Only the player knows. But his title is that he's a fucking wuss, you know, he hasn't got the right attitude. But if you go out with an injury and you play for ninety minutes and it's doing you more harm than good, you know, you're Braveheart, you're brilliant.

Players are willing to play with pain, if only, at times, to display an appropriate attitude.[6] There are times when players have doubts about their fitness, but are unable to express their doubts and feel constrained to say to managers (and sometimes to physiotherapists) that they are keen to play. For example, one senior Premiership player expressed the way in which he felt under pressure to agree to a painkilling injection to enable him to play in a forthcoming match. When asked whether he was given any options about whether or not to have the injection, the player responded as follows:

> Not really. I mean ... you are under a bit of pressure to take it [the injection] because you think, what does the manager say if I don't take it. I'm under pressure to take it because, if I don't, he probably looks at me as if you are a bit soft or you don't really want to go through it, or you don't want it badly enough. And you are put in that position sometimes.

When asked whether this situation occurs regularly for players at his club, the player replied: 'It definitely does here, which I think is a bad thing really. I think here, if you are not fit, and if the physiotherapist hasn't got you fit within four weeks, he thinks along the lines of injecting you.'

Without exception all the players interviewed said that they could not stand to miss games and would, if necessary, risk 'carrying' an injury. One former senior Premiership player described how, over several months, he had played with pain from a knee injury and, in attempting to compensate for the knee injury by changing his running style, had suffered one injury after another. The following is an extract from the transcript of the interview with this player:

> Player: Because you've got something that hurts, you are aware of it and you compensate naturally, probably unconsciously, and I was running in a different way. Changing my running style developed new injuries, so on top of one, when you are playing with an injury, then all of a sudden, you are playing with two injuries and then, you know, you get one right and then you've got another one ... you never give yourself enough time, I never give myself enough time.
> MR: Can you describe what it was like playing through these injuries?
> Player: You get familiar with it, any pain ... if you don't step back and ... get

out of the scenario, you kind of get used to the shit, I'm afraid, and that's what I was doing. I was compensating in other areas. I twisted my ankle in February last year, and that went on top of my knee and I'm compensating and then all of a sudden I'm getting bad toes. I'm getting bad toes 'cos I'm changing my running style ... and then all of a sudden my back's playing me up.

MR: How did you feel during this period?

Player: It was pretty depressing ... when you are getting up in the morning and you can't walk and all of a sudden you think to yourself 'Jesus, I've got to go to work today.' You know, it's like any job, if you can't do your job ... so it was kind of one thing on top of another and it's not a good feeling ... It's frustrating, but you get used to the pain and ... you keep on playing with the pain. That's the thing, you never say 'No, I'm not doing it.'

Later in the interview, he emphasized the continual pressure to return to play as quickly as possible:

We never gave it enough time. We were always chasing our tail with every injury that I've ever had. You know, there's always been a cup semi-final, or there's been a quarter-final in the cup or there's another [international] game ... you never give yourself time.

A willingness to play through pain and to be seen to possess a good attitude can lead players to mask their injuries in order to be fit for selection. In some circumstances, players will conceal the injury outright if they feel they can 'get away with it'. However, this is usually only the case with minor injuries, for example, groin strains and small muscle tears. For other players, being willing to play when injured may involve being prepared to have a painkilling injection (usually local anaesthetics), a cortisone injection, or taking non-steroidal anti-inflammatory drugs (for example, Ibuprofen and Voltarol), the use of which is widespread in football clubs. For example, one experienced player stated that at his present club, 'they give out [Ibu]profen like there's no tomorrow'. When asked how he coped with pain, another player, whose remarks were similar to many of the players interviewed, said: 'It was a case of grin and bear it really. I had tablets to sort of help it as well. It was just one of those stages where I think, "Get on with it".' In his (auto)biography, former Republic of Ireland international Tony Cascarino discusses his use of drugs which ensure he is 'fit' for selection. He reveals:

I've had two cortisone injections already this season. For the last eight years I've taken anti-inflammatory pills before and after every game. The pills play havoc with my stomach and scorch my arse with diarrhoea but when the ball hits the back of the net and the crowd chants my name, it seems a small price to pay.

(Kimmage 2000: 6)

Players are given painkilling injections to a lesser degree and, usually, only at critical points in the season. Some club doctors refuse outright to inject players using cortisone, whereas others seem more prepared to think in terms of injections, especially local anaesthetics, as an alternative strategy. Players are not usually consulted with regard to the implications of having an injection, are offered little advice and are rarely asked whether or not they are happy to be injected. One experienced player said that he had known a small number of players at his club who had refused to be injected and they had ended up in conflict with the manager. He went on to suggest that it would take 'a lot of bottle for someone to say no' if that course of action was proposed.

The dilemma for players of whether or not to be injected draws attention to a complex aspect of the attitude to playing with pain. Most of the players interviewed had been injected, enabling them to play, although all players spoke of their resistance to painkillers of all description (that is, injections and pills). One player, for example, spoke of a situation in which he had been injected twice before every game from late December until the end of the season in May. This player said that while he would avoid taking painkillers wherever possible – and at another point in the interview even claimed that he 'did not believe in them' – he rationalized his actions by suggesting that the stakes are a bit higher at Premiership level. In reality, this player expresses a dilemma faced by many others in that he understands that masking pain will not cure the clinical problem, but the decision not to accept a painkilling injection may lead, at best, to his temporary omission from the team and, at worst, to him being stigmatized as though he 'does not want it enough'. Thus, when asked whether players were able to make these decisions for themselves, the same player, as if to underscore his own attitude to playing with pain, said: 'Other players wouldn't actually play, they wouldn't carry injuries. They'd just say "no". *But they could play if they really wanted to.*'

There are considerable pressures on players to play with pain and injury: the evidence suggests that most are willing to conceal or mask an injury in order to remain in the starting line-up, even if this means having a painkilling injection. Former Newcastle United player Alan Gowling (1974: 208) suggests that:

> the club may want the [injured] player to play so desperately that they put pressure on the player to play. This pressure is generally not direct, but the player is placed in such a position that to refuse to play could have awkward repercussions in the future, or he may be made to feel that he is letting the lads down (a cardinal sin!).

However, as previously stated, one cannot explain these pressures in terms of 'external factors' alone, for there are also considerable pressures on players to reinforce their masculine identities. Throughout this discussion players have suggested that to appear to be unwilling to play with pain may lead their manager (physiotherapist or playing colleagues) to accuse them of being 'soft', of having 'no heart', of 'not really wanting it', or of being 'a poofter'. In the light of these comments, one might suggest that it is important that players develop 'appropriate' attitudes not only towards their occupation in general, but also towards their own bodies (see Messner 1990, 1992).

The importance of developing a 'good attitude' is impressed on young players from the moment they have contact with the coaching staff at clubs. This point is confirmed by the ethnographic research of Parker (1996a) who, whilst avoiding a direct discussion of the ways in which youth trainees cope with injury, highlights the significance of apprentice footballers being seen to possess or to develop a 'good professional attitude'. Many players in this study spoke of the differences between being established (that is, a first team regular) and of being young and inexperienced. The recurring suggestion is that young players are vulnerable to influence from significant others to a much greater degree than established players. This is not surprising. Further to this, young players are not only vulnerable, but are placed in positions whereby the act of not agreeing with advice would make them appear to others as disrespectful, as though they were not prepared to listen and, also, that they did not really *want* it enough. These types of exchanges are used as evidence by managers and youth coaches to draw conclusions with regard to the attitudes of young players in particular. Consequently, many players referred to situations earlier in their careers when they had accepted the advice of others unquestioningly. A former Premiership player, who had been advised to continue playing until the end of the season before undergoing an operation on his cartilage, said that at that time he did not have any doubts about whether he should have played on. He said: 'I was only sort of nineteen or twenty years old. I think at that stage you are pretty much guided by what your physio says to you ... whatever the physio says, you take as gospel.' The same player then referred to a situation in which he had been offered an injection in order to play. He responded to the question of whether or not he was happy to have a painkilling injection in the following way:

> If it got me through a game I'd go ahead and do it. As I say, at that time in my career, I just wanted to play and, if you are a young player you are pretty much guided by the physio. If he says take this tablet, you go ahead and take it. If they say we think you should do this, the players will do it.

Players describe individually different circumstances in which they respond to pain and injury; even so it is clear that the responses of players to pain are predictable on the basis of group membership (that is, as professional footballers), and that the *meanings* ascribed to injury are shared to greater or lesser degrees by all players as an aspect of the culture of football. In the process of interpreting what it means to be injured, players do not invent meanings, but rather are provided with meanings generated via direct experience or in the course of interaction among other players; in short, the inculcation of a 'good attitude' is not a passive social process. It is the organization of social relationships in football clubs which sustains, enforces, and reinforces conformity to particular attitudes to playing with pain and risking injury.

## Conclusion

A hallmark of traditional (Fordist) employment relations that held sway for much of the twentieth century was a bargain between the workers and employers in which workers traded loyalty and hard work for job security (Grint 2005). In professional football, the labour market has always been uncertain and, unlike conditions of work located in working-class industrial and manual occupations, players work hard and dutifully because of a pressing need to evince a dedication to an appropriate work ethic in the culture of professional football. Even when they have been left out of the starting line-up for a forthcoming match, there continues to be a critical need for players to display professionalism to their work. Thus, working without protest and with dedication – in training and in reserve team games – retains relevance for several reasons: because of a player's fear of job loss, because of the potential for negative references in the medium to long term, and because, in this highly contingent, 'masculinized' occupation, many believe that by reacting to the perceived indignity of rejection with renewed displays of hard work, players confirm in their minds and in those of their contemporaries that they are worthy of the status of professional footballer. A number of these points will be examined in detail in the chapters which follow.

This chapter has attempted to convey the significance and meaning invested in what, in professional football, is regarded as a 'good attitude'. The central difficulties of this task have been brought about by the ambiguous nature of the term and by the variety of ways in which the term is applied by coaches, managers and players in the context of football clubs. The respective attitudes and values of the players reflect the informal cultural norms, which emphasize the values of 'masculinity, active participation and victory' (Taylor 1970). These may guide behaviour and feelings and are an aspect of the taken for granted perspective in terms of how the game ought to be played and of how players are expected to conduct themselves. Failure to conform to the values can, for young players in particular, threaten career prospects, and for all players there may be unintended consequences in terms of status within the club. These values are embedded in professional football culture and for players they are unavoidable. In a number of instances, the internalization and belief in these values may help motivate players to confront risky circumstances (for example playing in pain and when injured) and while some players may experience fear or even anger, conformity to the informal but institutionalized norms may prevent them from displaying the real emotions they experience. In this manner, players reinforce the existing values, norms and power relations in professional football and maintain their hard-won status and sense of self among teammates, coaches and managers.

# Chapter 3

# Uncertainty and football injuries

Alan Mullery celebrated his thirtieth birthday on 23 November 1971. Not that he had anything to celebrate. By then he'd been out of action for a whole month. But long before that he'd obviously been struggling ... He'd been playing all season with stomach pains. He'd hoped he could play it out, that the pains would just fade away, but they hadn't. He'd been using a corset for some time ... This had helped slightly at first, but then the pains had grown worse ...

For several weeks he had deep heat treatment twice a day at the ground. The diagnosis was strained pelvic muscles. An X-ray had shown no break. There was no damage whatsoever to be seen. It was the sort of injury footballers hate most – where the cause isn't known, the injury can't be seen and there is no known time scale of treatment.

(Davies 1996: 168)

This extract describes a common problem for all professional footballers who sustain injuries. The particular injury discussed above is described as being the kind which nearly all players hate most. The precise reason why Alan Mullery's circumstances are described in such severe terms is the number of *uncertainties* which are bound up in this situation which present problems both to him and to significant others. For example, if Mullery is uncertain how long the injury will take to heal, he cannot predict in advance how many games he will be likely to miss. The ramifications of these types of uncertainty are manifold, but perhaps the principal consequence is that the footballer will be out of the 'action' (Goffman 1967). Furthermore, when footballers become injured in the course of playing, their daily activities alter and this is associated with the generation of a mixture of emotions and feelings, common among which are anxiety, frustration, guilt, anger, embarrassment and depression (Roderick *et al.* 2000; Young *et al.* 1994). These feelings may arise to varying degrees in distinct social contexts, for instance in different clubs, at different times in the season and at different stages in the player's career, yet all stem from adjustments in relations among players and managers, coaches, physiotherapists and other team members.

It is clear from the above quote and from the interviews conducted for this study that players fear becoming injured. Their fears are explainable in part as the result of the generation of a number of uncertainties. Thus, incurring a *disabling* injury has a number of well understood *meanings* for players. For example, an injury might mean that they will lose their place in the team and they may not be certain of regaining their position once the injury has recovered. They may fear that if the injury is severe and requires a long period of treatment and rehabilitation, the manager will replace them permanently, either by buying another player or by promoting a less established player from the reserves. Moreover, players may not be certain that the injury has been correctly diagnosed by the club's physiotherapist or doctor, or may not possess a precise understanding of how long recovery to full fitness will take. They may also fear the reaction of the manager and those of other players to their status as an injured player (Roderick *et al.* 2000; Young *et al.* 1994). Players fear being stigmatized as malingerers or, more bluntly, as 'soft'. And finally, although this list is not exhaustive, there may even exist uncertainties in terms of assurances regarding future contracts at their present club and potential clubs. Players become familiar with, and gain an understanding of, these fears and uncertainties in the course of their careers (especially their early careers), as they observe the constraints within which other, more established players are bound up and they talk to others about the consequences which may result from particular incidents. Before long, however, as players commence their professional careers, they experience at first hand the realities of being labelled 'injured'; it is these early insights and dealings with medical staff which provide the benchmarks for future encounters.

In the sociology of medicine literature, the concept of uncertainty has long been analysed as a central feature of day-to-day medical work, especially as it relates to the diagnosis and prognosis of a health problem (Adamson 1997; Calnan 1984; Davis 1960; Fox 1988; Roth 1963). Being ill and requiring medical treatment impacts on the lives of people in a multiplicity of ways and generates numerous types of uncertainties. Like professional footballers, many other people debate inwardly about what the effects of sickness will be for them in terms of, for example, their employment potential and the way in which others will treat them (Adamson 1997; Conrad 1987). These aspects of uncertainty are central in relation to professional football as well. Thus, the objects of this chapter are first to identify the myriad uncertainties experienced by players in the context of their occupation and, second, to understand the ways in which they try to cope during these indeterminate periods of time.

## The sociology of uncertainty

There are a number of categories of medical uncertainty found in the sociological literature (Conrad 1987). In the first instance there exists the uncertainty of sensing that something unusual is going on. For example, a person may be suffering from soreness or a vague discomfort. In some cases, an attempt to deal with this uncertainty may lead one to seek out medical advice immediately; however, it is well established that responses to pain vary according to cultural experiences (Annandale 2003). In order to understand how people come to consider themselves ill when they feel pain or discomfort, one must isolate some of the critical cultural *meanings* revolving round the perception of pain (Freidson 1970). The second category of uncertainty is referred to as medical or clinical uncertainty. In short, this uncertainty derives from medical encounters where the doctors or other medical personnel are unable to tell the patient what is causing the discomfort and, therefore, are unable to formulate a precise diagnosis (Calnan 1984). The third category of uncertainty is broad and stems from the diagnosis itself. Among other titles, it has come to be known as 'existential uncertainty' (Adamson 1997) and is central to the patient's experience of their medical problem. This term refers to a privately experienced awareness by patients that their future is undetermined. The unpredictable trajectories of many illnesses lead patients to ponder what it means to have a particular illness. Will they still be able to work? Will they need to change their lives? How will others treat them?

Unlike most members of the public (with some obvious exceptions including doctors, nurses, hospital staff), professional footballers come into contact with medically trained personnel each working day at the football club, usually the physiotherapist. The club physiotherapist is a central member of the non-playing staff who attends to the medical requirements of each player as necessary. If the physiotherapist is unable to make an accurate diagnosis, or if initial treatment proves insufficient, or if a player requires surgery or specialist treatment, the physiotherapist may refer the player on to the club doctor and then a sports medicine specialist. Most injuries sustained by players are examined in the first instance by the club physiotherapist, for they take care of the primary workplace health needs of players. Many of these injuries are non-serious (in that they cause only temporary discomfort) and occur during a match or training session. If the injury restricts mobility or is disabling, the affected area will receive medical attention almost immediately or, at least, come to the notice of the club physiotherapist. There is no sense of waiting to see what happens, that is, whether the pain or discomfort might subside, as might be the case with most other people. For *all* people, however, believing oneself to be ill (or injured in the case of players) does not in itself lead to the use of available medical services (Freidson 1970).

Some injuries, such as that reported in the extract on Alan Mullery, are not visible upon inspection and the cause cannot be immediately identified. Injuries of this nature can vary in seriousness and may be painful. It may be the case that a player is able to perform for a period of time with an injury of this type without a significant restriction either to speed or mobility and, despite experiencing discomfort, they may choose to *conceal* the injury from significant others. An established Division Two (i) player, for example, suggested that

> with experience, you can play a different type of game according to your limitations. If you are not 100 per cent fit or you've got a sore groin then you are maybe not going to be doing the closing down, the work rate. You are going

to be dropping off, looking for loose balls, that kind of thing, rather than going in to win balls. You play a different kind of game.

As the pain grows worse (as was the case with Alan Mullery) there comes a time when the player either cannot cope with the pain any more, or the injury becomes too disabling for the player to continue effectively. Consequently, there remains no other course of action other than to inform the physiotherapist of the problem. An inexperienced Division Two (i) player, who had suffered problems with the left side of his groin, described why he continued to play as follows:

> Player: I started feeling my groin on the left-hand side, and I started feeling it about the October time and I kept on playing with it, and eventually round about Christmas, I went to see the physiotherapist.
> MR: So you played through the pain then?
> Player: Yes, I played through it for quite some time without telling anyone.
> MR: How did you mask the pain at that time?
> Player: It's a funny thing the hernia. You can get through games, but you don't really give it your all. You can't stretch for certain balls, that sort of thing, but you can definitely get through it. First of all I didn't say anything and then it got worse and I gradually told people.
> MR: Why didn't you tell anyone straight away?
> Player: Why? Because I wanted to stay in the team. It's as straightforward as that.

This example was typical of the response of players who developed a problem, such as a groin strain, which did not restricted mobility significantly in the initial stages, or was not observed at first hand. Many players spoke of their reluctance to seek medical advice in the first instance (that is, when sensing something was wrong) in part because of what an injury could *mean* for them. These incidents provide model examples of the first type of uncertainty referred to in the sociology of medicine literature.

The second type of uncertainty, medical or clinical uncertainty, can arise when neither the player nor the physiotherapist, nor sometimes the club doctor, are sure of what is going on (Calnan 1984). Having sought the attention of the physiotherapist, players may suffer further anxieties about the injury and, centrally, whether or how long they will be *unfit for selection* in the team. The impact of this type of uncertainty can end, or be reduced, when the player is diagnosed as having a particular injury. In this connection, one veteran player, who had played in all four divisions, spoke of the period between 'breaking down' and being diagnosed in the following way:

> The worse thing is, say you have an operation and you get back to fitness, and get back out playing and training and you break down. You get yourself into all that condition and then straight after, when you know things are

wrong, that is the worst time. From breaking down until finding out why you've broken down, you are just in limbo. I have gone and had a real drink at this time, but as soon as I knew what was happening or whatever operation I needed, I could sort of focus myself again and get back at it. But it's when nobody knows what's going on, that's the worst time.

In many cases in which physiotherapists are made aware of problems, that is, discomfort or pain, players are expected to play on (during training or matches) to 'see how they get on'. In short, players are expected to test out their injury in the hope that in time, the pain will settle down, fade away and disappear. This type of normative behaviour is a more common constraint for younger, less established players. However, unless they are too severely disabled, all players are constrained to keep on playing with pain and in discomfort – as an aspect of displaying an appropriate 'attitude' to their work. It is only when the pain develops and significantly restricts mobility that a physiotherapist will remove players from training. The club physiotherapist, the club doctor and the players themselves are familiar with many injuries experienced in the course of playing. Even so, there are times when a diagnosis is not straightforward and an uncertain period ensues.

A third type of uncertainty can arise out of the diagnosis itself. While there may be a certain amount of relief for players at finding out what the problem is, they may at this time experience a new set of uncertainties. In sociological literature, these are known as 'existential uncertainties' (Adamson 1997) and they refer to an individual player's awareness that his future (at least in the short term) is undetermined. Unlike clinical uncertainties which are experienced by medical personnel as well as the player and significant others, existential uncertainties are experienced privately and are an aspect of the injury experience. It is clear that players dwell on considerations concerning what the injury *means* in terms of their future playing career. How long will the injury take to recover and when will the player be fit for selection? Will the injury heal and the body be as fit and strong as before? Is the physiotherapist positive he has diagnosed the problem correctly? How will the manager and players treat the unfit player whilst he is recovering? Will the manager buy a replacement? Invariably these questions do not have simple or immediate answers for players; the uncertainties endure and are incorporated into, and become a central aspect of, the experience of being injured. Pat Nevin (Nevin and Sik 1998: 25), the former Chelsea, Everton and Scottish international player, summarized this point as follows:

So all the players have this fear that they'll be seen as malingering. The manager is giving out signals that he believes it, and if you've been bought by a club, particularly if it has been for a lot of money, you're worried that the fans are going to start thinking it too ... In other words, it's a hotbed of paranoias. But on top of all that, way on top of everything else, whatever injury you've got – and it doesn't matter whether it's something like a medial-ligament strain, which everyone knows takes four weeks to heal, or something more serious, which is less easy to attach a timescale to – you always end up wondering whether you'll *ever* be the same again.

Sociologically speaking, what is most interesting about uncertainty in all the forms identified is how players manage it. The question of how players manage and deal with their injuries has been addressed by a number of sociologists. Nixon (1992, 1993), for example, employs a 'social network analysis' approach to examine the contexts that entrap elite athletes and constrain the range of alternative courses of action that they perceive are available to them. Applying a pro-feminist approach, Messner (1992), Sabo and Panepinto (1990) and Young *et al.* (1994) examine the risks of playing with pain and injury in terms of the way in which it leads to the validation of masculine and athletic identities. All of these studies focus on the manner in which athletes normalize (Albert 1999; Curry 1993), rationalize and legitimize their behaviour. They seek, that is, to understand the strategies developed by athletes in their attempts, in both the short and long term (Young *et al.* 1994) to restore what constitute, for them, compromised and diminishing notions of self. The following discussion attempts to examine the ways in which professional footballers construct a variety of strategies to deal practically with the uncertainties of injury.

## Coping with injury

Footballers conceive of their injuries largely in terms of 'putting in time' (Roth 1963) rather than in terms of the changes which occur physically. Thus, when discussing their injuries, players tend to point out how long they were out for and how many matches they had missed by way of summarizing what, medically speaking, might otherwise be understood as a complex sequence of physiological events. A young Division One (i) goalkeeper described the emphasis which is placed on time and in most cases the general urgency to return players to the first team. This urgency is expressed not only by individual players, but by all people who are connected with the 'health' of team members (Waddington *et al.* 1999). In the following example, the goalkeeper refers to the necessity to take advice from an appropriate surgeon and the differences such consultations can make:

> I think it does [make a difference] if you can get to see the right specialist, I mean some of the specialists who are around are not particularly sports orientated. They are specialists in that they treat Joe Bloggs who goes in, who's broken his ankle or leg. They are not particularly geared to dealing with sportspeople who really have got to get in, get it done and get back as quickly as possible.

The point being made is that specialists who are not familiar with the time-related constraints of professional sport cultures are perceived as not being able to meet the particular needs of footballers. The above player continues, asserting that:

> [some specialists] are on a different timetable and their knowledge is not quite as much at the cutting edge as it could be. I mean, there's a guy who comes away with the Welsh squad based in Cardiff who's set up a sports injury clinic and he's completely aimed at sportspeople. That's proved really successful for him and he's got a lot of respect. A lot of top players go to him and have treatment because they know he's right at the cutting edge of what can be achieved. I mean, if you get the wrong specialist it can take twice as long as it would with the right specialist, in terms of getting back. I mean, we've had problems with people at the club where specialists have stapled hernias and things like that and the staples have come undone, or where they just don't seem to have the appreciation of this is a sportsperson who's not going to be able to muddle through for a year and wait for it to heal properly. If they make a mess of it then the chances are that he's going to be coming back in to have it done again.

The central point is that medical specialists who deal with professional footballers require a heightened awareness of timing in order to gain players' confidence. This way of thinking is not born out of ignorance, but is a consequence of the culturally bound social situation in which players are tied. Thus, among the first concerns of all injured players when examined by club physiotherapists is to gain an indication of how long the injury will take to recover and when they will be fit for selection in the first team. In terms of many soft tissue injuries, players, physiotherapists and managers have a clear understanding of how long the player will take to recover.

Specific understandings of time periods are gained through experience and by discussions with older players or players who have experienced similar injuries. One finds that for many common injuries, for example, dead legs, strained muscles and sprained joints, players have a clear conception of how long it should be before they are ready to play again. A Division One player suggested that

> it's just experience, that's just a matter of knowing your own body, right, because you just naturally pick up those injuries through the career. You've had them before and you know how serious it is and how long it'll take.

Discussions among injured and fit players and physiotherapists regularly revolve round issues concerning how long they will be 'out', how long it will be before they can play again, how long it will be before they can jog or kick or start training with the squad. This discourse leads players to become increasingly familiar with particular types of recurring injuries; one might even propose that some older players may see themselves, or may be viewed by others, as 'mini-experts' (Waddington and Walker 1991). Their expertise is connected in a narrow sense to a developed awareness of time, rather than an understanding of, first, the way in which one's body repairs any damage or, second, appropriate medical practices.

As a consequence, players are able to construct particular understandings of certain injuries. As they become increasingly familiar with specific injuries, they are able to generate *timetables* (Roth 1963) concerning when certain events should occur; for example, when they will start to jog, sprint, begin ball work and tackling, etc. In other words, players, in an effort to define when certain things should happen to them, develop time-related benchmarks which mark the passage to fitness. These benchmarks serve to focus the minds of injured players and make them aware of whether they are ahead of, or behind, the socially constructed timetable. Players develop timetables in part as a method of gauging their own progress. Thus, thinking in terms of time-related benchmarks may assist a player's capability of predicting and controlling their immediate futures and leads, therefore, to a reduction of uncertainty.

To summarize this general point so far, one way in which all players tend to cope with the uncertainties generated when injured is to structure the time period through which uncertain events occur. This general principle applies to many aspects of the experience of injury for players. Even when the physiotherapist cannot be precise in terms of forecasting significant future dates, players, usually in combination with physiotherapists, will attempt to structure the immediate passage of time by generating short-term time-related goals. More serious or complex injuries are also understood in terms of blocks of time. As a consequence, the period of time spent receiving treatment and then rehabilitating from injury may become psychologically more manageable.

## The timing of surgery

Within professional football clubs, encounters between players and club physiotherapists tend to be quite prolonged and highly personalized, by comparison with nearly all doctor–patient relationships. For the most part injured players are in contact with the club physiotherapist(s) daily; their progress is assessed and monitored and is a source of constant discussion. It is during these 'focused encounters' (Goffman 1961) that players and physiotherapists negotiate and work out the details of treatment and rehabilitation timetables. As treatment progresses, both players and physiotherapists are better able to assess the speed of recovery and, thus, to reinterpret timetable benchmarks (Roth 1963). The ability of players to negotiate with physiotherapists about their treatment and to step up the intensity of their rehabilitation is one of the more striking and distinctive features of this 'doctor–patient' relationship. Taken as a whole, one might describe the injury 'career' as a bargaining process (Roth 1962) in which players, especially first team members, have a significant involvement in decision-making processes. While the ability of patients to negotiate with doctors should not be understated, many sociological examinations of medical relationships – between doctors and patients – argue that power resides with doctors (Coburn and Willis 2003). There exists a different balance of power among the social relations within football clubs. It is not unusual for players to discuss future pathways with medical staff or to be left with a choice of options in terms of the way their injury will be treated, some of which may involve a level of personal risk. This pattern of negotiation is conspicuously evident during discussions concerning the timing of surgery.

Compared with what might be termed 'normal' timetabling of surgery, the scheduling of operations for football players might be said to be relatively distinct. This distinctiveness is rooted in the fact that the people involved in organizing and deciding on the timing of surgery have different interests tied in with this decision-making process. In the first instance their interests may not necessarily be related to the immediate solution of the clinical problem or the long-term health of players. It is common practice for players and medical staff to have in mind a specific date to work towards which corresponds to an important match or, preferably, the close season. So, an operation might be postponed until the end of the season in order that the player can continue playing – carrying the injury – or he may request immediate surgery in order to be fit for a forthcoming match. In this way, players in part attempt to manage the uncertainties associated with injury. Some examples may help to illustrate this point.

An experienced former England international player stated that he had had no fewer than sixteen operations in his playing career and that, as is common in professional football, he had continued playing with most of these injuries and had postponed the surgery – to his knees, groin and shoulder – in each case until the close season. He explains:

> the injuries I was carrying weren't really interfering totally with my game ... so with my shoulder injury it was more painful at nights. Trying to sleep at night it had been very painful but I was getting through games with it.

The player said that the decision to *get through games* in this manner was left to him and that he was happy to continue; there was, he said, always an incentive to keep playing as the club was usually competing for a place in European competitions for the following season, or was doing well in cup competitions. For each of these injuries then the player, in conjunction with club medical staff, was able to put off the surgery and, if only in the short term, alleviate any uncertainties which may have been generated. A Division Two (i) player suggested that managers are keen for, and put pressure on, players to agree to delay necessary surgery. He said: 'The favourite thing for a manager is for players to get to the end of the season and then do the operation in the summer break. That's all that managers ideally want to happen.'

Alternatively, players and medical staff may decide that in specific circumstances – perhaps with an important cup match approaching, or maybe with the prospect of a relegation battle to come, or even sometimes in the early stages of a season – it is more appropriate either to undergo surgery immediately or for it to be timed for a break between important games. For example, a Division Two (i) defender, who had been taking anti-inflammatories and 'resting' rather than training in order to get through games for most of this season, described the reason he decided to press for an operation to his groin:

> Well, because we were having this FA Cup run, I thought to myself, if I don't get something done about it [the groin] soon, it might get to the point where I might not be able to play in the bigger games later on in the cup run. So I made the decision to go and get it done at that particular time [after the quarter-final] so it would allow me to get back for the semi-final game.

Describing a similar set of circumstances, another experienced Premiership player suggested that having a target date to aim for helped to focus his mind and gave him a goal to work towards. He said:

> I went over on my knee, and I thought I'd completely wrecked it ... when they diagnosed everything they said that I'd been lucky ... I went in [to hospital] on the Monday, Tuesday for an op, and I was back playing within two and half weeks so it was quite pleasing really to play in the Cup Final. I think the Cup Final had a bearing on it as well because that gave me more of a compulsive attitude to want to be fit for that.

The examples above typify the central point being made, namely that whether surgery is delayed until the end of the season or is timed in accordance with significant forthcoming cup or league matches, the uppermost consideration of players, managers and medical staff concerns availability to play, rather than the healing of the clinical problem and the player's long-term health. The timing of surgery in this fashion enables players to play – therefore reinforcing their sense of self and feelings of being wanted – yet, they are often in favour of these options as a way of offsetting, at least in the short term, the uncertainties associated with the injury they are carrying.

The general assumption noted at the beginning of this section is that relations between doctors and patients in NHS hospitals and general practice are 'asymmetrical' (Freidson 1970). Whilst there may be some similarities between the pressures footballers are able to exert on club doctors in terms of bargaining over the nature of treatment and the bargaining powers of 'ordinary' patients, players appear on the face of things to have much greater latitude in negotiating clinical decisions and treatment timetables. The process of negotiation and the decisions arrived at can only be understood against a backcloth of cultural expectations and assumptions with regard to the behaviour of players, managers and club medical staff. The patterns of behaviour identified may be more adequately understood if one thinks in terms of a culturally bound time clock which comes to be internalized by players, club physiotherapists and doctors (Waddington *et al.* 1999) and leads them in specific contexts to behave in 'appropriate' ways. These strategies – the construction of treatment and rehabilitation timetables and the timing of surgery – might be considered among the principal means by which players cope with the uncertainties associated with injury.

## Second opinions

The discussion thus far, which has focused on the way in which players cope with and manage these uncertainties, has been underpinned by conceptions of *time*. For instance, injured players must be seen to be doing everything possible to get back to 'fitness' in the shortest feasible time; and a central characteristic of the culture of football, as it relates to medical practice, concerns a strong and ever- present constraint for club physiotherapists and doctors to 'get players fit yesterday' (Waddington *et al.* 1999). All people involved in the management of injury in professional football are acutely aware of this constraint. Even so, there is a clear pattern evident in which, from time to time, players lose trust in their club physiotherapists. Furthermore it is clear that some club physiotherapists are stigmatized by players in terms of their competence, while others gain reputations in relation to diagnosing particular types of injuries – usually more complex injuries – observing relevant symptoms and treating clinical problems in a medically effective manner. A clear example of this was described by one Premiership player whose knee injury had 'broken down' a number of times. He said:

> I got to the stage where the physio was looking at me, he didn't know really what to do and I was fed up being round the club. People were looking at me as if to say 'oh he's broke down again' and so I just went away. I went back to the old physio I used to know at [my previous club] who was top class and I stayed away from the club for about six or seven weeks and I just solely worked with him. The physio at this club doesn't know that, I spoke to the manager about it ... and he sort of like said, 'Okay, I know the score with the physio here, go and get yourself sorted out.'

The player in question, who had played for a number of teams in all four divisions, described also how he lost trust with the expertise of his club physiotherapist – who was not qualified to a chartered standard – and their relationship had 'broken down' too, which had motivated him to seek alternative advice.

Relations between players and club physiotherapists can be highly personalized. Players whether injured or fit have contact with their club physiotherapists almost every day. Over time physiotherapists become familiar with most players at the club and conversely, players get to know the mannerisms and working practices of their physiotherapists. Like many other occupational settings where employees work closely with one another, there are pressures, especially on players, to be seen to be 'good patients' when injured; in other words, to co-operate with the demands and expectations of the physiotherapist in deed if not in thought. While some players have complete confidence in their club physiotherapist, others have suggested, some quite emphatically, that they do not trust their club physiotherapist to provide adequate medical support. Where this is the case and players are *uncertain* whether they will receive accurate diagnoses and rehabilitation programmes, they have tended to seek *second opinions*. In order not to undermine the authority of their club physiotherapist, or to be seen as 'bad patients', players tend to seek the advice of others without informing their club physiotherapist of their intention to do so.

When asked about whether they would seek a second opinion, many players suggested that it is not a course of action with which they felt comfortable. Most players said they felt guilty about going behind the 'back of the club' and that they felt they were, in some sense or other, letting their club physiotherapist down. That said, every player interviewed had either sought a second opinion or knew other players who had. Seeking second opinions and receiving treatment outside the club is a very common pattern of behaviour in professional football. Players are legally able to seek second opinions about, and treatment for, injuries. However, players who have sought treatment outside their clubs have experienced reprisals in terms of, for example, a distinct lack of 'equal treatment' thereafter. Seeking advice and treatment outside the club can generate tension and unpleasantness in the relationship between players and the club physiotherapist and/or doctor, which players attempt to avoid.

A veteran Division Two player described the following circumstances by way of explaining his decision to seek a second opinion:

> When I moved up to [a Division Two club] they had big problems. They had a guy who had really done no more than a first aid course, and so in terms of diagnosing what was actually wrong with people it was a massive problem. So many times the diagnosis was wrong and they would then be having a certain type of treatment or were told to rest, when clearly it was an operation that was needed to actually solve the problem. That became a difficult situation.

An experienced Premiership player, who knew colleagues who sought the assistance of other physiotherapists, suggested that at the beginning of his career a second opinion was not something that he would have considered. Now, with more than six years' experience, he would seek a second opinion if he did not 'have the confidence of the person who was in charge'; for him then, it was a matter of trust. This point was stressed most vividly by one experienced player who often sought outside assistance. When asked generally about meeting and getting to know physiotherapists at new clubs, he responded in the following way:

> You've got like your old school physios and you've got your physios that are up-together and who know what the score is and ... it's just basically trying to suss the person out. I mean, I've been lucky really because I've been to a good physio in my career and I know what's right and what's wrong in a way. I take him as a benchmark and it's a case of ... I often come here and then go back to the physio at [my previous club] and see him. He's okay, he takes me on, and he'll have a look at me, and I take more notice of what he says to me ... because I think half the battle is, if you trust the physio and he puts a bit of faith in your mind, you're halfway there.

The interview data indicate that players sought medical assistance from a variety of people whom they perceived as trustworthy and competent. The most common people among those to whom players turned – as the previous quote indicates – were physiotherapists from previous clubs.

A Division Three player described another common pattern of behaviour. When asked whether he knew of players who had sought second opinions without the consent of club physiotherapists, he replied that: 'A lot of players, who don't live near the club, but who live where they've been at clubs before, and they know the physio at that club, they would tend to go back to the physio that they know.' Not all players retain contacts with previous physiotherapists in this manner. Chartered physiotherapists who worked in private practices had treated a small number of players. Other contacts with chartered physiotherapists were of a more 'accidental' nature. For example, a Division One (i) goalkeeper, who was undertaking a part-time degree course, had attended a number of guest lectures given by a chartered physiotherapist who worked full time in another sport, with whom he had retained contact. Another experienced player said that when dropping off and picking up his child from school, he had become friendly with a mother who worked as a physiotherapist in a local NHS hospital. He said he often described his injuries to her – including the diagnosis of the club physiotherapist, who was not qualified to a chartered level – and the treatment he was receiving, and they would then discuss both the diagnosis and the rehabilitation programme. It was not, he claimed, that he did not trust the club physiotherapist; he wanted merely to ensure that he was not 'wasting time'. There are enough examples described in the interviews to conclude that seeking second opinions is a common pattern of behaviour among professional footballers. Moreover, players seek both advice and treatment and *conceal* this fact from their club physiotherapists.

In the view of the players, the underlying reason for this type of deception is straightforward. One experienced player, when asked about why players sought second opinions without informing club physiotherapists, responded by suggesting that players 'don't want to upset anyone'. Seeking medical advice outside the club is often viewed within the club as implying criticism of the club's facilities and medical personnel. Further to this, players do not want to be considered by physiotherapists, or even more managers, as *troublemakers*: that is, people who are not willing to listen, to take advice or to co-operate. Players like to be thought of as *good pros* who display 'good attitudes' to their work. A central aspect of a 'good attitude' in professional football is to appear to be respectful and to be prepared to listen. Young players learn that such attitudes extend not only to senior players and the management team but also to club medical staff. As a consequence, many players referred to situations in which, as inexperienced players, they had accepted unquestioningly the advice of physiotherapists and doctors – although many probably did not realize that alternatives existed – and had come to consider this way of behaving as appropriate, respectful and in their best interests. The balance of power among players, managers and club medical staff cannot be understood in economic terms alone, for explanations of why players come to conceal certain information from their club physiotherapists involve understanding an *emotional* dimension of this network of power relationships. In short, players feel a degree of guilt about not trusting their club physiotherapists. All the same, it is clear that any number of emotions generated are offset by the need for players to take the initiative – to take control for themselves – and to address any personal uncertainties they may be feeling.

In many of the interviews, players spoke in terms of 'faith' and 'trust' in accounts of medical relationships. It is proposed that these terms have slightly different meanings in professional football from those expressed by patients treated in NHS hospitals and by general practitioners. In the sociological literature concerned with issues of trust in medical encounters, 'good' doctors are perceived as having adept interpersonal skills. They are excellent communicators who 'talk things over' and have an 'ability to listen' (Lupton 1996). From the interviews with professional footballers it is clear that while these skills are not dismissed as irrelevant, they do not appear to be central concerns. Players perceive 'good' physiotherapists and doctors to be those who are concerned with getting them back to 'fitness' as quickly as possible: that is, who understand the time constraints and who minimize injury breakdown. If players lose trust in their club physiotherapists, as seems to be the case from time to time, they may seek to take control of the uncertainties generated by engaging in what is known, in sociological literature, as 'consumerist behaviour' (Lupton 1996), for example, reading up about their injury or consulting with different physiotherapists and doctors. Yet players do not seek out doctors in a manner similar to that of other consumers who exercise choice over, for example, hairdressers or restaurants; instead they are constrained to move covertly back and forth between their present club physiotherapists and other medical personnel whose skills they have sought.

## Conclusion

There are a great number of uncertainties experienced by players when they sustain injuries. These uncertainties vary from one situation to the next and may be related to factors such as the severity, complexity and visibility of the injury, the age and status of the player, the stage in the season and the importance of forthcoming matches, the orientation of managers towards injured players (Waddington *et al.* 1999) and the perceived competence of the physiotherapist. Some of these aspects have been discussed in this chapter. There are clear patterns discernible in the behaviour of players in terms of the ways in which they cope with and manage these uncertainties. These coping strategies – including the construction of treatment timetables, the timing of surgery and seeking second opinions – are considered most interesting sociologically as first they highlight the way players manage the power relationships in which they are bound up, and second they indicate the importance of understanding the emotions which arise out of the injury experience. Of importance also is the way in which conceptions of *time* tend to predominate in the minds not only of players and managers, but also of often highly qualified medical personnel. The time-related orientation of these people towards injuries leads them on many occasions to prioritize the short-term goal of getting players fit for selection for the first team, in spite of the consequences that this course of action may have for players' long-term health.

# Chapter 4

# Injuries, stigma and social identity[1]

From time to time players gain reputations among supporters, journalists and other 'outsiders' as being injury prone. Former England international midfielder Darren Anderton, for example, became known widely as 'Sick Note' because of a string of injuries which interrupted his playing career and which led him to play fewer than one hundred times in five seasons. Whilst this label may appear from the 'outside' as little more than a harmless joke, stigmas such as this have a number of unintended consequences for players. The networks of relationships in which players are bound up at their workplace involve not only associations with supporters but what, for them, are more central interdependencies: that is, relationships with managers, coaches, club physiotherapists and their team mates. It is these people who determine for the most part the extent to which players may be stigmatized, or the perceived magnitude of discrediting events. For players, therefore, stigma results from being identified as flawed, discredited or spoiled (Goffman 1963). The former Scotland international Pat Nevin has explained how injured players are made to feel as though they are, first, faking the full extent of their injury and, second, betraying their team mates:

> It's one of those things about 'the English Game' ... that players *almost always* come back too early. There is certainly a pressure from the clubs and a pressure from the management for them to do so. Liverpool under Shankly was an excellent example of this. Shankly apparently wouldn't talk to you if you were injured – he'd take your injury as a personal affront! It's true, it was no joke. You'd be going through all these personal traumas and fears, and your manager or coach is just making it worse by making you feel like a 'shammer' ...
>
> This has an effect on the player. Whether the feeling is the player's own paranoia or if it comes from the manager in a more calculated way, I don't know – it could be both – but you're made to feel a little bit of a cheat.
>
> (Nevin and Sik 1998: 88; italics in original)

It is clear that a number of fears are generated when players become injured. As has been stated already, the fears of players are complex and explanations of their vulnerabilities are contingent on a number of factors. Among them is a fear that they will be stigmatized as malingerers, or as a bit *soft*, or – to use Nevin's term – as 'cheats'. This fear is the principal focus of this chapter, the objects of which are to examine the ways in which professional footballers become, or perceive themselves as being, discredited and stigmatized by managers, physiotherapists or even other players and to understand how they, as players, contribute to processes of discrediting (Goffman 1963).

One former Division One player said of one of his managers, for example:

> He was a wild man. I think he put players under pressure ... If you didn't want to play because you had an injury then you were soft. You were soft if you didn't want to play. I suppose it could have been a form of emotional blackmail. He was a bit like that.

For other players, their fears are connected with the notion that they are letting down teammates, managers, coaches, supporters, as well as their family. One Premiership player, who during his second game for his new club received a serious knee injury which prevented him from playing for almost a year, clearly felt that, in some ill-defined but very real sense, he had let his new club down; in describing his injury and subsequent lengthy rehabilitation, he continually emphasized – as if to excuse his inability to make any playing contribution to the club – that the injury 'wasn't my fault'. As well as wanting to be seen to be working hard to recover from his long-term injury and in order to compensate for his lack of contribution to the club in terms of 'playing matches', this player undertook the responsibility of representing the club at official functions as often as possible. He 'felt bad' towards the club who had bought him and to the supporters who, he claims, have expectations of new arrivals. He wanted to be seen to be doing something by way of *contributing* to his new club.

Players do not want to be viewed by significant others – particularly by managers – as though, for one reason or other, they are stretching the truth in relation to an injury, and they do not want to be thought of as letting down their teammates. As a consequence players take action to avoid accusations of this nature, accusations which are an aspect of the process of stigmatization. In terms of injury experiences, this action consists primarily of playing through pain and injury, sometimes against their better judgement, as a way of displaying a characteristic which, among members of football clubs, is regarded as a 'good' professional attitude. Thus, playing through pain and ignoring injury is normalized (Curry 1993) and any behaviour which deviates from *the normal* is apt to offend, in Durkheim's (2001) terms, the 'collective sentiments' of other members of the football club. Moreover, the collective sentiments held by players, managers and physiotherapists in relation to injury are reinforced by their highlighting and discrediting of behaviour which, in their terms, is considered deviant. In addition, the daily schedule and routine for injured players in many clubs is often designed to be more demanding than 'normal' training (that is, training for 'fit' players) in terms of physical effort and time, in order to act as a disincentive for players to remain injured longer than necessary or for those who simply want, as it were, 'to step out of the firing line'. A short examination of the way in which the daily routine of players leads them first to recognize their status, albeit a temporary one, as 'non-producers' (Waddington *et al.* 1999) and second to experience a loss of self, is undertaken in this chapter.

## Swinging the lead

Without observable evidence, for example a broken bone, a dislocation or concussion, which indicates a player may be in pain, a club physiotherapist or manager can only know of a player's discomfort via communication with the player. Kotarba (1983: 133) suggests that pain-afflicted people appear quite normal in the absence of an observable disability or illness and remarks that 'secrecy is an essential property of the chronic pain experience'. Moreover, Kotarba (1983) suggests that a pain-afflicted person may be discredited if the 'critical audience' at hand (and in the case of professional football that audience may comprise the manager, coach, club physiotherapist and doctor and other players) has reason to believe that the speaker is falsely claiming pain in order to be relieved of unbearable role expectations. Many of the players who were interviewed for this study referred to incidents where they were simply disbelieved and spoke of circumstances in which other players had 'spun a yarn' or were otherwise accused of 'swinging the lead' in order to excuse themselves from, among other things, lost matches and hard endurance training.

Ideally players want their injuries and reports of discomfort and pain to be believed and viewed by significant others as genuine. They do not want to be considered as complainers, as 'soft' or as though they are not 'up for it' and nearly all players, but particularly younger, less experienced players, are constrained to 'manage the information' (Goffman 1963) they offer about themselves in order to avoid becoming discredited. One example, in which a player complained regularly of pain but was disbelieved, involved the young, inexperienced player on contract with Sunderland Association Football Club, Keiron Brady – referred to previously in Chapter 2. In this respect the point of relevance concerns the statement made by the youth team coach at Sunderland AFC, Malcolm Crosby, who, on viewing the youth player limping during a six-mile run, claimed that he did not believe there was something wrong with his leg. In his witness statement Brady makes the following remarks:

> He [Malcolm Crosby] told me he wasn't going to put up with any more nonsense. He told me that I couldn't stop and to keep going. He then sent the other players off in a different direction and he ran with me along the coast lecturing me about my attitude and telling me I just didn't like hard work.

The youth team manager, Malcolm Crosby, felt that the player – Brady – had an *attitude* problem.

It is clear from the interviews that players, club managers and even physiotherapists, make judgements, as well as medical diagnoses, on other players in relation to injury problems. These assessments may take a *moral* form when the player in question is considered by others to be injury prone, or to have an attitude problem in relation to stamina training, long journeys to away matches or important cup and league matches. These moral judgements are also made in relation to socially constructed *rules* concerning appropriate conduct associated with particular injuries; for example, one rule might be that players are expected to carry and play through 'minor' soft tissue injuries such as pulls and strains. Not playing through an injury of this type and therefore breaking this sub-cultural 'rule' can lead to the player becoming stigmatized (Goffman 1963). Moreover, moral evaluations are often guided by an interpretation of the player's behaviour based on pre-existing knowledge or even prejudice about him, as seems to be the case with the young Sunderland player, Brady. Thus, the moral evaluation of Brady has to do with an a priori interpretation of his past conduct which can render ineffective – as far as his manager and teammates are concerned – any legitimate medical diagnoses of symptoms by club physiotherapists or doctors. Similar cases in which employees have taken their employers to court in relation to, for instance, repetitive strain injuries, have been referred to as 'pilgrimages of pain' (Reid *et al.* 1991; Dodier 1985).

The issue for many players is not always that of managing interaction in which they have already been discredited – although this is clearly an issue for some – but rather to manage and control information in such a way that they avoid *becoming* discredited. In short all players might be thought of as 'discreditable' (Goffman 1963). When experiencing pain or discomfort, players are faced with a dilemma which is encapsulated in a quote from Goffman's (1963: 42) classic study of stigmas: 'To display or not to display; to tell or not to tell; to let on or not to let on; to lie or not to lie; and in each case, to whom, how, when, and where.' So for discreditable players – that is, those who sustain a number of injuries in succession or who experience continual bouts of pain – the problem is not that they must face prejudice against them, but that they must control information among managers and teammates who are prejudiced against players of the kind they can be revealed to be.

All players interviewed said they knew of 'cheats' and malingerers at both current and past clubs, yet predictably none recognized this behaviour in themselves. One Premiership club doctor suggested, in a manner similar to players, that a player under his care who gained a reputation among club staff for being injury prone consequently became the target of backhanded criticism. He said that the teammates of this player 'take the mickey out of him and they get irritated by him and they will start calling him a lazy bastard or whatever'. In fact this club doctor had few complimentary comments to make about this player –

who he said was not typical of the majority of players under his care – as the following quote demonstrates:

> He was a nightmare, but he was always being injured and off with one thing or another. We spent a lot of time and a lot of money trying to get him fit and we never could ... That sort of player was a hypochondriac.

He continued by raising questions concerning, among other things, the player's mental state:

> We have had players like that which, you know, the slightest knock, the slightest pain, they start complaining and saying they can't play. 'I can't play, there's too much pain', or 'It hurts me, I'll do more injury to myself.' You do get that. I can't abide it and find it difficult to understand personally. I think if you've been selected to play at that level [Premiership] then you want to play, you'd be positive, but in fact some of them, it comes from their background I suppose, their upbringing if you want to use those terms ... He was a case in point ... I told two managers, 'This guy is never going to be any good for this club', and even the consultants couldn't find anything wrong with him. He was scoped, examined, MRI scanned, he was everything and we just couldn't find anything wrong with him ... We never actually referred him for psychological help but you sometimes wonder.

Unlike the young Sunderland Association Football Club player Keiron Brady, referred to earlier, the club medical staff in this case could not provide evidence to indicate that this player wasn't a hypochondriac. Thus, the identity of this player is spoiled.

## Joking relationships and player banter

Among the behaviour most commonly described by footballers in relation to the management of injuries is the banter and humour directed at injured players, particularly those players who seem to be injured most frequently. All the interviewees recalled situations where they had joked at the expense of an injured player, or were themselves on the receiving end of jokes concerning their injuries. Joking of this nature – what players considered part and parcel of everyday banter – varies in terms of the time of season or the perceived importance of forthcoming matches, or the degree of severity of injury. A Division Three (i) player who had a long-term knee problem, for example, said when describing his present situation:

> It's quite amusing when players, like, you get the 'Man Friday' shout, which is my usual shout. I just train on Friday. You get, well one player suddenly got

about five different injuries in the space of about five weeks, you know, he got the mickey taken, you know for picking up an injury and for being a 'sick note' and things like this.

Such comments confirm Dodier's (1985) point that passing off remarks as jokes is a way to insinuate suspicion concerning proneness to injury without actually voicing it.

A former Division One (i) player suggested, in a less humorous tone, that 'some players were the butt of jokes [from other players] because of injuries most definitely. Players do not like other players who are constantly injured, they don't like that. They get irritated with them.' A young Division Two (i) player said that when he was injured, other players would jokingly insinuate that he was feigning injury to have a rest. They would say, 'Come on, you're having a laugh, aren't you. It's Monday morning, it's pissing down with rain and you've got a sore hamstring!' He went on to say that certain players at his club 'get slaughtered' during verbal exchanges such as this, especially if they sustain a number of injuries in succession. This type of banter among players is commonplace and appears in many cases to be double-edged. It seems important to understand that despite being couched in humorous and seemingly harmless terms, each joke contains a more serious implicit but generally understood meaning (Collinson 1988, 1992). These jokes may be alternatively recognized as veiled insults which are mediated through ambiguous 'piss-takes' and which imply that the injured player is either lazy or 'soft'. One experienced player echoed sentiments similar to those above in the following way:

> Yeah. There are players, those players get loads of stick for being injured, and the [other] players begin to doubt whether they're genuine injuries, or whether they just don't want to play, and that is definitely something that happens. Players are quick to pick up on things like that. 'Oh he doesn't fancy this trip', or 'it's Christmas' or 'Easter', or 'you've got something on'. We've got a lad at our place ... he's had three or four ankle injuries this year, so he's being called 'glass ankle' things like that, people do get stick for being injured.

Joking and snide remarks often deliver unpalatable messages with a softened impact (Collinson 1988). They are a means by which players, maybe unwittingly, seek to control those among their team perceived as not pulling their weight. The steady stream of cutting remarks experienced by players who are 'slaughtered' operates as a type of social control to minimize perceived malingering. Most players at some time become the target of jokes and banter among team-mates. It was claimed by most players that the banter is not serious. Indeed for some the banter was understood to be a source of team spirit which fostered camaraderie. Even so, sociologically it is clear that it is also a source of fear for players because it raises the threat of them becoming viewed as injury prone and as malingerers. The consequences of this type of banter were described by one former Division One player in some (emotional) detail, although the ways in which he became discredited were, for the most part, unrecognized by him. Even when describing his early career, he recalled the numerous injuries he sustained:

> I went to [my first professional club] and even at a young age I had a lot of soft tissue injuries. I had Achilles injuries, tendon injuries, calf injuries, hamstring injuries, groin injuries, even at an early stage ... All my career is littered with injuries. I have got so many photographs of me lying on the bed having treatment, probably more than actually when I played!

Like many other players interviewed, it is clear that he understood the way in which managers, physiotherapists and significant others develop impressions of players – impressions related in particular to their personalities and characteristics – especially those who are perceived to be injury prone. He stated that he tried to conceal his injuries from managers and physiotherapists:

> I have even pulled calf muscles just jogging and it got to the extent when I was at [a Division Two club] where I didn't like to tell people that I was injured. I got to the stage where I would go and have treatment at the [local] hospital and then come into training the next day. The situation would be, 'Oh [the player] isn't injured again!' I very much wanted to play all the time and when I got injured I wanted to see if I could get over the injuries without telling the manager or physiotherapist ... I tried to cover them up.

He suggested that some managers put pressure on him to play, but that, like most other players interviewed, he put the greatest pressure on himself to be available for selection. He could not seem to stem the injuries he sustained regularly both in matches and training and one manager even said to him, 'Oh, you can't be injured again, it must be all in your head.' In order to avoid this type of discrediting at one club, the player described a ritual he would carry out on a daily basis if necessary:

> I used to come in in the morning and I would go to the toilet and strap my calf up and put tracksuit bottoms on, and then we used to go out training and I would have to try and mask it. Sometimes there were situations where they would say that somebody had to go in goal, so I would go into goal to keep out of the way.

He said that he was ridiculed by teammates and that he could recall doubts being expressed about other players who were injured and whether or not they were 'swinging the lead' but, he continued, 'I would have hoped that they would have seen that I was genuine enough to see that I wanted desperately to get fit'. His desperation to be seen as genuine by significant others – to be seen to possess an appropriate 'attitude' – led him on a number of occasions to play against medical advice and to manufacture circumstances in which he could conceal his injuries. Underpinning his thoughts was a fundamental desire to play, but, further to this desire, the actions he described became more readily understandable, from a sociological standpoint, in terms of strategies to avoid being discredited:

> I was the butt of jokes and I had the mickey taken out of me. They would say, 'Oh you are not injured again!' I remember [a former colleague] saying to me once when I told him I had just pulled a muscle, 'You can't have pulled a muscle.' I said, 'I'm telling you, it has just gone now, my hamstring has just gone'. It was a bloody nightmare to be honest … you have been injured that many times that you don't want people to be saying, 'Oh, he's not injured again.' I would take a chance on playing when I wasn't probably 100 per cent fit. *I felt stigmatized throughout the injuries, that is why I took a chance.*

The joking and banter directed at this player may be viewed by some players in relation to the generation of team morale and high spirits 'among the lads', but for the player himself it had other unacknowledged and unintended effects. In terms of highlighting the subtleties of social control, the player in question, in order to avoid accusations of being soft or a malingerer, had on various occasions concealed his injuries by seeking out treatment at a local NHS hospital, strapped joints in the privacy of the changing room toilets and generally hidden injuries and their effects as best he could from others, even if this meant volunteering to go in goal. The joking and banter might be said to have the effect (or maybe unintended consequence) of social control (Collinson 1988) which leads players to conceal injuries and to play with pain in order not to be considered as having a 'bad attitude'; in short, banter directed at injured players reminds those who are 'fit' of the dangers of being viewed as 'a shammer'. Associated with this point – and a related aspect of football culture – is that players who are unable to play as a result of injury and who can, therefore, make no direct contribution to the team on the field of play, may be seen as being of little value to the club and may be ignored, or otherwise inconvenienced.

## Inconveniencing injured players

The special status of players who are injured and therefore unavailable for selection is expressed in a variety of ways, all of which have the effect of reminding injured players that, for as long as they are injured, they are of little use to the club. Of greater importance in terms of understanding processes of discreditation is the fact that, in most clubs, injured players have a daily routine which is significantly different from – and which is often deliberately designed to be less comfortable than – that of players who are fit. The following quote illustrates what, for injured players, might be taken as an example of a 'normal day':

> You have to report for 9:30 to the physio. Training usually starts at 10:30 for the fit players. You maybe have treatment, ice or something like that depending on what the injury is. We have treatment from 9:30 to 10:30, and then we will do some kind of circuit, upper body circuit or actually on the injury itself and be done for about 12:00. We report back in the afternoon for about 1:00 for some more treatment and then we go home ... We come in earlier and stay later to fit round the first team players. I mean the physio sometimes takes the fit players on sprinting or running sessions, and the injured players will fit round the fit players.

Of course, part of the different routine of injured players is related to the fact that they cannot take part in normal training sessions and that they require physiotherapy or other treatment. However, the different routine for injured players cannot be explained simply in terms of their need for specialist treatment for, in many clubs, the routine is deliberately designed to 'inconvenience' injured players and thus to act as a disincentive to them to remain on the injured list for one day longer than is absolutely necessary. This idea was expressed by a Division Two (i) goalkeeper who suggested that 'it's okay to make it difficult so that players don't want to be injured'. He elaborated on this point by suggesting that:

> I think it's a deliberate policy in one or two clubs to make it difficult in the treatment room and to make life uncomfortable so that players don't see it [being injured] as being an easy option and there are times when some young pros sometimes see it as an easy option when things are going badly. They think, 'Oh, I'll have two weeks here and step out of the firing line.'

One physiotherapist who had worked in two football clubs but who now works in another sport referred to the manner in which players are inconvenienced. To some extent he repeats the point made by the goalkeeper quoted above that players who are being treated are inconvenienced, although while the goalkeeper appears to think this procedure is necessary, the physiotherapist appears to think otherwise. He said:

> I've frequently had it said to me when I've worked at professional soccer clubs: 'Inconvenience the injured player. We don't want them too comfortable in the treatment room, sitting in the warm when the rest are out there in the cold.' There's this paranoia, I never could work it out, I don't know why it really exists.

Asked what this policy of 'inconveniencing' the injured player involved, he replied: 'Get them in earlier for training. Keep them after training has finished so that all of the fit players are going home and they have to stay behind for extra treatment.' A similar idea was expressed by another club physiotherapist who said, 'I think if a player is injured they have to work harder and longer and be inconvenienced.' He explained that he could not tolerate some players 'tossing it off, or taking the piss' and, therefore, injured players were made to 'work their nuts off ... so they'd rather train than be injured'. He added, by way of clarification, that:

> The players that we have to provide extra stimulus for, for want of a better word, have probably got some political thing going on at the club, with the manager or with the boys, or are not in the team basically. They're saying, 'I'm not going to train, I'm going to chuck my hamstring in', and we can't have that. So we don't have that by working them hard when they're injured.

Describing how injured players were 'inconvenienced', he said that 'you have to make it naughty' and added 'I will keep him [the injured player] here until the traffic builds up on the motorway'. Shortly after taking over at Tottenham Hotspur in 1998, George Graham was similarly reported to have introduced a system which involved keeping injured players at the ground until the build-up of traffic at the start of the rush hour on the M25. Reflecting on the changes he made when he was appointed as manager, Graham remarked that, 'I have never accused any player of putting on an injury but what can happen is that the treatment room becomes too comfortable.' He went to make the point that:

> When I arrived, I changed the treatment hours – the last session now finishes at 4 pm. That's just about when the M25 becomes absolutely hellish. It's surprising how many people now manage to get out of the treatment room well ahead of the rush hour.
>
> (*Observer* 12 February 2000)

Not all the players who were interviewed recognized that they were being 'inconvenienced'; some suggested that the daily timetables for injured and recovering players were designed by club physiotherapists with their best interests in mind. One former Premiership player, who retired because of a recurring knee problem, recalled the approach to treatment and rehabilitation of one of his physiotherapists in relation to a policy of deliberately separating fit and unfit players. He said:

> It was just a case of they [injured players] were working that hard, they were in at 9 o'clock, they were out running, they were in the gym after they'd done the running and then in the gym again after lunch. It was just a case of

you didn't see the first team because you were working as hard as you can yourself. I think that is the way to do it because if you've been out a while and then go back and thrust straight back into training with things a hundred miles an hour, you just can't physically keep up with it.

## Playing with injuries

To summarize thus far, the data collected for this study indicate that the vast majority of players are not malingerers. That said, the notion of malingering seems to be part of the mythology of professional football which is reproduced as an aspect of the occupational culture to ensure that players do not shirk. Ingham (1975: 365) suggests that the labelling of non-visible injuries in particular as 'faking' is an aspect of the occupational value of endurance, and goes on to make the point that the unnecessary hardships that athletes endure 'would not be tolerated by workers in other areas of commercial life'.

The commonly held view that injured professional footballers should be inconvenienced expresses a fear that they might feign injury – that is, view a period of injury as an 'easy option' – in order to avoid the rigours of training or playing. The interviews with present and former players suggest that such a fear is for the most part unfounded, for the central value of continuing to play, whenever possible, through pain and injury is also recognized and internalized by the players themselves; indeed, players learn from a relatively young age to 'normalize' (Curry 1993) pain and to accept playing with pain and injury as part of the life of a professional footballer. One player described the situation as follows: 'Players are so desperately keen to get back that ninety per cent of them come back to play long before they have made a full recovery. I am no different … there is desperation to show that you are keen.' One indication of players' willingness to play with injuries came in response to a question in which players were asked how many matches, in a full season, they played without any kind of pain or injury. Many players – and in particular senior players, who had often accumulated many injuries over the years – indicated that they played no more than five or six games in a season entirely free from injury and one senior player said: 'There's not one player goes out to play who's one hundred per cent fit.'

Without exception all players interviewed stated that they could not bear to miss matches and would play with an injury if possible. All players try to play on when injured during matches and both managers and physiotherapists expect players to continue where at all possible. Players admitted that they became impatient during treatment and rehabilitation and often returned to training and matches before they had fully recovered; they hope in part that this keenness to play is viewed by managers as a demonstration of their 'good attitude'. In these respects, the attitudes and behaviour of players reflect the importance attached to *active participation* as a central value in football culture. One physiotherapist, who had been working in the gym with a young player whose knee was injured, graphically illustrated the way in which this central value is brought home to young players in particular. The player had been working hard and had expressed some satisfaction with his gym work. The physiotherapist made it clear to the young player that working in the gym was of little importance:

> I said '[the manager] doesn't mind whether you're absolutely pathetic working in the gym as long as you're out there on a Saturday ... it doesn't matter if [the manager's] got Schwarzenegger working in the gymnasium ... he wants players out there on the pitch.' And the young player thought because he was working hard in the gym he was earning his money. Which is not the case. You earn your money by going out there and playing on the pitch. That's where you earn your money.

Players who had experienced a long-term injury spoke of a form of 'suffering' which develops out of their day-to-day life and is associated with a loss of self-esteem and self-confidence; that is, players who sustain long-term injuries lack the means necessary to support their positive self-image as players. In these situations, players may experience a variety of emotions, including guilt, depression and frustration. Serious injuries may result in a downward spiral in relation to self-image as players encounter diminished control over their daily lives. Some players indicated that, particularly if they were recovering from injury more slowly than had been anticipated, they felt discredited and blamed themselves for failing to meet time and fitness expectations. Other players reported that at some stage in their rehabilitation, the club manager and/or physiotherapist had lost patience with them, or at least had lost their initial sympathy. In addition, players with long-term injuries may experience a great deal of anxiety associated with the loss of their place in the team and the uncertainty surrounding future career prospects. Injury and the loss of their place in the team may also be associated, even in the short term, with financial losses (particularly through the loss of playing bonuses which, especially in lower division clubs, may be an important part of a player's total income) and, outside of the football context, with strained relationships with the player's partner or other family members.

## Suffering in silence? Players' experience of injury

For players with long-term injuries, the social conditions in which they exist contribute to their suffering a loss of self (Charmaz 2003). These social conditions include the way in which treatment and rehabilitation regimes restrict the day-to-day movements and 'free time' of players. Moreover, players begin to feel isolated and they develop, to greater or lesser degrees, a sense that they are becoming a burden both in and around the club and to others at home. These characteristics combine to limit the possibility for players to construct alternative valued self-images and relegate them to a marginal position in relation to the club's central activity. In the following section, patterns of 'suffering' are identified and analysed in terms of the ways in which they combine to produce a loss of self as a result of the player's inability to take part in the one activity which, above all others, sustains their positive self-image.

Badly injured players endure narrow, restricted lives which, for them, contrast sharply with those of their 'fit' counterparts who can contribute directly in terms of playing. Their injuries tend to become the sole focus of their lives as treatment, initial periods of discomfort and disability and the constraints of 'mundane' activities (physiotherapy treatment and rehabilitation exercises) structure and fill their days. Moreover, the tendency for club physiotherapists and managers to discredit players – and to treat them as though they were malingerers – may lead them, in turn, to adopt a more restricted demeanour around the club.

The course of serious injuries is often unpredictable and may foster uncertainty and fear in players. The unpredictability arises from 'grey' or uncertain periods of time in which players undergo and recuperate from operations, or when they attempt to progress too hastily, which is nearly always the case, and the injury breaks down or regresses to some degree. Consequently, players tend to develop *narrow* time frames which consist of good and bad or 'black' days and they may become focused on thoughts of 'just getting through the week'. In addition, players tend to *test* their injury constantly in the hope of detecting signs of improvement. The combination of direct restrictions and physical debility causes many players to experience frustration which may, when considered in light of the restrictive timetables and the lack of involvement for those injured in training and on match days, result in many feeling socially isolated. The tangible (or direct) restrictions on daily life and, consequently, the diminished sense of self which derives from their status as 'non-producers' (Waddington *et al.* 1999), can lead players to develop a sense of isolation from what are for them meaningful networks of social relationships. In short, spending their days on a restrictive treatment and rehabilitation programme is isolating: first, because the injury alone sets the player apart from others; second, because treatment tends to take place in separate locations; and thirdly, because the attention of players focuses on themselves (and their injuries) and they become self-examining and inwardly directed.

All the players interviewed spoke of feeling isolated and lonely during periods rehabilitating from injury. One Premiership player said, 'I've felt quite out on my own really for the last year and I've had some pretty depressing times, but you've just got to get on with it.' Another player from a small Division Three (i) club, who was asked to describe the emotions he felt during rehabilitation, said:

It's the worse thing ever being injured anyway. I'm like a bear with a sore head when I'm injured and that's fact. I just don't enjoy being injured at all. You are not with the lads, you are not playing, or anything like that. When people are saying 'When are you going to be fit?' you want to tell them what they want to hear, so you are always optimistic so they always put that thought in their mind. Then, when you are not, you feel as if you have let everybody down.

Reflecting upon his more serious injuries, one experienced player, who played in all four divisions, spoke of the fact that when other players go out to train, 'you are stuck in the gym doing your straight legs or what have you, and you are just left to yourself. It's a very lonely business to be perfectly truthful.'

The idea that the injured player is, at least for the duration of his injury, of little use to the club may be expressed in a variety of ways. For example, a former First Division player described the scenario at his club which involved the manager ignoring injured players, even when both were present together in the treatment room, in the following way: 'The manager was like any manager in those days. He didn't like you injured. He would ignore you. He would always talk to somebody else.' Perhaps surprisingly, such attitudes are still to be found amongst managers. A Division One (i) player said that some managers 'have a theory that injured players aren't worth spit basically ... You are no use to us if you are injured.' However, some managers were more sympathetic; the same player said that 'some managers always go out of their way to talk to you as an injured player'. One club doctor pointed out that the relationship between the manager and injured players varies from one manager to another: 'I mean it depends a little bit on the manager ... some managers obviously feel very uncomfortable with injured players, don't know what to say to them, feel as if they're being let down in some way.' Many players referred to experiences with managers whose managerial style was summed up by one England international player as 'roll your sleeves up and get on with it ... the old sergeant major jobs'. This player said that his current manager had been both sympathetic and helpful in relation to his injury problems, but that previous managers had been much less sympathetic: 'I am used to someone saying: "Are you not fit yet? What's the matter with you? I want you tomorrow. I want you Wednesday and then I want you Friday. Get your arse in gear."' Another player described the attitude of one of his former managers towards injured players as follows: 'You're not meant to be injured. You should be playing. You get paid to play. He totally ignored you when you were in the treatment room. His attitude was: 'You're no use to me any more.' He added that his present manager had a similar attitude:

My present manager is like that. I've heard him speaking to one of the players. He said: 'You're no use to me now, so what's the point in talking to you and seeing how you are.' I've been injured three weeks now and he's asked me for the first time today how I am, just as I'm getting back to fitness.

A similar point was made by one of the physiotherapists, who said that some managers took the view that: 'At the end of the day, you're a non-producer, as they say, if you're injured. You're not playing Saturday and you're no good to anyone. Some managers put it that way.' From an economic point of view, therefore, the players are the equivalent of *dead money*.

The lack of sympathy which some managers have for injured players may mean that, on occasions, managers may insist on players training even when they are injured. One senior Premiership player said that, following surgery on his knee, he had been advised by his surgeon not to run on hard surfaces before the knee had healed properly, but that his manager insisted that he took a full part in the training programme, which included running on a hard track. The player concerned was the club captain and, he said, the manager insisted that he 'set an example' to the other players.

The social isolation experienced by players seems most obvious in larger clubs, where players are able to 'lose themselves'. Clubs with smaller squads tend to be closer knit with players more intimate with the manager. Furthermore, it is only at a handful of clubs (although the number may be increasing slowly) that medical facilities are situated at the training ground, thus providing a greater opportunity for injured players to have contact with the manager and other players. In the light of the loneliness brought on by social and geographical isolation, a number of players suggested that the contacts which players do have with the manager and significant others throughout periods of rehabilitation can assume tremendous meaning. A number of younger players in particular have suggested that limited contact can make isolation bearable, if only in a limited way. One young interviewee spoke of the way in which contact with the manager might hinder 'actual' progress and may add a pressure in terms of time-related expectations. He said:

> Because that contact is minimal, whatever the manager does say to you, you sort of take it to heart. Like if he comes in one day and says, 'How are you getting on? Come on, you should be cracking on a bit now, you should be getting there now, you should be getting fit', you think, should I be getting there? Should I be getting fit? And because he's the manager and it is his decision about you at the end of the day, you might start questioning yourself. I don't feel right but, you know, should I be getting fitter?

Conversely, many players referred to banter with the other players as being significant in terms of making them feel, if only in a minor way, involved and a member of the team. One player, who had played in all four divisions, spoke of the relationship between fit players and the long-term injured, suggesting that:

> The one thing is, if you've got a serious injury, the last thing you want is people patting you on the back saying, 'Oh never mind.' You want to still be part of it, you want to be part of the lads as well. If you are out for several months, it's so easy to become totally detached.

Following closely upon their feelings of isolation, some players suggested that they had become a burden, to the manager, the physiotherapist or family members. For them these experiences were demeaning in terms of their self-confidence, principally because they felt that they had little power over their situations or the quality of their existence. For players who sustain severely disabling injuries, feelings of uselessness intensify as onerous and continuous obligations fall to wives, partners and other family members.

## Conclusion

The aim of this chapter has been to understand the ways in which the social relations of work in this 'prestigious' form of employment may have implications for players-as-workers in terms of the degree to which their claims to be injured or in pain are taken as 'genuine' (Bellaby 1990). The context of professional football is ideal for an examination of how injuries at work are produced through interpretive social interaction. In their work on 'corps de ballet', Turner and Wainwright (2003) devote attention to a habitus that evokes attitudes and dispositions in dancers such that they continue to dance in spite of the presence of pain and injury; thus, dancers continue to perform, which is, after all, their *raison d'être*. A similar habitus has developed among elite athletes for whom competing in pain is taken for granted (Wacquant 1995a). For some professional footballers, their preparedness to play hurt adds value to their symbolic capital (Bourdieu and Wacquant 1992), for they have established courageous and heroic selves through 'action' (Goffman 1967). Like dancers, footballers may retain symbolic capital well after their physical capacities have declined.

A central object of this discussion, which examines the shifting identities of injured players, focuses in part on how they may come to be discredited. The discrediting process experienced by players in certain social contexts is similar to the way in which other people – for example, people identified as possessing a mental illness or who possess a visible disability, single parents, AIDS victims (Charmaz, 2002) – who display pathological tendencies by deviating from norms may be open to stigma. Long-term injuries raise several dilemmas for players. First, players begin to consider the fragile and uncertain nature of their existence as professional footballers. Second, players depend more heavily on significant others to help them get through their time, both at home and around the club. They become inwardly directed and sensitive to the intentions and meanings of others towards them; they want to feel involved and to be valued. Yet, at the very time when these feelings develop, their ties to others are weakened, and isolation and loneliness intensify. Third, in a culture which emphasizes *playing* and which normalizes playing with pain and taking risks, those who do not *play* are denied, or deny themselves, the means necessary to sustain a meaningful life and a valued sense of self-identity.

## Chapter 5

# Transferring and the transformation of self

The relatively fragile nature of playing careers in professional football has been highlighted in the previous chapters in relation to the injuries sustained by players. During interview, other than periods of time inactive because of injury, the most vulnerable passages that arose for players were, first, when they were omitted from the starting line-up and, second, during job relocation. The central focus of this chapter therefore concerns the transferring of players from one club to another. The examination in this chapter will not involve a description of the mechanics of the process of transferring in terms of the general patterns of who speaks to whom and where and when, but instead will look at the way in which this process is initiated – that is, how it comes to be that a player is transferred in the first instance – and what a transfer means in terms of the player's sense of 'self'. The object of this chapter then is to relate the process of transferring, a significant turning point or clear 'objective' punctuation mark in the onward-moving career of a player, to transformations of identity and self-conception.

In this regard there are two central and related points to be made initially concerning the process of transferring: these were expressed by all the players interviewed, regardless of their status or of the clubs for whom they play. First, of those players who had moved to new clubs – two players interviewed had never experienced this process – all considered their moves to be positive in terms of their career development at the time of the transfer. In other words, they were 'happy' to leave their old club and pleased to join the new one. Second, when a player moves from one club to another, he moves to a club which desires his skills. It is this desire – the thought of being 'wanted' as expressed by the players – which strengthens his sense of self-worth and alleviates, if only periodically, the uncertainties which characterize the periods in which players transfer.

In cases where a player moves to a club of a higher status – in terms of league or league position, or even economic situation – he must learn to deal with the status transformation which such a move may bestow upon him. All players 'dream' of moves to *big* clubs and whilst there are anxieties associated with the 'high expectations' which, from the perspective of the player, such moves can generate, most, if not all, players perceive such moves 'positively'. Moreover, moves to *big* clubs involve what for a player is a 'positive' transformation of identity and status. They may also be thought of as benchmarks of 'progress' in terms of their career and in most cases may lead to an enhancement of 'self'. Not all types of transfer are as simple to describe. Most other moves are more complex in terms of a transformation of self, for they involve a period of *rejection* of one kind or another; for example, a player may be dropped from the first team for an extended period of time, or never really establish himself as a first team player, or even think he is being *used* in one way or another by the manager (and by 'the club' more generally). During these times players experience a heightened sense of uncertainty about their future and a loss of self-esteem and status. They feel unwanted, isolated from their teammates, let down – often by managers with whom they have attempted to identify and establish a relationship – and some, particularly older players, come to feel that they are treated like a 'commodity'. Players must learn to cope with this loss of self yet, as in periods of absence from the first team due to injury, they are denied access to the one activity that enables them to reinforce their sense of identity as players and which provides them with an opportunity to re-establish their sense of feeling needed and useful. Consequently, it is easier to understand why players come to view a move to another club in a 'positive' manner. Players need to feel 'wanted' and the new club offers them a fresh challenge and, most importantly, the feeling that their skills are indispensable.

## The 'big' move[1]

There are few aspects of the career of a professional footballer that were expressed in such straightforward terms by the interviewees as the movement of players (usually younger or lower division players) to what are perceived to be 'big' clubs. One experienced Division Two player, whose comment is suggestive of many others, said that 'every player playing in the lower divisions secretly yearns for the big move, but it doesn't come to many'. This point was born out by the research of Gowling (1974) who discovered that in the 1972–3 season, just sixteen per cent of all transfers involved players moving to clubs in higher divisions. This relatively small percentage is underscored by the figures found for the 1999–2000 season, in which approximately thirteen per cent of all transfers involved players moving to clubs in higher divisions. Of the players interviewed, those who had experienced this type of transfer spoke, as one might expect, only in 'positive' terms about their moves, even the moves that involved geographical relocation. For these players, their 'dream' had been fulfilled to some extent. A young Division One (i) player, for example, described his experiences in the following manner:

> Player: [My first club] is a decent ground and everything, a nice ground, but you go up to [the club to which he transferred] and it's unbelievable. Looking

around that place and the whole set-up there is fantastic really. It was like a different world from what I was used to so I was really impressed. They knew that and they offered me a good contract ... I wasn't going to ask for stupid money ... and they offered me that straight away and so I signed without any qualms, very little haggling really at all.

MR: So you were pleased with that move?

Player: Yeah, really chuffed with it. I was going to a massive club and I thought it was going to be my dream move ... I was really, really pleased with it, going into the Premiership was all I wanted to do. I was playing against people like Ian Wright and other people like that. I've always been a big Arsenal fan and we played against them in our third or fourth game. Arsenal at home: it was fantastic.

A former Division Three (i) player interviewed experienced an even more dramatic elevation in which he moved from a team which had recently been promoted from the Conference, for whom he played only fifteen times (scoring ten goals), to a Premiership club. Focusing at first on the financial dimension of the move, this player described how his salary increased by over 300 per cent; even so he realized that, by comparison to many other players in the Premier League, his new salary was only 'small fry'. He said that:

It is a lot of money. You've got to put things in reality. It is a lot of money to earn and that is great. I'd gone from two years earlier and not being wanted at a Division Four club to playing in the Premier League. It was just unbelievable.

When asked whether there were great differences between these clubs, he replied:

Yeah, when I think back now it's high profile ... Everybody wants to know you and you go to grounds and places like Anfield and there are 5,000 people milling about outside; you're getting off the coach and pushing through people and that's the way it was and it was good ... I think now the top Premiership footballers are not footballers they are superstars; the Beckhams, the Giggses, your Bergkamps. They are all superstars, and now when I started, I think it was '93 season ... it was good. I enjoyed it.

The examples above both describe situations in which players move to clubs in the FA Premier League. What was common for both of these players was that their moves came about, from their perspective, with little pre-warning and their acceptance of the contract offer occurred with little negotiation. In the case of the first player, he played for his former club in the first game of the Division One (i) season. He was transferred the following week in time to represent his new club in their opening game of the Premier League season the following Saturday. Both players expressed few reservations about the moves and, even when pressed, claimed their overriding emotion to be one of excitement in relation to the expectations of their new managers, teammates and supporters. The latter player in this connection said that, in fact, he put the greatest pressure on himself and remarked: 'I wanted to prove to myself that I was good enough at this level.'

Another inexperienced player who transferred from a Division Three (i) to a Division One (i) team also expressed this type of sentiment although his move, which will be described in more detail, was different from the other two in that he was receiving a great deal of praise for his performances and, in his words, he was 'looking for a move'. An understanding of the way in which this player came to be transferred is useful as it may be compared to the types of transfers to be described later, most of which involve periods in which the players experience 'rejection'. This Division Three (i) player was twenty-two years old and had played the first year of a two year contract. He said:

> I was doing okay, not blowing my own trumpet but the papers were writing nice things. I was shining in matches and people were linking me with other clubs and saying people are looking but it is all paper talk. You don't get any feedback from the manager and there's nothing definite ever said. You're never sure that anything is going to happen. You keep working and it came to the point where [my manager] wanted me to sign again, but I knew that that was the time and I was going to go ... And I made it clear to him that I wasn't going to sign another contract with them. I wanted to see what was going to happen.

The refusal to sign a new contract was a gamble for this player in a number of ways. The greatest danger for him would be for his contract to expire without other clubs showing any signs of interest. This situation would have been the worst case scenario insofar as his sense of self-esteem and confidence were concerned, for it would have meant that, for the time being at least, his assessment of his talents was misjudged. On another level, his manager may have questioned his loyalty to the club and his teammates may have cast doubts about his 'attitude'; in other words, suggesting that he possessed an over-inflated opinion of his own skills. The situation for this player developed 'favourably' and with one year of his contract still to run he received an offer to transfer to a Division One (i) club. When asked whether he thought he had taken a gamble, he explained his understanding of the situation in the following way:

> We were doing well and they liked me and I could have signed a good contract [with them] and I would have been quite content. It's a big move for me to move away from [my former club] which is not so far away from Middlesbrough where all my family live. I was moving quite a long way away

but it was a better deal and it was Division One football. I was never in any doubt to be honest that I was going to sign a contract. I never thought twice about it.

He had been in touch with a Professional Footballers' Association (PFA) representative who had advised that, relative to other players, the financial terms and conditions were appropriate for someone of his age and experience.

In a number of senses, the players who are transferred to 'big' clubs develop dominant self-images, akin to what Adler and Adler (1989) refer to as the 'gloried self', which is a consequence of individuals becoming imbued with celebrity. In some cases, players are raised to the status of stars and can regularly read their names and statements about their performances in local and national media. For many of the players, their move will have fulfilled their dreams; until then, they would not have interacted with people who accorded them such levels of importance and, for some, adulation. The players interviewed were profoundly affected by their moves and they all indicated that they 'grew in confidence'. An understanding of these types of moves is useful insofar as they highlight a number of central differences between the types of transfers experienced by players. In the case of 'big' moves, the players involved are usually ever-present in the first team of their clubs and speak of having few problems with fellow players or managers. The moves take place relatively quickly from the moment a transfer offer is received, although for some there may be a prior period of rumour and media speculation; in this regard, the player above refers to 'paper talk'. Most transfer offers are accepted immediately by the players (and in many cases by the respective clubs), almost certainly because they view the move as a means of career progress. The other types of transfer to be examined are more complex as they nearly all involve a period in which the player experiences a rejection of some nature.

## 'Doing is being'[2]

The types of transfers that will be examined in this section are those which involve a player being rejected, in one way or another, from the first team or the first team squad. Some players, for example, consider themselves to be established first team footballers whereas other, usually younger, professionals are endeavouring to become regulars. For nearly all players however, their careers are relatively short and the possibility of rejection is always upon them: a loss of form or the possibility of a younger, better player emerging from the youth team ranks are among the constantly problematic features of their occupational lives. The object of this section therefore is to explain how players come to maintain or adapt their 'self-conceptions' to changing circumstances and in relation to their new levels of involvement.

Unless players sustain an injury or are suspended, the only other time that they will be obliged to watch rather than play is when the manager does not select them. It was noted earlier that one of the basic cultural values in professional football is attached to *playing* and it was suggested that 'active' involvement in league and cup matches was the context in which the identities of players were instilled with meaning. Players are only able to sustain their sense of self (maybe their 'gloried selves') by playing in the first team, for it is only then that they have the opportunity to feel involved and to justify fully their status as a first team player to themselves and to others. This point is fundamental for players in relation to the process of transferring, as it is the case that being left out of the manager's plans for a forthcoming game may lead to a diminished sense of self for players as well as the generation of a large measure of uncertainty. In short, the major anchorage of self – his status as a performing member of the team – is severed and the trappings that serve to legitimize such ('powerful') self-definitions are withheld. The player now has a marginal position in relation to the central activity of the football club – first team football – and this is an indication, for him, that he is unwanted. Thus, players do not want to remain in situations where their skills are considered of marginal use and at this point (of realization) they may decide that their futures need to lie elsewhere.

Indeed, this type of comment was common among the players interviewed and one typical example was expressed by a Division One (i) player in the following way:

> If I'm not playing regularly when I think I should be I end up moving on really because I'm not prepared to sit in the reserves for months at a time. I think the type of player I am, I'm not the sort of superstar or anything like this, I'm just a steady sort of player. I don't have many fluctuations in my performance so if a manager goes off me I'll probably move on.

Another young Division One (i) player expressed similar views in relation to what he considered to be his marginal position at his club:

> I thought that I wasn't going to play so I thought that I had to leave the club and go to pastures greener sort of thing and find a new club that I'd have a decent chance of playing. I honestly didn't think I was going to play at [my present club] at that stage, so I thought I had to go. If I was going to have any sort of career then I had to get away.

This player said that his present contract had run out and, although the manager had offered him a new contract, he stated that: 'I wasn't featuring at all in [the manager's] plans'. He added:

> I was nineteen at that stage and I wasn't featuring. A lot of the lads my age and lads a year younger had all been thrown into first team games. I'd not had a look-in at all, so I was thinking that my future was lying elsewhere. I

wasn't going to sign at that stage. They offered me a reasonable contract for someone my age, but I thought I wasn't going to get a look-in, and all I wanted to do was play football. I didn't think I was going to have a chance at the first team ... I had nothing else lined up.

In fact, the manager of his team was sacked before he could find a new club and he was selected to start in the first eleven for every game by the newly appointed manager. Still, the views of this player are typical of many younger professionals who come to realize that they may need to leave their present club in order to progress in career terms. The next example, for instance, concerns another young Division One (i) player who had been sent out on loan at two separate clubs in consecutive months. In the following quote he explains how he came to realize that his position in relation to first team football was becoming increasingly marginal:

I think it dawned on me eventually. I must have come back from another loan spell at Crewe and then played virtually another full season at [his club] without making any headway into the first team, and then at the beginning of the next season there appeared three new signings who were all strikers and suddenly I'm thinking: 'Well, hold on, perhaps my days aren't exactly going to be here.' I don't need to be playing in the reserves. I've played three years in the reserves here so I've proved that I can play reserve team football. What I need to prove now is that I can play league football. Not three games, not ten games, but season upon season.

This young footballer played regularly in the reserve team but he came, in time, to consider this status, which he had formerly treated as one of progress, as a sign of stagnation. Hence, whether players are already established in first team football or whether they are progressing to that position, they can only maintain their identities either by continuing to play or by continuing, in their terms, to make progress towards their career goals. Being dropped from the first team because of a loss of form or failing to make headway in terms of first team appearances generates uncertainty and leads players to adopt strategies to remedy the situation. First and foremost among these strategies is for players to ask for a transfer to another club. Eamon Dunphy (1987) echoes these views in his *Diary of a Professional Footballer*. Having established himself in the first team (as well as playing international football with the Republic of Ireland), he is later repeatedly dropped from the first team at Millwall and expresses his thoughts – his disappointment – in the following way: 'There is nothing I can identify with any more. It is a new era, a new bunch of kids. And there is nothing there for me. The only question is how to get away' (Dunphy 1987: 143).

It may be argued from the perspective of players, therefore, that the transferring process is not set in motion when a player requests to be placed on the transfer list, or even when he is put on the transfer list by his manager (or 'the club'), for he will almost certainly have begun to consider his options in terms of first team football before then. Thus, the process of transferring may be said to be initiated when a player perceives that he may not be in the future plans of his manager and is omitted from the first eleven. For players, these uncertain times may be thought of as turning points in terms of their 'subjective' careers (Stebbins 1970) as they have few alternatives other than to take stock and re-evaluate their positions. The choices available are, by and large, already well known to them, for it is likely that they will have observed the transition of other players who have experienced similar episodes. It might be suggested that the kinds of incidents that precipitate the revision of their identity and status are likely at some time to befall, and therefore to be equally significant to, other players of the same generation. In a host of ways, players are prepared for what may happen to them, including the subtle warning signs and the types of feelings they may experience. Insofar as changes of identity and self-conception are asso-ciated with one's 'position', it might be argued that passages of status for professional footballers are socially patterned.

Over time, players learn – as part of the occupational culture of their group – to anchor their self-perceptions to 'playing'. For them, playing means being selected for the first team, for that is *where the action is* (Goffman 1967). Even younger professionals, who may be satisfied with making their mark in the reserve team at first, come to realize that they need to progress to the first team rather than stagnate at reserve team level. Thus, those footballers who consider themselves to be 'first team regulars' typically adopt an attitude to playing such that they are – as one experienced player put it – 'not prepared to sit in the reserves'. In this connection, Dunphy (1987: 157) said:

> I could never settle for reserve team football. I left Manchester United, when they were the greatest club in the country, to go to York so I could get first-team football. I'd go down to the third division now for first-team football.

The central point that he makes repeatedly throughout this section of his book, and one that underpins his general thoughts in terms of the process of transfer-ring, is that: 'I want to go somewhere where I can feel useful and wanted' (Dunphy 1987: 168).

Other players repeated the opinion that they wanted to feel useful and involved at the club at which they were employed. A Division One (i) player described a transfer which involved him moving down from Division One (i) to Division Two (i). When asked whether he thought this transfer was a 'posi-tive' move at that stage in his career he responded in the following way: 'Yeah, they were down a division, but yeah, cos I thought it was great. Somebody wanted me. I just wanted to go, you know, and play and know I was in the first team every week and wanted.' Another Division One (i) player reflected upon his career in terms of his motivations to perform suggesting that: 'As soon as I feel as though, when somebody says "I want you to play for me" my confidence goes woosh. *He wants me.* That's me anyway, my confidence grows ...' When asked to provide further examples of when other managers had instilled such confidence in him, this player went on to recount an occasion on which he considered it appropriate to confront a former manager, for whom he had a great deal of respect, about his decision to leave him out of the team. He stated that, if at all possible, he would avoid altercations with managers and had developed insecurity over time in terms of what *he thought* managers thought of him and his ability as a player. Thus, in relation to his considerations of 'feeling wanted' he said:

> He used to give me that all the time. Brilliant, you know. He left me out one game because he wanted to play three at the back, and I was unhappy. I said to myself, I've got to go and see the manager and have a confrontation with him. You know, I've got to go in and see him and ask why am I not playing. I've got to go in and be a little bit stroppy. But [my former manager] always knocked that out of me, so I couldn't go in with that attitude. So, I've tried my hardest and he went: 'Son, I love you. Don't worry about it. You'll play next week. I love you, come on. We need you.' And I'm saying to myself: 'We need you.' I walked out feeling a million dollars. I thought, I went in there to have a row with him and I came out feeling brilliant. And that's man management, isn't it!

In terms of understanding the process of transferring, the significance of the point that players want *to feel needed* lies in the fact that when they are dropped they must suddenly adapt themselves to the loss of sources of security and status: as far as they are concerned they are *involuntarily* deprived of a position in the team under circumstances which reflect unfavourably upon them and their capabilities. At these stages players begin to raise questions in their minds concerning whether they are in the future plans of their manager and whether or not they will remain in the first eleven, yet there are few people to whom players can turn in order to get responses to these questions. If these situations persist, players review their options and many feel that there are few alternatives other than to request a transfer to another club. So, feeling rejected, they – or their agents – search for other clubs with whom they will be able to re-establish their status as first team players. Consequently, few of the players interviewed spoke about their transfers to other clubs in anything other than positive terms. This pattern is understandable if one considers that a player is moving from a club with whom he has 'failed' to another, the manager of which has asked, and is willing to pay, for his services. Once again he feels wanted and useful and, moreover, he is among a new squad of players with whom he can restore his self-confidence.

## The non-person

In his classic study, *The presentation of self in everyday life*, Goffman (1959: 150) identified a number of 'discrepant roles', one of which he termed the 'non-person'. He suggests that some people are ascribed the status of a *non-person* when they are in social situations where they are physically and legitimately present, although lacking social acknowledgement; in similar vein, Ball (1976: 730) referred to people who were 'possibly receiving recognition as social object, but not as a social other'. When a player is rejected he can, to varying degrees, take on the status of a *non-person*: within professional football there have been a small number of highly publicized cases where players have been shunned as if absent. One notable incident in this connection involved former Newcastle United and England international Robert Lee, who discovered that he had not been allocated a squad number for the coming 1999–2000 season by Dutch manager Ruud Gullit. George Caulkin, writing in *The Times* (3 August 1999), said: 'As far as messages go, it was akin to turning up for work to find your desk has been cleared' and he added: 'It seems unquestionable that ejecting Lee is Gullit's intention'.

Hence, it is possible to identify a pattern of behaviour as a result of which the exit of a player from a football club may, in the words of one player, be 'hastened' by the actions of a manager. While managers may make their intentions known when selecting the first eleven, it seems that they also have subtle methods of undermining players such that they will eventually leave. A former Division One (i) player, for example, was asked to describe the way in which a transfer to a Premiership club came about. In setting the scene he spoke of his relationships with two former managers. He said:

> Player: I got on brilliant with [my former manager] so when he went, I felt he was betrayed by the club a little bit to be honest. He was forced to sell players that he brought through and he made a fortune for [my former club] and he didn't have any money to buy players ... they got rid of him and I was very unhappy. I thought he'd been dumped on basically ... And then [a new manager] came in and if they could get me out they would sort of take the money, I'd been there eight years.
>
> MR: What gave you that impression?
>
> Player: You just get feelings, it was just one of them feelings reading between the lines. Certainly there wasn't any conflict between us. I got on alright with him and he was fair enough, but I think he knew that I was [my former manager's] boy sort of thing, so I think he was quite happy when I went in the end. They got decent money.

This player is unable to articulate precisely his 'feelings' concerning the new manager although, like the player cited earlier who developed a 'paranoia' about what *he thought* managers were thinking about him, this player thought that the new manager believed that his loyalties lay with the former manager. It is clear that managers may marginalize players to varying degrees and make them feel unwanted. In these respects all managers must tread carefully for they risk shutting out members of the playing squad who may be *used* in a supporting role (i.e. as cover for players who may get injured). In this connection, managers attempt to 'manage' the emotions (Hochschild 1983) of their players since changes in power balances, brought on by feelings of rejection or failure, may lead to the emergence of personal and psychological conflicts for players. For some players – like Robert Lee, mentioned earlier – they are not so much 'cooled-out' (Goffman 1952) as completely ignored. For these players, feelings of 'power' are absent and, consequently, their options are limited to leaving the club or waiting in hope for a change of manager. The following extract comes from an interview with a former Division One (i) player who returns for pre-season training expecting to renegotiate a new contract:

> Player: Well, when I was at [my former club] I came back for what would have been coming round to my fourth season. We'd just been relegated from the First Division after a couple of seasons, and they got a new manager in who came from a Vauxhall Conference club, who hadn't managed in the League. I'd met him previously so I thought I'd be okay with him but he brought a lot of new players in particularly from non-league. I turned up for the first day of pre-season training and I didn't have any kit and I didn't have a kit number so I realized the writing was on the wall from day one ... I never even played a game for him.
> MR: How did you feel about that?
> Player: Oh, I was very angry, very disappointed because in the previous two years I'd probably played seventy-five to eighty games in Division One, and I was a far better player than the players he was bringing in. I mean I knew I was because they had been playing in the Vauxhall Conference or even below! And suddenly I was training on my own after three years of doing my best and training hard, because I was always fit. I couldn't believe it.

This player was bitter about this situation; to compound his disappointment and sense of rejection, he found himself isolated from the first team squad during training sessions. When asked to expand on these experiences, he replied:

> I was training on my own in pre-season: I just wasn't included in anything so I just went off and kept fit on my own. Just like, when the lads were playing a practice game, I was going round the pitch doing a twelve-minute run or something.

The manager treated him as if he was of no importance to the team and his previous self-defined status, that of first team player, no longer held true. The intentions of the new manager, like those of former Newcastle manager Ruud

Gullit, referred to above, seem clear: put simply, to eject the player. When asked what contact he had with the manager during this time he said:

> Player: The manager wasn't saying anything to me, he'd made it clear that it was time and that he'd let me know if anyone showed any interest. At the same time my contract was up and he offered me another year on the same money, so I'd have been on the same money for three years and I turned it down because I thought I deserved a rise, and so I expected to sit down and talk terms with him about a new contract but we never got that far. So as soon as it got towards the end of pre-season when clubs started showing interest, because friendly games start, I went and played a couple of trial games for a couple of clubs looking for a move.
>
> MR: When you were training on your own and it was clear to you that you weren't wanted, what did you say to the other players who had been there for some time?
>
> Player: It wasn't just me actually, there was about six of us who had turned up and we hadn't got any kit because he'd brought probably half a dozen players in ... I think I was the only one whose contract was up at that time as well, so some of the other lads were still included in training and that because they were in the middle of their contracts, so he might still need them.

So, in responding to the question of whether these experiences are common for players at this level of football, he said:

> It's a common experience I think. You speak to players and a lot of them, even if they haven't been treated like this, a lot of them have been at clubs where managers have treated players in the same way. I mean it wasn't nasty to me or anything like that, I mean it was just really, like you don't exist. You know, he doesn't say hello to you or anything but when you speak to him he's civil. I don't know, it's like a cold shoulder.

In summary, this player in interview describes a scenario that he considered common in professional football in which he loses a *status* – that of first team player – within the club, which for him was central to his sense of self and identity. He was instantly marginalized from his teammates, some of whom he considered to be second-rate, at a time when he believed he had a meaningful part to play in the team. There may be a number of players within a club who, at any one time, may be isolated by their managers and other members of staff or who at least may be subjected to feelings of isolation, but it is unlikely that they will remain unacknowledged by *all* team members as well. Yet, the idea of the 'non-person' (Goffman 1968), that is, someone who suffers *social* rejection, is significant in terms of the process of transferring insofar it sheds light on the feelings of rejection that players may experience and exposes the fragile nature of their existence and their identities as players. As soon as they are discarded they begin to reflect on and take stock of their positions relative to their contemporaries. They begin to generate feelings of uncertainty about their futures and if rejection is irrevocable, as in the case of the player who returned to work to find he was omitted from all aspects of pre-season training, they begin immediately to think in terms of their available options. In an occupational culture such as professional football, in which one's 'human being-ness' is evaluated by one's 'human doing-ness' (Ingham *et al.* 1999), being denied the right to exercise one's 'doing-ness' for any length of time generates frustration and anxiety. Added to this is the fact that the person who has the authority to deny a player a position in the first team – the manager of the football club – is the very person with whom that player is at pains to develop and maintain a working relationship. Thus, the sociological significance of the concept of the 'non-person' lies in the fact that this status position is more adequately understood as a consequence of changing power balances between a player and his manager.

## 'Sad tales'

The sense of rejection and loss experienced by a player when he is dropped in the first instance is 'cushioned' (Friedman 1990) by him to greater or lesser degrees. The concept of *cushioning* is similar to Goffman's (1952) idea of 'cooling out' *oneself* as adaptation to failure, although it refers more to a continuing set of less severe or crisis-like rejections which are a more regular and institutionalized aspect of an occupation such as professional football. In terms of the process of transferring, a player is better able to *cushion* his self-conception and to adapt to failure at one club for he knows from experience that he, like others before him, will be able to attain a new status, which perhaps differs from the one he lost or failed to gain, but which provides at least something or somebody for him to become. For a player who is moving to a club in a lower division, the alternative status position presented is a compromise of some kind, providing at least some of the trappings of his lost standing.

When a player transfers from one club to another he does so because, in the majority of cases, he has been 'rejected' by his manager. For all that, at no point in any interview for this study did a player express the opinion that he was not good enough at that level or that he did not play well enough and did not deserve his place in the team. In most cases, as will be indicated, the players interviewed attempted to rationalize the reasons for their transfer such that, via a combination of adjustment and 'cushioning' (Friedman 1990), they maintained their sense of self-esteem. In a number of cases, for example, they developed 'sad tales' (Goffman 1968) or 'cover stories' (Padavic 2005) in order to displace the blame for their rejection away from themselves or to generate 'distance' (Goffman 1961) for themselves from their rejector, hence saving face. For professional footballers, whose expectations and self-conceptions have been built up over some time, rejection by a manager is probably the most significant 'cause' of devaluation of self-esteem (provided the player is not so self-obsessed that he cannot perceive the opinions of others).

Using Goffman (1968) as a point of departure, it might be suggested that following times of transition or turning points, such as a process of transferring, a player may develop an image or view of himself which can be orally presented by way of explaining his present circumstances – that is, his rejection – to others: in short, a player will instigate a process of defining the self along defensible lines. In constructing an 'apologia' (Goffman 1968) of this nature, a player may be selective with, deny, or distort the facts in order to 'distance' himself from responsibility for *his* situation as it stands. The degree of detail of such 'apologias' varies, although from experiences, interactions and observation of others, players voice a number of occupational cultural sayings in an attempt to cushion and cope with their 'failure'. Typical in this regard are stock phrases that pertain to '*unlucky breaks*' and '*not* being in the right place at the right time'; in these circumstances the notion of 'luck' is used by way of an excuse (Gowling 1974). An apologia or 'sad tale' therefore is a method that players employ in order to explain their position in a way that is, for them, 'morally' appropriate (Goffman 1968). Thus, to explain the present state of affairs in terms of an 'unlucky break' is a legitimate way of expressing their disappointment concerning the way in which their circumstances unfold at a particular club.

For players, 'unlucky breaks' do seem to be important factors and contingencies in individual career progress and success, and may be of greater significance in an occupation in which there exists intense competition for scarce places in teams. The notion of *luck as an excuse* is but one of the apologias identified in this study: for example, when asked about experiences that may have changed his opinion of football, one former professional player, currently playing non-league, said:

> I think probably the hardest thing to understand when you go in [to professional football] is it is *purely about opinion*. Until you can take that on board you're always going to struggle, especially when you are not being picked and you think, 'I should be playing'. And you think, 'Well, hold on a minute. What have I done in training? How did I perform?' And you can see somebody else's point of view. I think that's the hardest thing to take on board.

Associated with the idea that professional football is 'purely about opinion' is the following remark by a Division One (i) player who was asked to recall his thoughts on the types of comments that had been made about his performances. He did not recall any specific point of view, but instead made the following point:

> You certainly take things to heart, like the slightest little comment and you go away thinking, 'What did he [the manager] mean by that?' They said something probably in pure innocence but you go away thinking they meant something else: you would worry about the slightest little thing. Obviously

in football there's a lot of 'if your face fits' and I think there is something in that to an extent. You want people to like you and think you're a good player and a good trainer.

Former Chelsea midfielder Eddie Newton discussed the success he had achieved under former managers Glenn Hoddle and Ruud Gullit, including four cup winners' medals. However Newton remarks on the arrival of new manager Gianluca Vialli in the following way:

> Sometimes your face doesn't fit. Whatever you do, it doesn't matter. I'd been through a lot of managers so I suppose it was inevitable that one of them would not like my face. From day one I knew I wouldn't be in his side.
>
> (*Guardian*, 7 January 2001)

Referring to the subjective – and therefore questionable – opinions of others is a convenient strategy for players in order for them to downplay, and divert attention away from having to account for, the level of their performances. In essence, the underlying idea that a player is hoping that significant others will accept is that under a different manager, whose opinion of his skills are more favourable, his *face would fit* and he could experience the benefits of success afforded a first team regular. Sociologically, then, 'being in the right place at the right time' means being among the 'right' people.

In this respect, a Division Three (i) player who had formerly played for a team in Division Two (i) said: 'Well, I left [my former club] because me and the manager started *bumping heads* really and it was just time to move on I think.' When asked whether they were 'bumping heads' because the manager was leaving him out of the starting eleven he replied: 'Yes, I mean he was right to do so in some cases but after a while I wasn't prepared to put up with it any more.' This statement of partial self-blame was the only one of its kind expressed among the interviews conducted for this study although it provides a good example of the way in which a player may distort the events that initiate the transferring process.

The final example involves a former Division Three player who was signed at the age of twenty from non-league football. The manager who signed him resigned almost immediately and a well-known former international player filled the position. The player said that in time he started to become unhappy at the club, explaining that the manager 'basically didn't think I would be good enough to be a centre-forward and started to play me at centre-half'. Following a three-month period during which the player received treatment for an ankle injury, the manager was sacked and a former player of the same club took up the position. The player returned to training to discover that the new manager, to use his own words, 'didn't rate me either and sent me out on loan to [a non-league team]'. When asked how it felt not to be rated by two managers in quick succession, the player replied in the following way:

> I was more disappointed with [my first manager in professional football], because he was a hero of mine when he was a player and I thought he might have taken the forwards and worked on us, which he didn't really do.

The player said that he had met his second manager by chance a few years later following a transfer to a club in the Conference. This second manager told him that his transfer away from the club wasn't anything personal, 'It was just he said, at the time he needed players he could rely on and he couldn't rely on me because of my inexperience.' The player concluded his descriptions of the events as follows:

> I felt hurt and I remember writing to the local paper about [my second manager], I said, 'He's let me go and I'm going to prove him wrong and I wish him no success at all in the game', which is a bit bitter and twisted, but when you're sort of twenty-one years of age that's the way you think. I saw him years later, and I've got nothing against him, it was a professional thing, and that's what I mean about football. Football is *purely about opinion*. There are people sometimes you like and dislike and it's not personal, it's a professional thing.

The last example presented augments the strategies identified so far, for the comments expressed by the player above illustrate the manner in which he responds to threats to his self-conception. In short, the strategy he employs is to *deny* the opinions of his ability as expressed by his former managers: a self-preserving 'rejection of one's rejectors' (Goffman 1968). Thus, in order to cushion himself from experiences of rejection and to adapt and defend the notion that he is worth something to somebody – an idea that has been built into his identity over time – a player may distort or deny the truth concerning the way in which he came to be transferred, or he may reject the opinions of his rejector(s), usually his manager. Consequently, the behaviour of a player may be understood more adequately in terms of the way he assists in a process of 'cooling out' in relation to his own failures.

## Conclusion

It would seem safe to conclude at this point that relationships between a manager and his players are potentially adversarial: a player validates his sense of self and identity by playing and contributing to the performance of the team, whereas the identity of a manager is maintained for the most part by winning matches. For players, the opportunity to play in games and achieve personal success may be more important than the overall success of the team (which may be composed of some players who are there by virtue of 'failure' and others who are there by virtue of 'success'). This chapter has examined more closely the process of transferring and contributed to an understanding of the fundamental ways in which professional footballers experience transformations of identity: that is, those socially patterned transformations that relate to what in other occupations might be understood in terms of 'promotion' and 'demotion'.

Players have few doubts about *big* moves since, for many, such transfers are what they have dreamed of achieving. Any anxieties they may harbour in this regard are outweighed by the challenge and the enhancement to self that accompany transfers of this nature. Players who experience a period of rejection prior to their transfer may have a more difficult period of identity transformation. Even so, in many cases they are able to cushion and adjust their self-conceptions to varying degrees of success through a combination of distorting or denying the truth or by rejecting the opinions of their rejectors, for many players recognize the subjective nature of team selection. A player is able to develop a *self-supporting* 'sad tale' (Goffman 1968) concerning the circumstances in which he came to be transferred in order to cushion or provide relief from the harsh realities associated with achieving career success in a professional sport in which regular and assured positions in teams are a scarce resource.

Throughout this chapter, individual players have tended to be treated in isolation. While the transformations of 'self' are socially patterned, the focus has been on the individual player in the main, to the neglect of his relationships to others. A sense of rejection or feelings of isolation, both of which are experienced subjectively, and transformations of identity more generally, are the outcome of interaction with others. With this thought in mind, one of the objects of Chapter 6 is to examine the people to whom players turn for advice and support when, for example, they have been dropped from the starting line-up or when they are deliberating over transfer offers.

# Chapter 6

# Transfer markets and informal grapevines[1]

The objects of this chapter are twofold. First, the intention is to explain how players develop informal networks of *friends* among their work colleagues. These *friendship* networks exist alongside the networks that players are bound up in by virtue of their employment, which include all work colleagues; however players will eventually lose direct contact with most teammates. Within their work networks, players develop relations that may be emotional – over time players make both enemies and friends. The high levels of competitive pressure for the limited places in the first eleven can lead to rivalries and even conflict among 'teammates'. By contrast, friendship networks are comprised of people 'inside' the game to whom players turn during times of uncertainty and who will offer support. The second object is to understand the way in which friendship networks can facilitate the process of transferring. Networks of this kind are useful for making new associations. This examination will look closely at the mechanics of the process of transferring in terms of the general patterns of who speaks to whom, where and when.

The identity of a player, as a *non-person*, a *reject* or maybe as a *superstar*, is gained via interaction with others. The sociological problem which lies at the heart of this chapter therefore relates to an understanding of the social relations of support systems for players. The idea is not to treat players in isolation, but to look at professional footballers as *homines aperti* (Elias 1978) such that their identities stem from the nature of their relationships among people 'inside' the game. Thus, the questions addressed concern whether players receive support from others in their team and the nature of this support. Who do they talk to when they are dropped from the starting line-up? When do players know about potential transfers and who tells them? An important point of this chapter will be to gain an understanding of the patterns of informal or unofficial lines of communication among players, coaches and player agents, as they relate to the process of transferring.

## The development of friendship networks

The interview data indicate that most first team players do not discuss their team selection circumstances with other players in their team. If they have not been selected to start in the first eleven for a forthcoming match, or if they are unsettled by their current situation and are reviewing their options, players tend to keep their opinions about their own state of affairs to themselves, particularly within the football club. The flip side of this scenario is that players do not enquire about the inner thoughts of those who are omitted from the first team, nor do they think it is their place to ask such questions in 'public' settings – what might be referred to as 'gossip centres' (Tebbutt and Marchington 1997) – such as changing and treatment rooms. Most concern themselves with keeping safe their own position in the team. There are exceptions to this rule, some of which will be examined in the course of this chapter. Notwithstanding the initial comment about the reluctance of players to openly display their reactions to issues of selection, it would be naïve to suggest that players do not talk about their performances or the performances of others or about matches in general, for talking points of this type are debated continually. For all that, there is a distinction on the whole between the discussions among squad members that relate to individual performances in matches and in training and of transfer gossip in general and the way in which a player may personally deliberate over future career developments. These points could have been included in Chapter 2, concerning occupational culture, for the 'attitude' that underpins the approach of players to the plight of others may be summarized in the following way: as one experienced player put it, 'think about yourself first and worry about the rest later'.[2]

While it is the case that some players seek out the opinions of others concerning their performance in a game, they are far less likely to examine their anxieties and the pros and cons of potential transfers with other squad members with whom there exist internal rivalries. Thus, it might be argued that solidarity among, and support systems for, players within the club – the type of which may exist informally for employees in other occupations (Collinson 2000) – is undermined by ruthless competition for places. For example, one former Premiership player spoke of his experiences of rivalry among players in the following way. He said:

> despite the fact that me and you might have to be friendly on the field and off the field, if we're playing for the same position I'll do my utmost to make sure I'm the first person. So, as I always say, you don't have many friends in football, but you have a lot of acquaintances.

Magee (1998) notes similarly that players coming from leagues outside England find it difficult to get 'real' friends. He quotes Danish international Claus Thomsen, who remarks that 'you can't really be close to anyone because you are not quite sure that they are friends ... it's very difficult to get very close friends in football' (Magee 1998: 129).

Regardless of the high levels of competition and the underpinning emphasis on individualism, friendships do develop, particularly if players have come through the youth ranks together. Alan Gowling (1974) demonstrates that among a squad of players, particular friendships develop that are likely to be structured in terms of age, playing experience, length of time at the club or with previous clubs, or even travel circumstances to and from the training ground. Parker (1996a) discusses the age-related friendship 'cliques' that were formed by the apprentices in his study of the youth training scheme. Back *et al.* (2001: 151) examine the development of social networks among black Afro-Caribbean players who, it is suggested, 'stick together' and don't easily 'mix' or 'fit in'. In their study they suggest that such perceptions held among players more generally are reinforced to some extent by the development of black friendship networks within the community of professional players. In this respect, Back *et al.* (2001: 151) make the following point:

> Friendship groups which are white, black or mixtures of black and white players pervade the dressing rooms of clubs up and down the country but are rarely discussed in public or considered as problematic unless they are exclusively made up of black or foreign members. Indeed the creation of supportive communities of players from ethnic minority backgrounds might be more readily understood than the alternative formulations in the context of the difficulties encountered by black players over the years.

At this point one may put forward the argument that individual players may be more willing to disclose their uncertainties and fears among a group such as this than they would in the context of the club dressing room.[3] In addition, it is in these 'closed' contexts where players feel able and are more likely to involve themselves with the circumstances and feelings of others. To examine this hypothesis, the following examples are included in order to demonstrate the types of people with whom a player may talk about personal issues.

The ability of young professionals to provide immediate support for each other will alter rapidly as soon as a number of players are released, or one of them transfers away from the club. Traditionally, few apprentices are offered professional contracts (see Parker 1996a) and those who sign new terms may be drawn closer as a consequence of their collective experience. Those who are released and who are offered contracts elsewhere must find new people whom they can trust or contact friends, who may be former colleagues, at other clubs.

A Division One (i) player, in this connection, spoke of a small group of people 'within the game', but not at his present club, to whom he turned when he had previously been uncertain about what his next move might be. The network described by this player includes players from former clubs with whom he had developed a close relationship. On this occasion the members of his 'network' responded in the following, and in his opinion unhelpful, way:

I was anxious, even when I was speaking to people, you know, players whose opinion I valued, they'd say: 'You'll be all right son, oh don't worry you'll be all right, you'll definitely get a club no problem.' But I was thinking 'well, yes I should get a club', but you're still twitching a little bit, a bit nervy.

As players get older and move from one club to the next they meet other people 'inside the game' with whom they develop friendships, who provide support in the form of advice or words of comfort. Over time, players build up a network of people in whom they can place their trust: a network that may include current and former playing colleagues, player agents, former managers and coaches. These networks may be spread across a number of leagues and in addition may assist an unsettled player for, as agent Bill McMurdo has pointed out: 'Players recommend other players to managers informally all the time' (*Guardian*, 22 January 2000). So, players develop relationships with a number of significant 'insiders' in whom they can confide their personal thoughts. This network will also facilitate a process of transferring upon which a player may embark.

Players may express their thoughts to their wives or partners more openly – a point dealt with later in this book – but in the context of the 'gossip centres' within the football club, such as the changing rooms, the physiotherapy room and the training ground, there is a tendency for players to react to disappointment, upsets and uncertainties with humour (Collinson 1988). For example, a former Division One (i) player who was ignored and treated as a 'non-person' (Goffman 1959) by his manager, made the following point with regard to the presentation of self. He said: 'We were all disappointed *but you don't show that in the dressing room*, because everybody's been there and everyone knows what it's like so, you know, it usually gets treated with sort of humour and that.' Similarly, humour was used by players to deal with other potentially difficult situations. For instance, a former Premiership player referred to the fact that players at his club considered a second change of manager in quick succession as farcical. He said: 'It became almost a standing joke. The lads would laugh about it, but people were worried. At the backs of their minds, it's a subconscious thing, no one is happy with the situation.' An agent interviewed for this study commented on the ups and downs experienced by players by suggesting that, while humour was an important aspect of dressing room banter, 'they have to be macho because the persona of all players is that they have this *hard front*'. In the light of the requirement for humour as one means by which players may save face and maintain a 'hard front' (Collinson 1988), the problem of the social relations of player support systems might be explainable, in part, if one considers it in the following manner.

When players are faced with personal disappointment and uncertainty they must manage the impressions that significant others receive (Goffman 1959). In the company of their teammates, players, in accordance with their masculine occupational culture, are expected not to complain but to laugh along with the group banter that may be directed at them and to be seen to work enthusiastically to regain their former status.[4] In other words, in 'frontstage regions' (Goffman 1959), workplace humour of this kind may assist players in appearing to accept what for them is a fearful situation, whilst avoiding their surrender of self among teammates, enabling them to maintain a 'hard front'. 'Backstage', players will be anxious and may feel as though they have failed. Players observe other teammates being dropped from the team from the first moment they sign a full-time contract and from this instant they begin to learn informally the occupationally 'accept-able' ways in which to react. The process of informal socialization for young players centrally involves learning to deal with the fears and uncertainties associated with their work, particularly in terms of 'presentation of self' (Goffman 1959). They must learn also how to react appropriately to players who are dropped or face outright rejection. In time, there is nothing new to learn as such for they see regularly the transition of other players who experience periods of rejection, some of whom leave in search of first team football elsewhere.

## Informal practices and transferring

The significance of the above discussion is that player support systems are char-acteristically informal and often involve former work colleagues who now play for, or are connected in some manner with, other clubs. Players are more likely to discuss their circumstances or personal unhappiness among people who belong to their developing friendship networks. Friendship networks are useful for players insofar as they enable them to make contacts with other 'insiders', some of whom may have extensive webs of contacts. Thus, in terms of the process of transfer-ring, mediators between two networks that are only weakly connected are often indispensable links in the chain of information regarding available players.

The majority of transfers are organized using a mixture of formal and informal procedures. For instance, the procedure of 'tapping' – 'illegally' contacting a player with a view to signing them – would be one example of an informal or unofficial practice. The informal and in some instances illegal practices that are identified in this chapter are underpinned by the networks of contacts which players develop throughout their careers. These contacts may include former playing colleagues, player agents and coaches and managers under and/or with whom the player may have played.

It is an established sociological point that organizations are constituted by the interplay between official and unofficial practices of participants (Watson 1995). The industrial relations literature indicates that an informal structure of social relations inevitably emerges alongside the formal one in workplaces (Auster 1996; Grint 2005). Even practices that are 'against the rules' or are illegal are often viewed sociologically as integral to the daily social organiza-tion of work. Thus, practices that break rules are not always abnormal nor do they necessarily constitute a threat to the interests of those people who are bound up with workplace activities. Some deviations from the formal system may be so commonplace that 'unwritten laws' and informal associations are established (Watson 1995).

There is a great deal of excellent sociological research concerning the networks developed instrumentally by employees in particular occupations. For example, in his study of the occupation of boxers, Wacquant (1998) examines the job descriptions of boxing matchmakers, who he refers to as 'fleshpeddlers'. Of importance for matchmakers, according to Wacquant (1998), is their nexus of personal contacts through which information about the boxing scene and particular boxers flows. The focus for both Faulkner (1971) and Blair (2001) concerns people involved in the entertainment business, many of whom – like professional footballers – are on short-term fixed contracts. Faulkner (1971) suggests that the kind of career which a musician will have mainly depends on their ability and willingness to fit into an existing network of informal relationships among performers, composers, conductors and the hiring contactors. In her piece entitled 'You're only as good as your last job', Blair (2001) indicates similarly that people working in the British film industry, as well as those attempting to gain access to it, hear of and secure work through a variety of types of personal contact who provide recommendations. Blair suggests that an employer would, rightly or wrongly, view a recommended person as presenting lower risk than a completely unknown individual. What is true of workplaces more generally also applies to the work practices in professional football, particularly in relation to the process of transferring.

In professional football, managers and club chairmen may have in mind players whose contracts they want to renew and extend and those whose contracts they intend to terminate. They may have some idea of the players they want to sign from other clubs, perhaps for a fee, in order to strengthen their chances of success. Official procedures exist by which club administrators are formally required to abide when signing players, whether they are dealing with existing club players or others who currently play for and are contracted with other clubs. Even so, the interview data obtained for this book indicate that the 'real work' related to signing players and the process of transferring happens despite the formal procedures. The object of this section then is to examine the informal networks that players form over time that may be used to initiate and subsequently facilitate the process of transferring and to *cut through* the formal transfer procedures.

Sociologists interested in the social organization of work have for some time examined the issue of conflict (and the forms that conflict may take) between employers and managers and their employees, as well as conflict among employees (Grint 2005). The problems of employee subordination and the various forms of 'resistance' to that subordination are common themes and have been the focus of scrutiny (Collinson 2000). Whilst remaining cautious not to overgeneralize, most studies have been concerned with identifying 'oppositional' practices and the development of a counter-culture by employees which involves informal – sometimes illegal – procedures that are intended to win back for them a greater measure of control over their work (Collinson 2000). In part, this resistance involves a degree of 'defence of self' (Watson 1995). Other studies have examined the unofficial practices of managers in business and industrial sectors. A number of these studies, for example the classic research undertaken by Gouldner (1964), illustrate how unofficial rule-breaking may in fact help to meet the ends that those rules were originally intended to serve. Yet, attempting to interpret the informal practices identified in professional football solely as forms of resistance to the power exerted by managers would be a mistake in the light of the interview data obtained.

It would be inaccurate to interpret informal practices solely as oppositional in nature as many of the unofficial associations are experienced as co-operative rather than a source of conflict. The same transfer deal may have positive consequences for some people bound up in the move and, concurrently, it may have negative spin-offs for others. So, the networks of relationships that develop may not only be useful for players but for other network members as well, including management. For example, a network of contacts may be beneficial for agents in order for their players to move regularly, although they don't want their players-as-clients to feel constantly unsettled. The value of a player may drop if he doesn't exhibit a level of 'stickability' and he – and his agent – may gain the reputation of being a troublemaker. The informal networks or grapevines may be useful for club managers too. For instance, they may employ the practice of 'tapping' players – or their agents – who may be unsettled or are close to the end of their contracts. Managers may also fall back on their networks in order to acquire players on a temporary or permanent basis: for instance, if their squad is weakened by injury. As managers move from club to club they develop co-operative associations with former players, some of whom in time become managers and coaches, from whom they can request assistance. All players and managers develop and are members of informal networks. So a player who uses a friend or acquaintance to initiate a move may benefit directly or indirectly from the associations developed within the game by that contact. The following examples indicate the ways in which the majority of players and coaches working in professional football secure work for themselves, at some stage in their career, through a variety of personal associates who perform functions such as providing recommendations.

In his doctoral thesis, Magee (1998) highlights the principal ways in which transfers can be initiated – what he terms the 'points of recruitment' – namely, 'tapping', scouting, agents, advisors, sponsors and the grapevine. He refers initially to a 'tapping' system, which is a system that can be defined, in short, as 'illegal' communication.[5] Managers and coaches contact players, and in some instances agents, informally with the intention of discovering whether or not a player would consider transferring to their club. Magee (1998: 100) suggests that '"tapping" is a common practice that most clubs follow'. An agent interviewed for this study expressed a similar point of view. When asked how transfers are initiated the agent responded in the following way: 'What they [the clubs] are supposed to do is to contact the club [with whom the player is contracted]. Invariably they contact the agent to ask whether the player would be interested.' There have been a number of accusations of illegal transfer activities, principally tapping, referred to in the national press. For example, former Manchester United player and Dutch international Jaap Stam stated in The Mirror (13 September 2001) that he was 'tapped up' by the Manchester United manager Sir Alex Ferguson. Stam acknowledged in the interview that the *illegal*, and therefore 'highly dangerous', get-togethers have become an 'accepted part of the game'. Confirming the commonality of 'tapping' as a central feature of processes of transferring, journalist Matt Dickenson (*The Times*, 2 June 2005), remarking on the saga involving Arsenal player and England international Ashley Cole and Chelsea FC, comments in the following way:

> The practice of 'tapping-up' will continue, but perhaps not with the same brazenness that led Chelsea and Ashley Cole to that fateful meeting in London's Royal Park Hotel on January 27. No one expects clubs and managers to start following the rule book to the letter, but the message sent out by the FA Premier League's disciplinary commission yesterday in meting out record financial punishments for the offence was that miscreants had better not get caught.

In his autobiographical diary, Eamon Dunphy refers to an illegal phone call he received from a former playing colleague, Theo Foley, who was keen to sign him, but wanted to be sure that he hadn't 'lost interest in the game'. Dunphy mentions this illegal contact as follows:

> I was sitting at home this evening when the phone went. It was Theo Foley, the Charlton manager, and an old teammate from the Irish team ... 'What is the problem at Millwall?' I told him that I wanted to get away.
>
> (Dunphy 1987: 165)

This informal 'testing of the water' – as one experienced footballer expressed it – extends not only to players but also to the recruitment of other personnel employed as football-related members of the club. For example, one physiotherapist,[6] describing how he moved from a Division Three (i) club to a Premier League club, explained that after one year at the smaller club he had 'one of the classic phone calls that you get in professional football, which was: "We have not had this conversation, but if our physiotherapist leaves at the end of this season, would you be interested in working for us?"' Another physiotherapist explained how he moved from a Division Three (i) to a Division One (i) club: 'The manager [of the Division One club] just rang me and said "I fancy a change" [of physiotherapist] ... it was totally illegal.'

A number of players referred to 'classic' phone calls similar to the ones described above. For instance, one young Division One (i) player, who had not at that point established himself as a first team regular, described the period in which he was deciding where his future lay. The following interview extract concerns the period during which he was contacted by a former coach who had recommended him to other managers:

> Player: I didn't think I was going to have a chance at the first team, I had nothing else lined up, [a former coach] was assistant to [my former manager] and when he left the club he phoned me up and said, 'Look, I've got these clubs sorted out for you. Don't sign your contract. I can get you here, get you there.'
> MR: Are players contacted like this normally?
> Player: Yeah, it quite often goes on.

Contacts generally serve the function of directly offering a job opportunity, informing a player of a potential job opportunity, or recommending a player to a third party. In this connection, having a person who can recommend the 'attitude' and abilities of a player is important. Younger players who may be peripheral members of the squad are subject to greater uncertainty and longer spells out of the manager's first eleven. Their contact networks tend to be limited, for they will not have had the opportunities to gain and to build on a favourable reputation among their peers in terms of their individual qualities or their commitment to their work. Thus, friends and ex-colleagues remain influential for established players throughout their careers, for they are the people in a position to comment on the quality of an individual player's work and, in time, they become one of the dominant forms of contact used to secure employment. Blair (2003) identifies similar forms of contact in her study of networks of interdependence in the UK film industry.

Magee (1998: 100) highlights 'the grapevine' as a central 'point of recruitment' in professional football and, in this regard, he suggests that: 'Football is often described as a "who-you-know" sport.' In his discussion he examines each 'point of recruitment' separately: he does not tell us whether there is any overlap between them. Furthermore, he does not shed light on whether the initial contacts made through 'the grapevine', whether by an agent or a former playing colleague, are legal or illegal in terms of FIFA regulations. It is certainly the case that managers tend to view a recommended player as presenting a lower risk than one who is completely unknown or lesser known (see McGovern 2000 and 2002). Leverage in the labour market for players is strongly affected by pre-existing relationships with others in the 'industry'. But Magee's tendency to discuss the 'points of recruitment' as distinct elements in the transferring process is not supported by the data collected for this study, for official and unofficial procedures are often bound up in the same transfer. For example, many players are 'tapped' via a contact, who may be a former playing colleague or an agent (who may also be a former playing colleague), who is a part of 'the grapevine', as has been illustrated above.

## Availability and time

Of course there are *legal* types of contact made constantly between managers and players (or approaches to players by club scouts), which are sanctioned by the clubs with whom the player is contracted – unless, that is, the player is out of contract.[7] In these instances, prior knowledge of the player by the manager, or receiving a recommendation from a contact, is still important in terms of recruitment. A number of players interviewed for this study explained how managers for whom they had previously been young professionals had recruited them. For example, when asked how his transfer came about, one former Premier League player responded in the following way:

> It was completely out of the blue. The Premier League didn't start till a week later so I'd done my pre-season and played the first game with [my former club]. [The Premier League club] were up in Scotland on a pre-season tour and they played Hearts and got stuffed. So [the former manager] got in touch completely out of the blue and said, 'Look, we're desperate for a centre-half. Come up and talk.' I went up and signed that day.

Another former Premier League player described a very similar scenario. He said:

> [My former manager] became manager of [a Division Two club]. He phoned me up at about ten o'clock at night. I was in my house. He said, 'Would you want to play for me again?' I said 'Yes, definitely.' He said, 'Get in the car tomorrow, you're coming up.' So I was signed the next day. It was unbelievable.

Both the moves described above had been timely for the players involved, in that managerial changes were afoot at their present clubs. Further, for the players and managers involved, these kinds of transfers represented a reduced risk for they were not negotiating with completely unknown individuals.[8] Consequently, any uncertainties which could be generated during these indeterminate times in players' careers may be dispelled to some degree.

The point demonstrated is that while connections may be comparatively weak and may arise for players unexpectedly, they may still prove to be crucial in terms of opportunities for employment at professional football clubs. Further to this, there are other, arguably indirect, forms of contact that may be means by which a player is offered an opportunity to transfer, such as a recommendation through a third party. For example, a former Premier League player, whose contract had only two weeks to run, was becoming increasingly desperate to find a club during the 1997 close season. Despite the efforts of his agent – with whom he was losing faith – he eventually asked his father's solicitor to fax the clubs with whom, by chance, he had formerly undertaken some work. After months of uncertainty, which were made more worrying by the birth of his first child, he spoke to and subsequently signed for a Division One (i) club via a contact of the solicitor. There may be a number of other patterns in terms of the way in which a player or manager initiates a process of transferring. Crucially, however, all the examples provided, which are representative of those described by the interviewees for this book, demonstrate the importance of the development of a network of contacts for professional footballers, even if the player is not deliberately – perhaps instrumentally – attempting to cultivate such ties. The significance of the relational patterns illustrated in these examples cannot be overstated for they are central in terms of the work opportunities available to players throughout their careers. Playing contracts can be short and most players have to re-secure their positions or find new clubs on a regular basis. A high level of interdependence exists among players for they work in close (and 'closed') environments; the constraint to maintain and develop good reputations as reliable professionals among colleagues is experienced on an ongoing basis. The relatively high level of interconnectedness of professional football, an industry in which personnel move from club to club on a relatively regular basis, may be demonstrated further in the following example. This involves an experienced Division One (i) player who was reunited with a former manager with whom he had previously experienced some difficulties:

> I came back off my honeymoon and the fella who'd made me train on my own at [a former club] had taken over as the manager. So, I was thinking that I was ready to move on again, because of the way he treated me the time before. I'd met him in the meantime and sort of spoke to him and had been civil to him. I always had a feeling that I would come across him again and so at the start of the season, once again, he's brought a couple of centre-halves with him so I was expecting not to be included. But as it was I played and played very well.

An understanding of time should be allied to an appreciation of the social relations of transferring. Without overstating this point, the opportunity for a player to move from one club to another may also be contingent on a number of time-related factors, not least of which is the moment when a manager decides he needs another player. *Available* candidates are reviewed and a manager may decide upon a player who possesses the skills and abilities he requires. Players who are looking to transfer must hope that their availability coincides with the point at which the manager begins his search for a replacement. The player who is selected by the manager as possessing the relevant talents may, or may not, want to move, for he may have alternative options. Thus, certain players may be identified as second or third choices, although they may not know that they are likely targets. An agent interviewed for this study made the following remarks in this connection:

Your player [the player of the agent] may not be a manager's first choice. He may be his second or third. It may well be that an agent can push a player on a Monday, but the club has someone else in mind at that time. That player [the manager's first choice] may decide not to sign, so by the end of the week, all of a sudden, the manager is looking to his other choices. So the circumstances can change in a day.

Thus, opportunities for players to transfer may arise unexpectedly. In Chapter 5, the views of a number of players were that, among management, it is necessary for your 'face to fit' and players must cope with the simple reality that certain managers have a tendency to sign particular types of players (McGovern 2002).[9] In terms of the process of transferring, it is not only necessary to be identified as someone who possesses a 'good attitude', it is also necessary to be available at the right time.

## Conclusion

Throughout their careers, the rewards available to professional footballers are in short supply for all but the most elite players. This fact brings to light a basic paradox for managers of the organization of football squads: namely, that those who are officially intended to work co-operatively and to achieve specific, management-defined ends, may find themselves in conflict, or direct competition, with each other. In these circumstances, the uncertainties and competitive pressures for places in the first eleven – pressures experienced by all but the most secure players – are central for understanding the informal lines of communication among players, managers, coaches and agents. Over time, players develop 'informal' networks of significant insiders in whom they can place their trust. As a general rule they tend not to confide in current teammates with whom there may be internal rivalries. These contact (or friendship) networks are also highly significant in relation to the process of transferring.

Transfers are organized using a mixture of official and unofficial procedures. It is too simplistic to suggest, as is often asserted, that the practices of agents undermine the efficiency of the transfer system. Players, agents and managers, all of whom may have interests at stake in the same transfer deal, must adhere to official practices, at least publicly. Unofficial and sometimes illegal action – such as 'tapping' – may in some cases help to meet the interests (for players, managers and club directors) that those rules were originally intended to serve.

There are complex permutations of movement between football clubs by players, managers and coaches. Access to and movement within professional football clubs are strongly influenced by connections developed within the industry, even if those associations are not fostered with this specific intention in mind. Friends 'within' the game prove to be important mediators of opportunities to move and the importance of such friendship networks continues throughout the career of a player; they are, then, highly significant in relation to labour mobility. Ex-colleagues, for instance, become important as players become established as first team regulars for securing work through activities such as offering jobs directly, recommending individuals via a third party or providing information.

# Chapter 7

# Control and the process of transferring

Among the portrayals of contemporary professional football there exists a widespread perception that modern players earn vast amounts of money and, with the assistance of 'influential' agents, are able to dictate to club managers and directors in terms of salaries, length of contracts and other conditions of employment. There has been an increasing focus on the issue of 'player power' in print media since the landmark 1963 Eastham case, but particularly since the formation of the English Premier League and most notably the 1995 Bosman ruling. For example, Nick Townsend (The *Independent*, 8 November 1998) suggests that 'the scales of influence have swung significantly away from the clubs to the players. Once regarded almost like serfs of feudal landlords, they [the players] now have clout like never before.' There are numerous other articles in which managers and chairmen refer to 'player power' and the 'declining importance of contractual obligations' (see Greenfield and Osborn 2000). But are players (and their agents) able to wield such control over clubs in terms of the process of transferring, as is commonly suggested?

Magee (1998: 115) suggests that 'there are certain players whose talent is sought after and they can subsequently control the system. Such players can be termed "the exploiter".' By contrast there are players who have few choices and, according to Magee, 'are not in a position to determine their future. These players can be referred to as "the exploited"' (Magee 1998: 115). If one imagines, as Magee does, that these ideal types – the 'exploiter' and the 'exploited' – are positioned at the extremes of a continuum, then players who are labelled 'the marketable' occupy middle positions. The 'marketable' are players who are viewed as club 'assets' (Magee 1998: 116), with a market value which club managers and directors may be able to 'exploit' for their own interests if an appropriate situation arises. Marketable players may be sold in order to generate capital and to relieve financial pressure. It is clear that these three ideal types must be considered in relational terms for players are never in, or out of, full control and, over time, their position on this continuum will change as they grow older, suffer injuries and as opinions of their playing performances alter.

Magee's initial discussion of the levels of control that players are able to wield, in terms of the direction of their careers and specifically in relation to the process of transferring, raises many sociological questions.[1] Thus, one may legitimately ask over whom or what do 'the exploiters' have control? For one can only have a degree of control over the actions and intentions of oneself and others. Who is controlling 'the exploited'? Are players who find themselves in relatively weak positions being 'used' by managers, or agents, or club directors – or a combination of all three – who may be furthering their own interests? In what ways are players able to *resist* the attempts of others to control the direction of their careers? Do 'marketable' players have a choice when their club directors are attempting to sell them in order to raise capital? Can a deal between football clubs be agreed upon lawfully without the consent of the player? Moreover, to what degree do the wives and partners of players have veto powers when it comes to decisions concerning, for example, whether or not to accept a transfer offer that involves geographical relocation for them and their family? What is the nature of the input provided by the club doctors who perform medical examinations prior to players signing their contracts? And finally, although these questions are by no means exhaustive, are issues of control in part dependent on the orientations of players to their work as professional footballers? Does it matter whether players consider themselves to be working 'off' their occupation as footballers rather than working 'for' football, in the sense that Weber (1965) uses these terms?[2] In other words, do players' perceptions of their ability to control their next transfer depend on whether, on balance, they view their work solely as a means by which to make ends meet, or as a way in which they can fulfil their dreams and achieve occupational goals?

In short, the sociological problem that lies at the heart of this chapter concerns the social relations of control which contour the job mobility experiences of professional footballers. Specifically, the objects of this chapter are, first, to understand who possesses greater or lesser ability to control the process of transferring and, second, to examine the nature and forms of their control. The discussion that follows is set against the backdrop of the previous chapters that examine transformations of self and self-conceptions as players transfer, and the way in which informal networks facilitate movement between clubs. Thus, the way in which players 'cushion' their sense of self from workplace realities such as rejection and the means by which they develop informal networks which, among other things, may assist movement from one club to the next, are, for players, attempts to resist the control exerted by other people (club managers, agents, club directors, partners and wives) who are bound up in interweaving decision-making processes about the direction in which their careers are heading. This chapter focuses on the social constraints experienced by players as they make decisions about future transfers.

## Control and labour processes

Debates about the concept of 'control' have a long history, particularly for sociologists interested in the nature of work and labour processes (Thompson 1983). There is a great deal written about forms of control initiated by management and resistance by employees to managerial controls (see Collinson 2000; Grint 2005; Watson 1995). This body of research indicates that organizational control involves various types of work-based regulations including technical, bureaucratic and professional regulations, controls aimed at reducing or making unimportant employees' resistance, controls which attempt to discipline the potential maverick, and efforts to establish and disseminate the legitimacy of the organization with all its inequalities and deprivations (Salaman 1981). Nevertheless, within organizations, employers and those in formal controlling positions – such as football managers – are able to exercise a significant degree of control over subordinate members – in this instance, the players – by virtue of their control over desired resources. For professional footballers, the desired resources equate not only to improved financial conditions, but also, and perhaps more importantly, to opportunities to lengthen and improve contracts and to gain or confirm playing status and build reputations. Managers have control over sanctions too: this is observable in terms of less favourable treatment and, ultimately, rejection. In a number of occupational settings, research indicates that workers who experience, for example, the insecurities of short-term contracts, subordination and deprivation of opportunities – in professional football one might think in terms of a lack of exposure to first team football – are likely to demonstrate some resistance to what are, for them, oppressive controls (Collinson 2000).

Managers and managerial styles found in professional football are noted for inflexibility and authoritarianism respectively (Parker 1996a; Tomlinson 1983; Wagg 1984). It is suggested that authoritarian forms of control (of the kind employed by managers in order to call into line players who show signs of indiscipline or insubordination) rely mainly on financial rewards, penalties and threats such as rejection for their effectiveness, whereas normative forms of control (that relate to the possession of a 'good attitude') attempt to 'shape work culture and workers' subjectivity in order to ensure compliance' (Ezzy 2001). Normative forms of control are central in Tomlinson's (1983) examination of the structures of control within football culture, a 'speculative' but sociologically pertinent article constructed using mainly the autobiographies of certain professional footballers who played in the 1970s. Tomlinson focuses on club culture as a form of social control, a point that is born out in Chapter 2 of this study on the attitudes to work in professional football. He suggests that the characteristics of football culture relate more to 'adolescent play' and 'juvenile giggles' than shop floor resistance – although such embedded counter-cultures can involve 'horseplay' and 'banana time' (Watson 1995) – and goes on to make the point that: 'Boys will be boys in football culture because the structures of control allow them to be little else' (Tomlinson 1983: 173). Tomlinson (1983) outlines three potential ways in which 'football culture', an occupational culture in which relations of domination are constructed and reproduced among club personnel over time, constrains the behaviour and social activities of players. He states:

> First, structures of control in the club position the player rigidly at the bottom of the hierarchy. Second, the playing group is predictably fluid; the bulk of the team can disappear within weeks, for various reasons, to be replaced by a new crop. And third, the collectivist dimensions of the culture of the player are directed, on the whole, towards essentially harmless laughs and jokes.
>
> (Tomlinson 1983: 173)

The notion of control in the workplace, the related debates located in the literature on labour processes, and Tomlinson's excellent discussion of football culture as a form of control, provide a backcloth against which to examine issues of control as they relate to processes of transferring.

For professional footballers, the process of transferring may come to signify what, for some players, might be considered a turning point, or at least a benchmark by which 'outsiders' may assess the direction or trajectory of their careers. At times, a transfer may be considered a fateful moment (Giddens 1991) for players insofar as the move may indicate to them and to others a sudden rise or fall in fortunes. The research data collected indicate that there are few occasions in which players are able to control their destiny. Historically it may be possible to identify certain gifted players whose statuses were such that they were able to choose which club they would like to play for or the conditions of their playing contract. More commonly, as indicated by these research data, the choices available to players are constrained in a number of ways.

## Retain or transfer?

The legal regulations of the 'transfer system' in English professional football are the principal means by which the actions and intentions of players are controlled when moving from one club to another. These regulations also constrain the plans of managers and directors who attempt to buy and sell players. The legislation relating to the transfer system in professional football has always appeared 'odd' to outsiders (Foster 2001). The 'retain and transfer' system, which is the name given to the first set of rules relating to job mobility in professional football, 'is without parallel in the history of British industrial relations' (Sloane 1969: 181). The transfer system can be traced to a clause inserted in the regulations of the FA in 1885 which required all players to be registered annually with the Association. The clause, designed to protect smaller clubs by preventing players from club-hopping, instead resulted in the registration becoming something to be bought and sold in its own right (Morrow 1999). Thus, it resulted in the creation of a transfer market. At the end of each playing season a player would be placed on either a 'retained list' or the 'transfer list' on the club's terms, the only proviso being that the terms be no lower than the agreed minimum wages and conditions. Effectively, clubs holding a player's registration had a monopoly over him in that any transfer required, most importantly of all, the consent of the club holding the player's registration.

Prior to the case of the former Newcastle United player and England international George Eastham, in 1963, the 'retain and transfer' system operated in almost all instances to the benefit of the club – that is, the club directors – who possessed the registration of players. For example, former England international Sir Stanley Matthews remarked on one year contracts as follows:

> Before the [1939–45] war, and also just after the war, you would get a letter saying 'Stoke City', and addressed to you: 'Dear Mr. Matthews, we've decided to retain you for the following year, your wage is so-and-so.' Or they say, 'Sorry you are on offer for a free transfer.' We had no say. We were more or less like slaves in those days. I asked for a transfer one year before the war. I was turned down, so the club held you. You were tied. You couldn't do anything about it.
>
> (Taylor and Ward 1995: 38)

T.G. Jones, a Welsh international, referred to a situation in which his club, Everton, did not listen to his appeals that, at the age of thirty-one, he couldn't afford to be playing in the reserve side. He said:

> Well, I had no situation at all. I know that Matt Busby wanted me at Manchester United. I know that Tom Whittaker wanted me at the Arsenal. I'd been told this from good sources and one of them – I won't mention who it was – came to me and said, 'Tom, you're wasting your time. You're on the transfer list but they won't transfer you. They've put you on the transfer list to make you happy, and that's where you're going to stay.'
>
> (Taylor and Ward 1995: 38)

Tomlinson (1983: 155) argues that, 'Players were in many ways powerless' and he cites the cases of former England internationals Wilf Mannion and Tom Finney who, he claims, 'were controlled to the point of being someone else's property'.

From the initial legalization for professional footballers drawn up in 1885 to the Eastham case in 1963, the balance of power was heavily in favour of club directors in terms of all club matters including team selection and the purchasing of new talent. The players in question dealt directly with the club chairmen and/or directors. It wasn't until the 1950s that football club managers increasingly began to take control of team affairs and thus became accountable for team performances (Wagg 1984). Wagg (1984) states that a number of clubs did not appoint a 'manager', in the modern sense of this term, until after 1945, and the title 'secretary–manager' served well into the 1950s; Arsenal, for example, did not alter the title until 1956. Prior to 1963, it would appear that for players the process of transferring – or the negotiating and signing of a new contract – was a particularly 'us' and 'them', bipolar affair. From the viewpoint of the player, he was being sold or released to a club and, with or without his consent, the two clubs involved negotiated a deal that best suited their interests, financial or otherwise. The 'career' interests of the player were not of paramount concern for club directors; still, players were not without power, even prior to 1963. For example, T.G. Jones, who had requested a transfer from Everton as mentioned above, decided that he wasn't missed, even when he played on Saturdays for Hawarden Grammar School Old Boys, and despite being captain of Wales. He said:

> They didn't even ask where I had gone. I said, 'Well, if you won't let me go, I'm afraid that I will walk out and play non-league football,' because I'd already had a business offer from the men who ran Pwllheli Football Club ... Their attitude was 'No one leaves Everton.' And I did. It cost them a lot of money.
>
> (Taylor and Ward 1995: 39)

Even in circumstances in which players are much less able to constrain the actions of the more powerful club directors, players do have some power, for the directors have at least to take the player's actions into account. In these examples, in which power differentials between players and the club directors are very great, the directors had not only a higher degree of control over players, but also a higher degree of control over the processes of transferring as such. For transfers prior to 1963, it is possible to understand the course of the transfer largely in terms of the plans and intentions of club directors.

In reality, few (if any) transfers can be characterized sociologically as bipolar, for they involve multiple groups of people who all may have different interests at stake; thus, expressed in simplified terms, all transfers involve at least the existing employer club, the employee player and the would-be employer club. So, following the end of the maximum wage in 1961 and the Eastham case in 1963, the perception of players of the *multipolar* nature of the process of transferring came more sharply into focus as club directors were stopped from retaining a player's registration when out of contract. Subsequently, between 1963 and 1995, modified versions of the 'retain and transfer' system existed. In this period – a time period from which data concerning player transfers have been obtained for this book – players were not unconditionally free to negotiate a contract with a different club unless they were given a 'free transfer' by their employing club (Gardiner *et al.* 1998). In essence, the new transfer conditions required clubs either to grant 'freedom of contract' – in this case the player is literally a 'free' agent who can move to a new club on whatever terms he or his agent can negotiate – or, alternatively, the club could retain him as a registered player by offering a new deal on terms no less advantageous than the expired contract. With respect to the latter circumstances, the player is 'free' to negotiate a move to another club but this is subject to the club agreeing a transfer fee. In a large number of cases, as will be demonstrated, a player's desire to move may be frustrated if other clubs are not prepared to pay the required or prescribed transfer fee. Moreover, a player may submit to pressure to sign a new contract with a club to regain some security of employment (Gardiner *et al.* 1998).

## Freedom of contract

Freedom of contract might be considered to be among the principal means by which *players* have been enabled to make their own decisions about the trajectories of their careers. Magee (1998) suggests that, for players, 'freedom of contract' is generally regarded as a position of strength when bargaining for new employment and this view is supported, in part, by former Charlton Athletic player Garry Nelson. Nelson (1996: 262) comments that: '"Freedom of contract" has made it possible for players to let their contracts expire and yet put themselves in an enhanced bargaining position. Consistently good form should clearly earn appropriate reward.' Nelson (1996: 262) discusses the different perspectives possessed by players, but particularly those who are more experienced, and directors who are bound up in contract negotiations, in the following way:

> With players who are doing the business well enough to justify the original outlay on them and justify their first team selection, the club will not want the contract to expire. Every attempt will be made to offer a new one that is sufficiently attractive for the player to want to sign. But he (and certainly, where applicable, his agent!) will appreciate that he is negotiating from a position of strength. What he now considers 'attractive' may be a considerable escalation on his previous terms.

Nelson is not untypical of the majority of observers who have commented on transferring and changes to employment laws as they relate to football, insofar as he tends to focus on *player power* and the manner in which, in many cases, this has been bolstered.

So, an 'exploiter' (Magee 1998) such as Sol Campbell, for example, who signed for English Premier League club Arsenal, cannot be blamed, according to Paul Hayward, for 'playing the market to his own spectacular advantage' (*Daily Telegraph*, 30 May 2001). Hayward makes the point that 'Campbell's demands at Tottenham reflect the destructive player-power threatening football'. The twenty-six year old England international was able to turn down an improved offer from the Premier League club for whom he was formerly contracted, Tottenham Hotspur, and negotiate a new and vastly improved four-year contract with Arsenal, via his agent, Sky Andrew, without the concern of a transfer fee. Campbell was able to take advantage of the 1995 Bosman case which rules that transfer fees for players out of contract are illegal under European law. Thus, from 1995, players out of contract could move without a transfer fee. The distinctiveness of the example of Campbell relates to his power and status. That is, at twenty-six years old, he was among the wealthier and more financially secure Premier League players (he was reputed to be earning £6.5 million per year). Moreover he had a developing global reputation; he turned down offers from Inter Milan, Barcelona and Bayern Munich (*Daily Telegraph*, 2 July 2001) before signing for Arsenal in the English Premier League. One might suggest that, since he possessed the higher power ratio, he was able to exploit the rules of transferring to his advantage; that is, to a much greater degree than most of his predecessors prior to 1995, he was able, in part, to control the process of transferring in which he was bound up.

Campbell's higher power ratio is understandable, since he was rated among the best in his position, he was relatively young and a club hoping to sign him would deal directly with him (and his agent) for he was *out of contract*: he was 'on a Bosman', as is common parlance among professional footballers. Thus, any club wanting to secure his talents would have to submit to his demands to a greater degree than he would have to submit to theirs. But even players who do not possess high power ratios of a more 'obvious' or celebrated nature may decide to let their contracts expire in order for them to become 'free agents'. So, players who do not think they are a part of the plans of their manager may decide to find a new club, even if that means taking a cut in wages or playing in a lower division, to acquire regular first team football. Alternatively, a young and ambitious player with a building reputation may decide against signing a renewed and, quite possibly, improved contract with their present club in a lower division so as to attract attention from 'clubs' of a higher status.

For example, a young Division Three (i) player stated that he had made it clear to his manager that he was not going to sign a new contract after he was made aware that 'two or three clubs were interested in me to the extent that a scout was coming to watch me on a regular basis'. Unfortunately this player shattered his shoulder blade in a game and an offer never materialized. However, he went on to comment that, 'from what I've been told by people in the game, if I'd done alright in that game then there was going to be a firm bid on the table by the end of the week'. This young player could not be described as being 'in control' of his destiny, but by not signing a new contract with his present club he embarked on a riskier course of action in order to pursue the occupational goal of playing at the highest possible standard.

All the players discussed thus far appear to be in – albeit temporary – positions of power, although the sources of their power may differ. For example, players who could be labelled 'exploiters' are perceived or perceive themselves to be *in form*: Nelson (1996: 262) refers, in this connection, to 'players who are doing the business'. One might suggest also that their sense of self as professional footballers is strong for they recognize that more than one club would like to employ them. Furthermore, all the players are, or are becoming, available in terms of 'freedom of contract', a context that, for them, is considered one of strength. Prospective clubs would not necessarily need to go through the process of 'tapping' and would not, therefore, pay a transfer fee. Even so, while the players considered above are of different ages and statuses, they are all able to use the factors mentioned as bargaining chips in order to locate themselves in enhanced negotiating positions. Whilst earning wages from playing is fundamental for all professionals, these players are also able to exploit their circumstances to pursue occupational goals.

Not all players however are able to exploit the social circumstances in which they are bound up in advantageous ways. Players who are out of form or favour (or who are not paid 'substantial wages'), or whose contract is not renewed, may have to find new clubs in order to revive their careers. Furthermore, a player whose contract is terminating at the end of the season but who has not been informed of whether he is to be offered new contractual terms, is likely to experience increasing psychological insecurities. These circumstances are more meaningful for older players who, by and large, have a greater number of responsibilities in terms of, for example, wives, children and mortgages, and who therefore possess a heightened awareness of job security. One experienced Division One (i) player whose contract was terminating at the end of the season in which he was interviewed, expressed his feelings about the indeterminate position in which he found himself as follows:

> Oh God, yes, it frightens me to death, you know, my contract running out at the end of the season. It's coming too quick ... I've got to get everything ready, all my qualifications behind me. I've got to get my pension all sorted out so I can finish when I'm thirty-five and then I can try and get a job that I want to do. But these last two years, I just feel as though things have come too quick, which is a nightmare ... I've got to be able to pay the mortgage.

The player said that in most circumstances having *freedom of contract* was 'a good thing', but at his age (thirty years) he needed to keep playing. When asked how he resolved the problem of feeling as though he was in a *state of limbo*, he replied:

> People keep saying to me, 'Oh, you'll get a club, no problem.' I'm not looking to leave but my contract runs out at the end of the season so I'm waiting for them to make up their minds. They haven't offered me a new contract at the moment and I can talk to other clubs in January. It's quite stressful, you know, but you just keep it to yourself.

Asked whether he talked to anyone *outside* the club the player made the following point:

I speak to my girlfriend. In fact, recently, I said to her, 'You know we could be living in a shed at the end of the garden at the end of this year.' I've got a five year plan, up until I'm thirty-five, and if I keep getting a contract we should be all right.

Unlike the previous examples, which highlighted the career status concerns of (mainly younger) players who are looking to increase their reputations and fulfil occupational dreams, this older player, by contrast, prioritized contractual security at least until his thirty-fifth birthday as the focus of his attention. One might suggest that he is playing 'off' rather than 'for' professional football; and, like other players interviewed, he neither desires, nor attempts to achieve, the status of 'freedom of contract'. For many it is forced upon them at a time when they are seeking to extend job security for themselves and dependants.

The above example is typical of a number of interviewees who described the time period leading up to the expiry date of their playing contracts. For many of these (mainly) older players, the prospect or imposition of 'freedom of contract' does not strengthen their capacity to achieve enhanced control over the process of transferring and, consequently, over the directions of their careers. Younger players may struggle to perceive the likely course of such negotiations and, hence, their career moves, for they have limited reputations and networks of contacts in the game, while other players may struggle to establish themselves as first team regulars. The ability of all these players, young and old, to gain a degree of control is limited insofar as they are constrained by the choices they perceive are available to them. Some of the players interviewed, for example, suggested that they thought that certain managers withheld information about prospective clubs whose attention had been drawn by recent good performances. So, if only one club shows an interest in a player then he (and/or his agent) is constrained to deal solely with representatives from this club. A former Division One (i) player, now playing for a club in Division Three (i), said that he hadn't signed the contract which was offered to him and that he wasn't included in the pre-season tour to Malta. The player had to find another club in this period as, according to his manager, he wasn't figuring in any future plans. He said that three managers approached him at this time but his choices were constrained and he described the circumstances as follows:

So the manager of [the club for whom he eventually signed] at the time phoned me and asked me to go up there. I think I also spoke to the managers of [two Division Three clubs] as well. I didn't go to [one of the Division Three clubs] because it was too far, as I was happy living where I was. So, the other two clubs were my only real choices because they were within commuting distance.

This player went on to express his thoughts about this move, suggesting that:

> I was happy to sign for [the manager] because it was still within commuting distance of [my home town], which was important to me. I didn't want to uproot across the country unless somebody was prepared to pay me a lot more money, which they weren't.

A number of mainly older players discussed the geographical constraints in relation to potential transfers, for many were not prepared to 'uproot' suddenly, move their families and relocate to an area in which they had no friendship ties. One experienced player, now retired, said that in his experience it was common for players to buy or rent accommodation during the week and return to their families at the weekends and after matches.

Another experienced player, who had played for clubs in Divisions One (i), Two (i) and Three (i), talked of his mental deliberations leading up to the point when a decision was made concerning his future. He recounts also his actions and refers, indirectly, to his (in)ability, in the early stages of bargaining, to control the course of contract negotiations. In the following account, the player describes the sequence of events and makes reference to the Bosman ruling, which had come into effect in that season:

> I didn't know whether it was out of fear or maybe it was because it was the last year of my contract again, but I was playing very well. Come Christmas time I had played every game and [the manager] made me captain. We were well up in the league all season and at the end of the season we got into the play-offs and I tried to negotiate a new contract, as I was in the first wave of this Bosman ruling. They offered me a new contract, effectively they offered me another fifty quid a week, and I wanted more money. I felt I deserved it because I'd been on the same money for two years, I think. Plus they'd been spending more money on players' wages in the last twelve months, plus I was captain of the team that had got to the play-offs and I thought, you know, I deserved to be at least on equal levels with them. So I haggled, I spoke to the chairman once and then I haggled with the manager for about three months and I couldn't get anywhere.

He said that throughout the summer close season a number of clubs had contacted him concerning a potential move away, for he was now 'free' from contract constraints – he was 'on a Bosman'. He went on to explain the difficulties that may arise for players who are *free agents* and those who find themselves in circumstances similar to the one described above:

> I spoke to [two Division Three clubs] but, because there were so many players available, they were all reluctant to commit themselves. They were all offering two or three month contracts and basically I thought it was ridiculous. I mean effectively it's a two or three month trial for a thirty-two year

old defender who's played a couple of hundred league games. I wasn't prepared to do that.

When asked how he coped during this period he said:

> It was difficult. It was a stressful summer really because of the uncertainty
> with the situation at my current club. I didn't seem to be getting anywhere
> with the manager which didn't surprise me after my previous experiences
> with him. It was awful to be honest ... I've been playing professional football
> for about the last fifteen years and you get to thirty-two and you realize that
> you are never going to be a millionaire or play for Manchester United and all
> that. But I've got the brains to go on and do something else.

The occupational position of *free agent* – otherwise interpreted as unemployed –
for this player does not generate the 'advantageous' effects which may transpire
for other players, such as England international Sol Campbell, mentioned earlier,
for this player does not possess the power differentials to control either the contract negotiations or the process of transferring in which he is embedded.

Experienced players, such as the one quoted above, might be labelled 'the
exploited' using Magee's terminology: it might be argued that there exists a fine
balance between possessing 'freedom of contract' and age, for some older players
expressed the thought that they felt 'used and discarded'. The Bosman ruling and
its ability to enable certain players (exploiters) to enhance their bargaining position has received a great deal of attention from the media while few people have
commented on the negative consequences of this ruling from the point of view of
players whose power position is less strong. A former Premier League player, for
instance, made the following remarks when asked whether he considered the
1995 ruling to be advantageous for players:

> It is if you're at the top of the tree. The biggest thing is if you're talking about
> the Bosman ruling, I remember, last year there were just under 600 pros
> available on free transfer, whether that's through the Bosman ruling, players
> being over twenty-four, out of contract, or clubs freeing them, or what have
> you. It is good if you're in a situation where you know you've got four, five or
> six clubs after you, or if you're Dennis Bergkamp or Michael Owen. But if
> you're like Joe Soap who's played in the Division Two or Three for ten years,
> then it doesn't really do you any favours ... it's good if you're the cream of the
> crop and it's good if lower league clubs want you, but if nobody wants you
> then I'm not sure it's a good thing.

The player quoted above reaffirms a point expressed earlier concerning the desire
for all players to be and to feel 'wanted', as even in the context of the Bosman ruling, that is, post-1995, players who are not wanted may find themselves

unemployed or with few alternatives other than to accept their first and possibly only contract offer.

It seems to be the case, from the interview data collected and from statements made in the media, that transfer processes post-1963, but particularly post-Bosman, that is, post-1995, typically involve more people. Writing in the *Guardian* (8 September 2001), Vivek Chaudhary claims that transfers are more complicated than ever, and makes the following comparative point: 'Transfers used to involve a telephone call from one club manager to another. With the game becoming more global and international transfers increasing, the number of people involved in the buying and selling of players has also multiplied.' Chaudhary quotes the agent Rachel Anderson, to the effect that: 'The whole transfer system has become an incredibly complicated industry. Quite often you have a deal and several parties want to get involved. It's getting worse because the money is greater.' So, as the number of people involved in transfer processes grows, the individual player may not only find negotiations increasingly opaque and uncontrollable, but also he becomes gradually aware of his inability to understand and control them. This may in part explain why players have come increasingly to employ agents to act on their behalf.

Throughout the history of professional football, power ratios involving club personnel have usually been extremely unequal; thus, club directors with relatively great authority and control have exercised their power over team managers and players to the full, often unscrupulously for their own purposes. From the first day that a player signs for a club, he has a degree of power relative to the manager (and club directors) as long as he is considered to be valuable in playing terms. But players can lose power, particularly if they sustain a bad injury, or lose form, as *all* players do. If there is a change of manager, for example, a player who is not in the plans of the new manager may find that he is starved of exposure to first team football: his status and sense of self as a first team regular may diminish. But even though the club manager and club directors may have power over the player, the player is not altogether powerless: the power of the player is in proportion to the manager's dependence on the level of performance achieved by the player and, hence, the team. For all that, there are other people who may find themselves bound up in the broader process of transferring and, in this context, may also possess a degree of relative power. It is to the first of these – agents – that attention now turns.

## The role of agents in professional football

One of the first significant transfer debates since the formation of the English Premier League centred on whether Sol Campbell would remain with Tottenham Hotspur at the end of the 2000–2001 season or whether he would succumb to the advances of Arsenal, Manchester United or Bayern Munich, among others. The media presented Campbell as a player who could take his pick of prospective clubs. When asked about his future at Tottenham Hotspur and his conditions for staying, Campbell said: 'They just have to convince me that they're as ambitious as I am' (*Daily Telegraph*, 26 March 2001). The bargaining power that players such as Campbell have at their disposal is considerable and vastly superior to that which was available to their predecessors. Now, in a seller's market, a number of players in the current FA Premier League can secure their financial future in a single contract. One aspect which this transfer process highlighted was the centrality of agents who are employed by players-as-clients to represent and act as broker for them during contract negotiations. Thus, a developing aspect of the modern game is the prevalence of agents. Over the last few years, they have been increasingly able to form relationships with the prized professionals in the top leagues of Europe. Many top players – it is estimated that at least eighty per cent of Premiership players – now employ agents to represent them. No longer do they have to negotiate their own contracts with club managers or chairmen. This position of influence has enabled agents to have a significant effect on the movement of players between clubs. So how has this situation come about?

Football agents are commonly seen to be a new phenomenon. In fact, they were active in the scouting and recruiting of players on behalf of clubs following the legalization of professional football in 1885. The use of agents declined somewhat in the early years of the twentieth century as clubs developed their own scouting networks, although they have never completely disappeared from the game. Nevertheless, the *entrepreneurial* agents (Taylor 1999) of this earlier period were distinct from the type that Premiership players such as Ashley Cole and Michael Owen might employ today. Whereas the former represented the clubs, the latter represent the players. As recently as the 1960s and early 1970s, the use of agents by players was largely confined to what might be described as extraneous commercial ventures. It was not until the mid-1970s that players began to turn to people 'outside' the game for professional advice on contract and transfer negotiations. In the subsequent period there has been a discernible shift in the bargaining power between players and clubs, a shift which has been facilitated and, at times, exploited by agents. These changes to the labour relations of professional football are partially attributable to modifications in the structure of players' contracts and in the transfer system, the principal changes being the landmark Eastham case in 1963, alterations to 'freedom of contract' law in the late 1970s, and, of course, the Bosman ruling in 1995.

In light of these transformations, what range of services can a Premiership player expect from his FIFA licensed agent?[3] One such agent described his duties in the following terms:

> It's not just their contracts. That is just a tiny part of the job of an agent, I think they (players) need to be aware of how to work with the media and to get the media to work for them and not be confrontational, and how to capitalize their income after they finish playing.

The Professional Footballers' Association (PFA) is also able to offer its full support to players. One of its licensed agents characterized its approach as follows: 'We have management agreements with players and within that we can look after every aspect from representing them in their contract negotiations, looking after their commercial interests, legal, accountancy, everything.' As another agent put it, 'this task is considerably easier if you are operating in a seller's and not a buyer's market'. Agents see the marketing of a player as essential if his profile and stand-alone value are to be effectively exploited. They may also organize items such as personal insurance; many are granted power of attorney. In addition to offering financial advice, there is an overarching responsibility for agents to offer career guidance. Therefore, the nature of the relationship between a player and his agent is one in which the player invests a great deal of trust.

The life of a professional footballer is one in which a great deal of uncertainty is generated. There are few players who can guarantee that they will be selected in the first eleven from one week to the next. Even the most gifted players or those with immense experience will at some stage experience rejection. Historically, there have been few advisers to whom players could turn in order to talk through their problems. The macho personae of most players lead them to 'put a brave face on it' when things turn sour and to conceal their feelings of anger or hurt. So, whereas thirty or so years ago most players handled their affairs alone and may have felt isolated in the process, the majority of Premiership professionals now employ agents. Indeed, some may seek the advice and support of their agents on a daily basis. It tends to be a relationship which recognizes few boundaries in terms of the levels of intimacy involved.

Players are keen to be represented by an agent they can trust, someone who will relieve them of the burden of negotiating with the very person – the manager – who will be selecting them to play in the first team and with whom they have already formed or will have to develop a working relationship. Many players have spoken of the pressurized situations in which they have been placed with regard to contract negotiations. An older, former Premiership player, currently playing in Division One (i), when asked to reflect upon his experiences of negotiating with club personnel, said, 'even at this stage now, it's all little games, contracts. They try to put pressure on you, get you in their environment, that's how it works.' Agents share this understanding of 'how it works'. In this connection, one licensed agent said: 'It's not a level playing field when they [players] go talking to managers about contracts. The manager has all the information, a player doesn't. It's an unequal struggle.' Another agent was more forthright about the need for players to be represented. He said:

> Players need agents because they [players] say, 'yes' to everything. If a manager says to a player, 'I'm going to offer you this because we don't pay any other players any more than that', how can a player tell his gaffer, who is going to pick him for the next game, that he doesn't believe him ... players

can't afford to let personality get in the way of negotiation whereas I solely represent them.

As will become apparent, such representation can also have its problematic side.

Few agents work alone. Many of the early agents who began as solo operators, notably Jon Smith, Tony Stephens and Jon Holmes, have either combined forces, or now work for large marketing groups such as SFX Entertainment, subsequently acquired by the US media firm, Clear Channel. But even those who continue to work for themselves (many of whom are former players) usually employ a number of assistants (who may also be former players) to act on their behalf. The 'bigger' businesses are able to handle more clients, although some single agents are reported to have as many as sixty contracted players. One agent, who represents twenty-one players, is of the view that

> you can't have any more than that and look after them. I mean twenty-one is a lot to deal with, you know, just phoning them every week. If you can imagine how long that can take, it's a lot of time.

In the view of this agent, those who deal with larger numbers 'treat their players as commodities ... they focus solely on the buck'. According to former professional footballer Ray Bloomfield, who now works as a football consultant and adviser to licensed agents:

> now you get a lot of players signed up willy-nilly by agents, but if they're not in the first team at 19 or 20, they're left in limbo because the agent hasn't got time to deal with them. You could spend an entire week dealing with one player, so the agents neglect the ones that need help and focus on their big stars.
>
> (Taylor 1999)

More worrying, however, was the situation described by the PFA licensed agent referred to earlier, who said:

> what the agents will do is latch on to their prize and they will wrap themselves around them, because that prize then opens the doors to other prospective clients within that club. They'll do a hell of a lot for them and then they'll do absolutely nothing for those who aren't regularly stripped [selected for the first team].

He added that,

> a lot of agents scatter their contracts around. They sign people up, but you won't see them for months and months. And then suddenly one of the players

begins to do well and there's a bit of speculation and then the agents come back in ... We also have players being sued by agents who sign the players up, who have nothing to do with them and suddenly they'll see a piece in the press about a player. The player thinks, 'I haven't seen him for such a long time, I can't remember signing a contract. I'll go to somebody else.' He signs and suddenly the original agent sues. That's the way they operate.

To summarize, the problem as far as agents are concerned is finding and signing players who have the capability to earn money: a potential *cash cow* for the agent. However, the problem for players is to find an agent in whom they can place their trust and who won't treat them, to quote the former Portsmouth and Derby County manager Jim Smith, 'as a meal ticket' (*The Times*, 4 February 2000). Thus, the player–agent relationship is characterized by these potentially divergent interests. The negative image that clubs tend to have of agents emanates from their reputation for unsettling players and encouraging them to be more nomadic. To quote Jim Smith again: 'The last thing agents want is for their client to stay 10 years at one club. They are engineering a different society' (*The Times*, 4 February 2000). Smith's view of agents is given some credibility in the light of particular high profile incidents. For example, in January 2005, Arsenal player and England international Ashley Cole, and his agent Jonathan Barrett, met officials from Chelsea FC with a view to a possible transfer, even though Cole had two-and-a-half years remaining on his five year contract – an illicit 'tapping' scenario in which Cole was accused of engineering a move to Chelsea. For his part in the saga, Cole was fined £100,000 – the equivalent of four weeks' wages. Sir Philip Otton QC, chairman of the FA Premier League's disciplinary commission, stated in his report that he had treated Cole leniently, for he accepted that Cole had been 'manipulated to a large extent by his agent [Jonathan Barrett]' (*The Times*, 2 June 2005).

Ray Bloomfield, the football consultant quoted earlier, offers some support for this view, when he says that he avoids working with certain agents as a number of them 'just cause disruption ... if a player gets left out of a team, his agent might nurture his grievance, play on his ego so that the player comes to think that it's not his fault' (Taylor 1999). In contrast, the licensed agent Rachel Anderson's response to the claim that agents encourage players to transfer at regular intervals, is: 'Well, they must like the aggravation ... It's much, much easier to renegotiate an existing contract' (Taylor 1999). However, when asked about whether she would advise an out-of-favour player to move on, she replied:

He has no choice. They put him in the reserves, have him training with the kids, it's demoralizing. I'd tell him to wait a while if a new manager has come in, but if there's a personality clash, divorce is the only way out.

(Taylor 1999)

While there is some general agreement concerning the necessity for players to have someone brokering their deals, opinions on what constitutes appropriate representation diverge. It can be the case that the level of dependency which develops between some players and their agents makes the former vulnerable to exploitation by the latter. Some agents not only negotiate on behalf of their clients; they often do so in their absence. This leaves open the possibility of covert manoeuvering between the agent and the club which may be at variance with the player's interests. For example, the PFA licensed agent referred to relations between agents and the clubs as 'laughable'. He elaborated:

> You know prominent managers, high profile club chairmen or vice-chairmen as the case may be, talk about combating the activities of agents. It's because of the clubs that the agents have thrived; the clubs are in cahoots with the agents. I mean you go to games, you will see agents in and out of boardrooms. They scream when they feel that an agent is unsettling one of their players and yet they'll do anything for them when they are looking to get a player from another club.

He went on to point out that 'they [the clubs] pay agents and this is totally against all the regulations. We have now got legal cases going on looking to support players who have been stitched up by their agents.' To underscore this point he made reference to an interchange he heard at a seminar: 'Somebody was giving a talk about his discussions with an agent who was being paid by two clubs and the player. He asked this agent, "Whose interests do you represent?" The agent replied, "Well my own to begin with".' It seems that in order to feather their own nests some agents may, on a formal level, be representing their client's career interests while simultaneously, on an informal level, they may be in a position to take advantage of the need of a club to attract or dispose of players. In the course of contract negotiations there are likely to be numerous opportunities for agents to exploit the situation for their own gain. In such cases, they are, in effect, operating as 'double agents'. However, too strong a focus on these more dubious activities should not be allowed to detract from the numerous positive benefits that representation by agents has brought for players. Much of their good work in relation to pensions, personal insurance and education remains unacknowledged by many in the football industry.

## Club doctors and physiotherapists

The majority of players who transfer from one club to another do so against a backdrop of injuries. Information pertaining to their medical history is important for prospective club executives prior to them signing a contract. Few club directors would want to invest club capital in a player – a potential club asset – whose health is in question. Medical history is an important aspect of player transfers and is relevant in any discussion of who possesses an ability to control the process of transferring.

Club doctors and physiotherapists are drawn into the process of transferring insofar as medical examinations are a usual feature of this form of job relocation. As a result, club managers and directors are drawn into the realm of medical consultation, a context in which, one may assume, they relinquish a significant degree of control to the medical practitioners upon whom they rely for a *professional* opinion of the players they examine. There is a general assumption in encounters between practitioners and their clients that 'doctor knows best' (Oakley 1980). Medical practitioners are members of a professional body[4] and possess, by virtue of their formally recognized status, an official mandate to apply their knowledge and values, as Waddington (1996) notes, free from 'external control'. Freidson (1970) has written about forms of 'client control' in medical relationships and how one of the tasks of medical professionals is to persuade 'the client' to follow their advice. The clients in the case of professional football include the manager and club director. Even so, the advice of medical practitioners is not always trusted (Lupton 1996), and in the context of professional football medical practitioners may themselves be subject to control by powerful *clients* (Freidson 1970) – in this instance club directors and managers – particularly as many are part-time employees of the club (see Waddington *et al.* 1999). For example, club directors and managers may experience pressure from club supporters to be seen to be actively attempting to purchase new players to strengthen the football squad. This pressure may consequently be deflected onto club doctors and physiotherapists to pass fit a potential player whose long- or even medium-term health may be in question. Moreover, the pressure felt by club directors may be such that they feel unable to act on the advice provided by the club doctor, hence undermining the legitimacy of the doctor's position. In such circumstances, club doctors and physiotherapists who apply their professional medical understandings come to be 'clients' themselves, having neither exclusive nor final responsibility for the information they provide. Ultimate authority lies with the club directors. Under these 'patronage' relationships (Johnston 1972), club doctors may serve and advance the interests of club directors and managers. A particularly striking example of this latter circumstance is cited later.[5]

What constitutes a player 'medical' is a matter of debate. For instance, when asked whether or not he met the club doctors in person prior to signing contracts at respective clubs, a former Premiership player made the following remark:

> No. Well I say that, I met some of them. I'm thinking of the medicals that you do at [a Premiership club], I don't think it was the club doctor that did it, I think it was the physio that did the tests. At [another Premiership club] I think it was the same, the physio took you to all the places you had to go to. It was the doctor here at [a Division One club] in conjunction with the

physio, but there are different levels of medical the higher up you get if you see what I mean. Obviously at [a Premiership club] it was a lot more in-depth.

A definitive description of a player medical is not possible based on data gathered for this study, yet, according to the player quoted above, they may alter from one club to the next. Neither is it possible to say conclusively whether or not the advice offered by a medical practitioner is taken into account. Even so, it would appear to be the case that player medicals are a common feature of transfer processes.

It is usual to read in the print media about player *medicals* as transfer negotiations between club directors and managers, agents and players conclude. On some (albeit rare) occasions, advice provided can lead some club directors to reject an offer from a selling club. For example, former Newcastle United player and Northern Ireland international Keith Gillespie failed a medical prior to a proposed £3.5 million move to Middlesbrough (*Daily Telegraph*, 3 August 1998). The central problem and one that appears relatively commonly was that Gillespie had an existing ankle injury which would take, it was estimated by the buying club's doctor, a further two months from the start of the new football season to repair fully. Clearly, Middlesbrough didn't want to buy a player who could not contribute to performances and was, therefore, a 'non-producer' (Waddington *et al.* 1999). Similar circumstances arose for Dutch international and former PSV Eindhoven centre-forward Ruud van Nistelrooy whose potential British record £18.5 million transfer to Manchester United fell through following an injury to his right knee. Van Nistelrooy sustained the injury prior to Manchester United officials completing contract negotiations. The Manchester United manager Sir Alex Ferguson remarked that: 'Nothing will be sorted out until the boy comes over next week and has a medical on his knee ligament injury and we sort out other things' (*Daily Telegraph*, 26 April 2000). The medical test revealed that he had not fully recovered from his knee injury and it was reported that Sir Alex Ferguson asked to see van Nistelrooy *in action* before completing the deal. Again, the Manchester United directors didn't want to purchase a player who could not contribute to team performances. The most common interjection of medical staff in terms of the process of transferring appears when players have existing injuries, the extent of which requires specialist medical opinion in terms of future matches missed. What is sociologically interesting about van Nistelrooy is that he has performed at the highest domestic and international levels and could be considered among the types of 'powerful' players who, according to Magee's (1998) criteria, is typical of an 'exploiter'. Even so, social circumstances beyond his control have constrained his ability to manage the direction of his career at this particular juncture.

It is not only in contexts related to purchasing players that medical practitioners may be bound up in transfer processes, willingly or otherwise. For example, an experienced, former international player interviewed for this study provided a striking example of unprofessional conduct on the part of the club doctor. In this incident (reported in Waddington and Roderick 2002) the club doctor at this Premiership club was clearly acting as an agent on behalf of the club and used confidential medical information about the player to advance the interests of the club over and against those of the player. The player described what happened as follows:

> The club doctor, in my opinion, totally compromised his situation. I'd had [an operation] and my contract was up at the end of the season ... I was approached by [three leading English clubs], Atletico Madrid and Lyon. Three or four weeks later, when I was talking to these clubs, I got summoned to the club doctor's ... the club doctor called me and said would I go round to his house ... I arrived there and he was there with the surgeon who did my operation ... the surgeon wasn't particularly happy about being there. He [the club doctor] said, 'You're thinking about leaving the club this summer?' I said, 'Yes'. He said, 'Well, the surgeon has told us that you've only got another year at the most to play football. If we make that common knowledge, no club in the world would pay millions of pounds for you.' I said, 'Well, what are you telling me?' He said, 'Well, if you're thinking of leaving the club and we made that common knowledge, then ... no-one would buy you.' So ... I ended up agreeing a new deal to stay.

The incident described by the player had taken place several years previously and, at the time of the interview, the player was still playing for the same club. The player said that he thought the club doctor was probably acting under great pressure, not in this case from the manager but from the club chairman, but he added that this did not excuse the doctor's behaviour: 'He was probably under great pressure to do that, but he's done wrong.'

The purpose of this discussion has been to describe some of the ways in which football club medical staff may be bound up in transfer processes. Their primary purpose relates to player medical examinations and the interpretation of results, although their involvement may stretch further as exhibited by the example of the club doctor described above who acted as an agent on behalf of the club. This latter example is useful for it highlights the complexity of the power ratios among people involved in transfer negotiations, specifically club doctors, who are 'powerful agents' in their own *professional* right and their clients who, in this particular instance, may also be their employers.

## Wives and partners[6]

In most football clubs in England, the formal employment positions such as player, manager, coach, physiotherapist and director are well established; from one club to the next one is able to identify relatively easily the people who occupy these positions. Although players will already be familiar with the structures of power among these relationships when they transfer to new clubs, specific personnel are able to shape these power relations because in professional football job descriptions are not precise – in fact, in many football clubs there is an absence of job descriptions (see Waddington *et al.* 1999). The perception by players of their own positions of power relative to other players alters, for instance, as they sustain injuries or are dropped because of a loss of form; these changing personal circumstances may lead to the generation of *personal* issues for them. When they move to a new club their sense of their *own* power may become re-established. The pertinence of this point at this juncture relates to the fact that the process of transferring not only has an impact upon the player, but also upon his wife or partner and children. On a broader level, the partner[7] and family of a player are also bound up among the network of relations which characterize professional football: they experience too the effects of changing balances of power.

Former Republic of Ireland international Tony Cascarino provides a good illustration of the way in which the family members of players are affected by the player's profession in his revealing (auto)biography, *Full Time* (Kimmage 2000). The following extract relates to a period shortly after he transferred from Celtic in Glasgow to Chelsea Football Club:

> We moved to London but the cataclysm continued at Chelsea. I was booed at Stamford Bridge on the day I made my debut, and then Michael came home from school one afternoon and inflicted the cruelest blow of all. The boys in his class had been talking about me. 'You're not very good, Dad, are you?' he said. How do you respond to something like that? What do you say to your six-year-old son? That his friends are wrong? That there's a lot more to the game than what they hear from their dads? What's your defence when you're thirty-one years old and your career is in freefall? There was nothing to do but swallow hard and resolve to make him proud.
>
> (Kimmage 2000: 5)

Thus, an examination of the consequences of a process of transferring may lead to a more adequate understanding of the interconnections between the home, work and family life for players.

In Chapter 6, the informal networks developed by players were examined, although their networks involve individuals who might be said to be part and parcel of the 'football industry', for instance, agents. The household, however, provides an appropriate focus from which to examine the interdependence between 'home' and 'work'. Although it is not possible to undertake a full examination of these links in this book, it would be inappropriate to view the 'home', 'work' and 'family life' as discrete subjects. As Bonney and Love (1991) suggest, it would be non-sociological to perceive the household as a 'black box' from which decisions concerning, in this instance, a player's career emanate. In this section, the very public spheres of work and the private spheres of day-to-day domestic life and relationships are not considered separately, but are recognized as overlapping and interdependent.

Of course, at the heart of this question is the significance of the partner in relation to the process of transferring. More specifically, the focus concerns the degree of relative power of partners to impact on decision-making processes relating to transferring, often involving geographical relocation. This is the 'problem' addressed in this section. From data collected during the interviews and from various secondary sources, one might argue that job relocation is a key issue for the partners of players. Labour market migration is a relatively rare event – with less than three per cent of couples making such moves in any one year (Bruegel 1996) – yet in the context of professional football simultaneous job and geographical relocation is commonplace for one or all members of a family.

In mainstream sociological and psychological literature there are a number of studies which focus on the changes to levels of stress that may be produced in the course of job relocation (Luo and Cooper 1990; Martin 1999; Munton 1990). According to this body of literature, job relocation refers to the process of a simultaneous job and geographical move. It is generally thought to be the case that moving job and house can both be stressful life events but when they co-occur, as is often the case for professional footballers, it is hypothesized that high levels of stress are experienced by the relocator and his or her family (Munton 1990). Relocation, or job transfer, in particular, can have profound effects upon the lives of individuals and families. It can require changes in children's schools, partners' jobs and also provoke difficulties associated with selling and buying property in changing housing markets. This small but growing body of literature, which has been undertaken mostly by psychologists of work, draws a number of conclusions which are relevant for the study of professional footballers and their movement from one club to another. For example, it is generally assumed that job relocations resemble other commonly regarded stressful life events. In particular, they disrupt routines of daily life, are accompanied by changes in social context and provoke feelings of anxiety, uncertainty, loss of control as well as challenge (Munton and West 1995). There are three 'factors' that are commonly implicated by psychologists as 'causes' of relocation stress: age, sex and whether the relocator has a family. In particular, having a child is associated with greater levels of relocation stress.

The social relationships between work and the home should be viewed as a process, changing over time as people develop through their life span. A central issue in the job relocation literature concerns the effects such a move has on the partner of the relocating employee, sometimes referred to as the 'trailing spouse' (Martin 1996). The often-cited reason for greater stress levels for females – as the 'trailing spouse' – is that they feel isolated when they move, are bored, lonely and lack a social network. In addition, they typically spend long periods of time at the new home and/or taking care of children and, in a significant number of cases, are charged with settling chores (Luo and Cooper 1990). By contrast, relocating male employees benefit from social interaction in the workplace. Consequently, levels of stress experienced by men decrease whereas with women they tend to stay the same (Martin 1996). It could be argued that since relocators often move to better jobs or because they are promoted, the anticipated 'negative' effects associated with the move are counterbalanced by an improved work situation. The general literature in this specific area suggests that while people questioned in past surveys viewed job relocation as an opportunity for new job challenges and future career enhancement, and were unwilling to turn down a transfer for fear of jeopardizing their career, nowadays over sixty per cent of people refuse a move at some time in their careers because of the potential disruption it may cause (Munton 1990). There is little doubt that job relocation is a common career contingency for professional football players. Moreover, for nearly all the players interviewed for this book, transferring to another club, whether or not it involved geographical relocation, is viewed more in terms of an opportunity than a potential disruption. So, a central issue in the job relocation literature concerns the (often unintended) consequences such a move has on the partner of the relocating employee; it is these consequences which may constrain and enable the behaviour of partners in terms of the process of transferring.

The issue of relocation in the context of professional football is interesting as, from the viewpoint of a player, transferring to a new club is usually considered in positive terms. A transfer presents a player with the opportunity to re-establish his identity as a first team regular and to feel wanted, characteristics which underpin his sense of 'self'. In this regard, consideration should also be given to the stage reached by the player in his career and whether, on balance, he considers himself to be playing 'for' football, or playing 'off' football. Both scenarios may lead a player to consider a move which necessitates geographical relocation. According to Ortiz (1997), who has undertaken one of the few studies of partners of professional athletes, many wives and partners of players have come to terms with the fact that their husbands are 'married' to their sports careers first and to them second. Insofar as the partners of professional footballers are concerned the problem may be viewed from an alternative perspective. For example, it may be the case that they are tied to their husbands economically and, thus, recognize the need to relocate in order to secure an income, regardless of whether or not they wish to do so. The reaction to a move involving relocation may also relate to the degree to which the wife or partner 'identifies' with the playing career of the player (Thompson 1999). So, they may feel as though they must avoid overt conflict when discussing a potential transfer by suppressing their own wishes. Given the typically short-term nature of football contracts and, relatively speaking, overall playing careers, the partner may place prime importance on the career of the player, and forfeit or 'trade-off' (Jarvis 1999) their personal desires. That said, a decision made by a player and his partner about moving to seek work following redundancy from a club, which may involve a step down in status for the player, is a very different kind of decision from one which relates to a promotion to the big time. It may be argued that the pressures on them to acquiesce to a mobile lifestyle are both economic and cultural. The cultural norm that married couples live together,[8] wedded to the traditional notion that a wife follows her husband wherever his work takes him, has been historically very strong and very significant in this context.

Since the Bosman ruling in 1995, the activities of the partners of professional footballers have been more closely scrutinized; interest in particular relationships and infamous incidents have come to be amplified by the media. This interest relates, in part, to the celebrity status achieved (Rojek 2001) by a number of elite Premier League players. There has also been a media-led rising of interest in the wives and partners of high profile professional footballers, since midway through the 1990s. Arguably the zenith of this interest was the ITV drama entitled *Footballers' Wives*. The women in this series were characterized as variations on a well known stereotype with qualities including bleached blonde hair, sparkly nails and all-year tans, and were presented wearing revealing clothes in many scenes. Missing on this shortlist however is the anonymity 'expected' (Thompson 1999) of wives and partners in many circumstances of their husbands' sports career. This point has been substantiated by McKensie (1999: 234) who claims that among the important lessons she learnt as wife of an American footballer was that 'in the world where I lived most of my life, I was an afterthought at best, and my existence was acknowledged only because of my connection to my NFL husband'. Yet, in professional football in England, interest in the wives and partners of players has increased since the well publicized partnership of Real Madrid player and England international David Beckham, and pop star Victoria Adams, better known as Posh Spice of the pop group the Spice Girls. Alyson Rudd (2000) states in *The Times Football Handbook* that, of late: 'Some wives are prepared to give interviews, some have careers and some are more famous than their husbands.' Alongside the plentiful images of celebrity partnerships between players and pop stars, actresses and other public figures, there have been a number of meaningful articles and interviews exploring the daily lives of wives and partners who do not crave the limelight in their own right.

### Commuting relationships

Among the most notable episodes in which a wife was considered to have influenced the process of transferring was that involving former Premiership defender David Unsworth, and his wife Jayne Unsworth. Previously a player with Everton in the north-west, Unsworth was keen to move from London-based West Ham to a Premiership club further north. Unsworth was quoted in the *Daily Telegraph* (30 July 1998) saying that, 'my wife and I are uncomfortable living down there [London]'. Despite renewed interest from Premiership club Everton, Unsworth agreed to a £3 million offer from Aston Villa. On his arrival at Aston Villa, Unsworth asked the manager at this time, John Gregory, permission to live on Merseyside, which meant a daily round trip of 230 miles to attend training. After only five days Unsworth informed John Gregory that he had made a mistake and that he wanted to be released from his contract in order to rejoin Everton, the club where he began his career. Alyson Rudd (*The Times*, 1 October 2000) commenting on the male domination of professional football, suggests that 'football is in a time warp' and, in this connection, she wrote: 'When David Unsworth dared to adhere to his wife's wishes and admitted his move to Aston Villa was a mistake because Mrs Unsworth wanted to live back on Merseyside, there was outrage.' Rudd went on to suggest that this 'outrage' would not compare to the outcry 'if players started letting their wives decide where they should play'. Reacting angrily to Unsworth's transfer request, the Aston Villa manager John Gregory suggested that the player and his wife had laboured under the erroneous belief that Birmingham was almost as close to Liverpool as Bolton. When asked about the transfer request, Gregory quipped to journalists that unforeseen late homecomings had apparently led Jayne 'to throw the dinner in the bin'. He went on to say that: 'We all know who wears the trousers in that house' (*Daily Telegraph*, 30 July 1998).

The example involving David Unsworth is useful for it alludes to a number of patterns that are sociologically pertinent for enhancing an understanding of, first, the way in which players transfer from one club to another and, second, more general changes between males and females in the social spheres of 'work' and 'home'. It seems clear from his comments that the Aston Villa manager John Gregory possessed an unambiguous idea of the behavioural expectations of the partners of professional footballers. His comments reflect traditional dominant male attitudes in general in which segregated gender roles lie at the heart of expectations.[9] One can assume that Gregory does not think it is the place of partners to interfere in football or career-related decisions. Even so, it is clear from the example of David and Jayne Unsworth that, to some degree, partners *are* influential. It may be that, in the context of professional football, there has been some eradicating of the longstanding expectation that partners should adopt the role of the 'trailing wife' (Bruegel 1996; Martin 1996). Players may decide to travel long distances each day to the football club – as was the case with David Unsworth – or to buy or rent a flat and live part of each week away from the family in order to play and train.

The argument presented in this section is not that there has been a major shift from the traditional expectation of the 'trailing wife' to a situation in which all players and their partners consider initially some form of *commuting* relationship. The prevailing situation for many – probably a majority of – partners (and their children) is that they continue to relocate with the player when he transfers to a new club, particularly over major distances. Writing in the *Sunday Times* (13 January 2002), Richard Woods and Rachel Dobson claim that 'young and far-from-rich wives have found their lives uprooted at a few days' notice when their footballer husbands have been transferred from one end of the country to another'. Vicky Wilson, engaged to former Darlington Town player Phil Brumwell, said that relocating twice in one year was expensive and disruptive, 'but it's part of life for a footballer's family' (*Daily Mirror*, 3 January 2002). A former Premiership defender, interviewed for this book, made the following observation when asked how his wife adjusted to a move north:

> She loved it straight away. She's very outgoing and makes friends easily. Talking to other players it can be really difficult for the wives, a lot of them don't settle and get homesick. I can honestly say that when it comes to my football, not that I wouldn't worry about [my wife], but I know that I can go anywhere and she would come with me and we'd be happy and it wouldn't be a problem. She gets on with people and mixes really well, but for a lot of players it must be hard, they think that they can't move too far away because of the wife – David Unsworth scenario.

These examples highlight how transferring may impact on the lives of the partners of professional footballers (and their children). One can suggest, on the basis of the interview data and the anecdotal evidence collected, that there is a cultural expectation that job relocation is a part of the game to which players and their families must adapt. The lives of the partners can be dominated by the player's work to some degree, particularly if they are tied to him economically. Many partners relinquish a significant degree of control over their own employment prospects, their lifestyles as well as their identities. When a player transfers from one club to another, there can be a great deal of disruption for his partner. For the player, the mobile lifestyle has a thread of continuity, precisely because each move relates to their work, and at each club they have new workmates with whom they can connect immediately. A recently retired former Premiership player expressed this point succinctly. When asked whether transferring posed a problem for players and their families, he said:

> I don't think it is a problem for the players. Because when a player joins a new club he's got twenty new friends, his teammates. It's hard on the families though, especially the wives. I mean I've heard of wives who get clinically depressed about things. I mean they might move into a village. She doesn't know anybody. She might have young babies. They can get very fed up. The lad's out training every morning, having a laugh with his new teammates. And it's not really difficult for him. But tasks like getting the kids into new schools, I mean, that's all put on the wives. It can be very difficult for them.

The options available for players and their families are not simply a matter of personal choice, but are linked to tight job markets which, for many players, reduce the opportunity to choose positions in specific locations. A consequence of this apparent lack of choice is that players may be constrained to move significant distances in order to play first team football. For the partners of players, such transfers, in previous eras, have resulted almost automatically in geographical relocation if such a move was considered necessary.

It is hypothesized here that the expectation that partners (and children) will 'trail' the player *without* hesitation is diminishing. Where it is reasonably possible for them to do so, it is normal for a player (particularly those with families) to travel each day to his new club in order to avoid the hassle and stress of relocating. For all that, while many families will continue to trail, there exists a trend in which players and their partners are increasingly coming to decide upon a 'commuting relationship' for the duration of the player's contract. In this context a commuting relationship relates not only to someone who travels long distances to work each day, but also to couples who live apart for one or more days each week (Gerstel and Gross 1984). A recently retired Premiership player referred to this trend in the following way:

> Player: The thing with being a footballer's wife is you've got to be prepared to move. I can never really understand wives who say they don't want to move but you hear about so many marriages where the wife stays in her home town and the player moves about and stays in hotels during the week and comes back at the weekends.
> MR: Does that scenario occur regularly?
> Player: A lot of that goes on because a lot of wives are so stubborn. They won't move. I just can't understand it. If you're a family you go where the work is: you go together.

This player provides an indication of the prevalence of commuting relationships and, concurrently, the traditional expectations males place on partners. Despite these traditional expectations, partners have at their disposal a degree of persuasive power and some – like Jayne Unsworth – can bring to bear a great deal of pressure when negotiating. Adding substance to this comment is a statement expressed by a former Division One (i) player, who replied to a question about whether transferring was a problem for partners as follows:

> Even the latest thing with David Unsworth, when he went to Villa, wanting a move back to Everton. The press latched on to the fact that it was his wife who wanted to get back. He denies this but they do have a big say. I mean, a player comes home from training and the wife is moaning that the area is horrible. 'Get me back to wherever' … What I'm saying is that it has an influence about what the player decides to do with his career. If your home life is not happy then it will affect you. If you're coming home from training and things aren't right, you can't relax. It plays on your mind.

Players and their partners may try to resolve this dilemma by renting or buying a flat, or by arranging for the player to stay with family, close to his new club. The apparent reluctance on the part of the partners of professional footballers to relocate – in defiance of traditional expectations – may be partially explained by reference, first, to the proximity of social and kin networks and, second, to what Gerstel and Gross (1984) refer to in their work on commuter marriages as 'the effect of feminism'.

### Social networks

A number of wives and partners have suggested that that they are unwilling to leave their networks of friends, family and other forms of social support (such as schools and childcare) at a time in the history of professional football in which more players are transferring more regularly. Much of the anecdotal evidence provided in the print media indicates that partners find it difficult to leave friends and family: they often experience feelings of isolation, are burdened with the logistics of relocating and struggle to settle in unfamiliar settings. The view of Victoria Margetson, for example, wife of experienced goalkeeper Martyn Margetson, is typical of a number of statements made in interview by the partners of players. She explains her experiences as follows:

> After eight years, Martyn moved to Southend. We were settled in Manchester, so it was very hard. It's not like when other people move. You've only a week to find a house. It was quite hard leaving my friends and family. I felt quite isolated in Southend. I couldn't work because Matthew [their son] was only eight months old and it was hard to meet new people
>
> (*Daily Mirror*, 3 January 2002)

The uncertain circumstances that may quickly materialize for partners can generate a great deal of anxiety, particularly for those already familiar with the initial isolation and disruption that are characteristic of player transfers.

Ann Lee, the wife of former Nottingham Forest player Jason Lee, for instance, exhibited such anxiety at the prospect of leaving Nottingham, the city in which their family – including three children, two of whom were in school – were now settled. Interviewed for a television documentary on players' wives, Ann Lee said:

> I don't know what I'm going to do now. I really do want to stay here, but I also want to be with Jason. I want Jason to come home everyday and that's not going to happen if I stay here ... but Nottingham is where I'd love to bring my kids up.
>
> (Channel Four, *Cutting Edge*, 11 November 1997)

While the patterns of interaction between the couple are unclear in terms of how they decide upon their future living arrangements, Ann Lee informs the interviewer of their final decision at a later point in the documentary. She states:

> The club want Jason to move nearer Watford. A forty-five minute drive which is understandable. But I really want to live in Nottingham. So he's going to be staying at his mum's in London. He'll definitely be coming home on Sundays and I hope to think he's going to come home on his days off as well. I don't want to be a single-parent family but I also want to be happy where I live.
>
> (Channel Four, *Cutting Edge*, 11 November 1997)

While Ann Lee displayed a strong symbolic attachment to Nottingham as 'a place', her sentiments are arguably better understood in terms of the networks of friends and acquaintances and preferred schools and childcare options, which are tied to familiar locations and which in turn foster 'rootedness' (Hanson and Pratt 1995). The rootedness experienced by wives and partners may be augmented by the fact that many struggle to find and maintain friends, due to the fact that their husbands are thought of as public figures. The prospect of having to make new friends is not one relished by many (Webb 1998). For Jason and Ann Lee, the 'costs' of setting up separate living arrangements were unknown, for this was the first time they had been in a position to make such a decision. It seems likely that this is the type of resolution that is being reached by increasing numbers of professional footballers and their partners.

Another pattern was identified by a Division One (i) player who transferred from a club situated in a city in the north of England to one in the home counties where, relatively speaking, the cost of living and, in particular, house prices, are higher. The player explained how economic circumstances constrained him to live the majority of each week away from his wife and children. The following is a short extract from his interview:

> Player: I discussed the move with my wife and a lot of people in the game, friends whose opinion I value in the game ... I was still living in [my home town] with my wife and family, two kids, and the move to [the southern city] would mean I'd have to stay there during the week and come back up to [my home town] at the weekends.
> MR: Did your wife consider moving down?
> Player: No, not at the time. We couldn't afford the house prices. Financially it just wasn't possible.
> MR: How did you feel about that situation?
> Player: It wasn't an easy situation. I was constantly travelling between [my home town] and [the southern city]. You know, I hated leaving home on a Monday and couldn't wait to return after games.

After one season, this player moved on to a club in the south-west of England where he was joined by his wife and children. His wife worked as a nurse and she was able to find employment at a local hospital relatively easily. This player said that 'you don't often get players' wives who have their own careers'. That said, their dual *earning* partnership, as opposed to a dual *career* one, may have led to relocation being less of an obstacle for this player's wife, who was instantly able to contribute financially to the upkeep of their family.

Social and kin networks operate at local and national levels and must be considered as interdependent in terms of understanding transfer processes. In other words, at a parochial level, domestic and social support and knowledge of local schools, friends and acquaintances and neighbours, may foster 'rootedness' (Hanson and Pratt 1995) among family members. Against this backdrop of familiarity and stability, one must consider the (usually) narrow employment market which characterizes professional football. A player may therefore feel constrained to make uneasy career decisions during periods in which he may have few alternative employment options and few, if any, alternative employment skills. For some players, these feelings may be augmented by a heightened sensitivity in terms of equality when negotiating with their partners about the future living arrangements for their family, an orientation which may be explained, in part, in terms of changing balances of power between the sexes.

### The effects of feminism

The reluctance on the part of partners to relocate is demonstrated by the number of examples of players who agreed that they would either travel each day to, or buy or rent a flat in the location of, their new club. This feature provides an indication of a changing balance of power between players and their partners in relation to decision-making about whether or not to accept a transfer offer. This pattern may also be a sign of a change in 'attitude' on the part of the partners towards first, their husband's career and second, their own aspirations. These patterns would be consistent with other research which suggests that younger women hold less traditional attitudes to the gendered divisions of labour, both at work and at home (Newell 2000). A major factor facilitating the decision to commute probably relates in part to the legitimate demands of partners for greater individual freedom and personal choice, although these changes probably relate more to middle-class women than to women from other, particularly lower-class, social groups (Newell 2000). Any analysis of a decision to commute reached by a player and his partner cannot be explained separately from an understanding of the long series of earlier decisions, commitments and experiences from which such resolutions emerge. Thus, one would need to understand more about what Jarvis (1999: 231) refers to as 'the situatedness of household strategies': in short, an understanding of time, place and history of household decision-making. The changing balance of power between the sexes in England has had a number of intended and unintended consequences. Two such consequences of relevance here have been an equalizing of household duties and a realization on the part of women that they can achieve life goals which may be alternative to, or even encompass, traditional expectations in terms of the gendered *divisioning* of labour (Oakley 1990; Newell 2000). Household negotiations and the resultant decisions should be understood in the context of broader social changes.

The shifting orientations of players to their work as they experience long-term injury, rejection and changing life circumstances impact on the partners of players as an aspect of their interdependence in which they are bound up. One may question whether and at what point in her life history a partner thinks mostly about her husband and his playing career, about her children and their schooling, or about herself and the quality of her life. The job of professional footballer is among a number of occupations in which the workers may be defined as 'public figures'. Being a 'public figure' essentially means being defined in terms of work for the purposes of almost all social contacts (Finch 1983). And if public figures are 'contaminated' (Banton 1964) by their work, insofar as they can never really leave their work at the workplace – they are rarely 'off duty' so to speak – it is also true that their partners experience some of the consequences of being a public figure, but without having been paid to be one. Thus, the partner of a footballer can be defined by his work and they are both given a vicarious public figure identity. A partner can never erase what has come to be known as the *'wife of'* identity (Finch 1983).

This comment is substantiated by Ann Lee – quoted earlier – who describes succinctly her attempts to develop her own identity and, hence, her self-esteem. Deliberating about 'what I want out of life' and issues of self-improvement, she states:

> I'm taking Maths and English GCSE which is what I should have done at school, but I tossed it off. But now I need them ... I'd like to be someone, I don't want no dead end job. I think it's about time I put my contribution into this family. I don't want to be known as Jason Lee's wife. I want to be Ann 'the whatever'. I want to be somebody.
>
> (*Cutting Edge*, Channel Four, 11 November 1997)

Suzy Barnes, wife of former Liverpool player and England international John Barnes, confirms the sentiments expressed by Ann Lee. She says that when John Barnes was transferred from Watford to Liverpool it was a very difficult period in which she felt 'very isolated'. She and their three-year-old son moved to Merseyside initially, but then returned south in order to be among 'all my old friends' (Webb 1998: 182). In the following quote, she describes how, over the course of the next two seasons, she managed to develop her 'own life':

We actually spent two years apart commuting up and down the motorway but in a way it was good as it gave me some space and the chance to develop my own personality. For the first time ever I was on my own, no mum to lean on, no John. Footballers are high maintenance and it's very easy to stay in the background, making preparations, waiting for them to come back home – it can be soul destroying ... But then I turned it round and decided not to spend the time waiting but to see it as my own time ... I developed my own life and John had to fit in with me ... I became so much stronger, more independent.

(Webb 1998: 182)

The sentiments expressed by Ann Lee and Suzy Barnes are, it is suggested, indicative of a change in attitude on their part towards their husbands' work and their own aspirations.

Information relating to other partners included in this section suggests that Ann Lee and Suzy Barnes may not be alone in terms of exercising their 'power' during processes of transferring. As the examples included in this section have indicated, many of the partners of professional footballers are also coming to decide against relinquishing control over aspects such as their own employment prospects, their lifestyles and, to varying degrees, their personal identities. The ways in which their changing orientations are manifest relate to their percep-tions of the legitimacy of their power which they are able to exercise when negotiating about the 'situatedness' (Jarvis 1999) of living arrangements, partic-ularly when their husbands are either considering, or are in the process of, transferring from one club to another.

## Conclusion

The problem addressed in this chapter concerns the relative power of players in relation to the process of transferring. In short, the patterns of interaction among the personnel who are typically involved in transfer processes are identified, in the first instance, against a backcloth of the changing legal regulations of the 'transfer system'. One aspect of this analysis is the changing distribution of power among club directors, managers and players. In addition, this analysis includes agents, club doctors and physiotherapists, as well as the partners of players who are also imbued with a degree of relative power by virtue of their ties to players and to football clubs. It is clear that some people involved in the course of trans-fer processes are more powerful than others. Magee (1998) refers to 'exploiters' by which he means the players who are able to use the regulations of the transfer system for their own advantage. Still, among the networks of relations identified in this chapter, the relative power of players to steer the activities of others may depend on factors such as their age and the work-related reputations they develop. Some players are considered very powerful in the sense that they are in strong negotiating positions, while others may have few, if any, alternative choices. In some circumstances the balance of power appears to be firmly in the hands of the club directors who are able to control the process of transferring largely in terms of their own plans and intentions; however, neither club directors, nor managers, nor players can act arbitrarily or do as they please. All parties bound up in a process of transferring must at least take into account the actions of the others involved and they must abide – officially at least – by the regulations laid down in the contracts which all parties sign. Club directors and managers for instance rely on the levels of performance achieved by their players and this in turn can be a means by which they – the players – can exercise a degree of power over their employers. Conversely, club managers can utilize the threat of rejection as a means of exercising power over players who need 'pulling into line'. An examination of the dynamic balances of power among the network of interdependent relations which characterize professional football – which includes agents, club doctors, physiotherapists and the partners of players – is essential if one is to understand adequately the movement of players from one club to another.

## Chapter 8

# The fate of idealism in professional football

In a chapter entitled 'A Dream Come True', journalist David Conn (1997) discusses the ambitions and lifestyles of modern professional footballers in the 1990s; he undertakes this task in part by examining the career experiences of Newcastle United player and former England international Alan Shearer. Yet for Conn the title of the chapter is something of an irony. At face value the title implies that for many boys in England, a career as a professional footballer would indeed be perceived as a 'dream' means of making a living. One of the central points of Conn's chapter however is that accompanying the economic and commercial changes that have occurred in the organization of professional football – larger television and sponsorship deals and more agents – there has been an unintended and gradual decline, or even loss of understanding on the part of players, of the meaning of being a 'footballer'. In other words, Conn (1997: 229) suggests it is difficult for contemporary players to keep their dreams alive; he illustrates this point forcefully in the following way: 'The players are only the symptoms of football's more general loss, commodities simultaneously overpaid and ruthlessly dealt with, in danger of losing their love of the game, loyalty to the club, the bond with supporters.' Despite Alan Shearer's career achievements, Conn views his experiences as a type of 'tragedy'. On the one hand Shearer has been liberated from 'oppression, haggling [and] insecurity at 35',[1] but on the other hand Conn suggests that:

> on the day he achieved his childhood ambition [signing for Newcastle United] ... he seemed like he was doing a job. Remembering his media training. Smiling the smile. As if the hard business of realising his dream had, at only 26, removed his capacity to dream at all, replaced it with agents and negotiations and deals and the crisp, dry matter of contract.
>
> (Conn 1997: 230)

Conn's analysis is interesting sociologically, for he refers to players as commodities and implies that, wittingly or otherwise, they collude in a process of commodification. This view is echoed by former England international centre-

forward Les Ferdinand. Interviewed by Conn (1997: 226) about the issue of loyalty shown to professional footballers, Ferdinand remarks that: 'To clubs you're
just a commodity ... They'll sell you at the drop of a hat.' Although Conn is probably wrong to claim that players are overpaid – many of the players interviewed
for this study are, or were, paid only modest salaries, for most do not achieve
national celebrity status – he is arguably correct to allude to the lack of sincerity
displayed when footballers, like Alan Shearer, 'smile the smile'. In a similar manner to Wright Mills (1951) in relation to his discussion of 'the personality
market', Conn (1997) highlights a pattern in which, in the broad context of
work, 'the smile' of a footballer could be perceived as 'a commercialized lure'.
Shearer sells his labour, energy and skill to his employers, like all other players,
and it could be argued that he sacrifices his 'social personality' to a multitude of
customers. In the course of their work, the 'presentation of self' (Goffman 1959)
of footballers becomes an instrument employed by them for an alien purpose and,
consequently, they engage in a self-estranging process. Calculated displays of
feelings in the context of work, such as 'the smile', are probably what Hochschild
(1983) had in mind when she discussed the *use value* of emotion work. So, while
Conn (1997) refers specifically to 'the smile', he does not mention the process
through which players, such as Alan Shearer, learn *to use* emotional displays or
gain an understanding of the occupational contexts in which they are practical.
Additionally, Conn fails to ask whether players recognize the part they play in
their self-alienation and what the consequences are for those who continually
engage in this type of *instrumental* behaviour.

In his ethnographic study entitled *Chasing the Big-Time*, Parker (1996a) examines the thoughts of young trainees about their 'work'. He describes the way in
which various aspects of football apprenticeships lead many of them to realize
that the life of a professional footballer is not solely about issues of fame, conspicuous consumption and fortune.[2] He suggests that young players learn quickly
about the seriousness of workplace pressures, in contrast to the perceived financial and prestigious benefits of careers in football upon which media portrayals
tend to focus, and he identifies dimensions of the occupational culture – namely
authoritarianism, seriousness and pressure – which serve 'to modify trainee perceptions of life within professional football' (Parker 1996a: 95). In short, Parker
identifies many occupational practices and demands experienced by trainees to
varying degrees, and likens their overall introduction to the professional game to
a process of 'mortification' (Goffman 1968). Many aspirants do not progress
beyond their apprenticeships to achieve the status of professional player. Only a
small number, comparatively speaking, are offered a professional contract.

The problem of how to conceptualize how a player such as Alan Shearer can
develop from being an individual who *dreams* of success, for whom the professional game could be considered a 'calling', to one who recognizes, albeit not in
these terms, that he is economically dispensable and that an informal, yet important part of his job is seeming to others to 'love the job', might be addressed by

employing aspects of Max Weber's discussion of 'politics as a vocation' (1965). Put simply, Weber suggests that there are two ways of making politics one's vocation, although one might consider a host of other occupations in this vein. He proposes that: 'Either one lives "for" politics or one lives "off" politics' (Weber 1965: 84). Weber does not introduce a false dichotomy here, for he recognizes that people who are 'sincere' about their work, at least in the first instance, live both 'for' and 'off' their work in practice, whether or not they recognize this state of affairs. So it could be said that the occupation and means of subsistence is a 'central life interest' of players who live 'for' football, those for whom football provides internal meaning (Dubin *et al.* 1976). Thus the income that derives from their work may not be a key concern in the early phases of their career. Still, while Shearer may be fulfilling a dream by signing for Newcastle United, the club he supported as a schoolboy, it is Conn's (1997: 230) contention that, sooner or later, what counts is 'the crisp, dry matter of contract'. In other words, the internal change implied by Conn (and Parker) is that in time, players come to realize that football is not solely a route to fortune and celebrity status, but a source of income which will pay a mortgage and provide for their partners and families. On balance, a player who strives to make the professional game a permanent source of income lives 'off' football. The data collected for this study indicate that the overwhelming majority of players come to recognize *in time* that they are making a living 'off' football and come to be less concerned with fulfilling dreams.

The temporal dimension hinted at above is important because so many of the experiences of professional players relate to periods of time in one way or another; thus the players interviewed talk, in direct and indirect ways, of the time remaining on contracts, certain and uncertain passages of time associated with particular types of injury, periods of time out of the starting line-up and their age (as a socially constructed category of time). All these aspects of the careers of players generate uncertainty in some measure: this uncertainty may be compounded by factors such as the age of a player or the stage and/or status he reaches in his career. Many of these dimensions of uncertainty have been discussed in previous chapters; even so, one very important aspect of these examinations of the turning points in their careers has been relatively absent. In simple terms this aspect can be expressed in the following question: over the course of their careers, what unintended consequences are generated for those players who, often in public contexts, experience, time after time, periods of uncertainty and anxiety in relation to their future as players? In other words, do the ups and downs of their existence as professional football players alter the way in which they view football as a profession and their approach to their careers? The problem therefore is to explain how players come to perceive themselves as professionals and how these views, their work perspectives and orientations, change through the course of their careers.

Many of the players interviewed related their thoughts and feelings to moments in the course of their careers in which they believed they began to gain a clearer understanding of their position and status relative to their contemporaries. Key or fateful moments in their lives, connected directly or indirectly to injuries and contracts, as well as factors 'external' to their careers such as getting married and starting a family, lead players to develop an awareness of the insecurities which are integral aspects of their occupation. For some, this developing awareness coincides with moments when they feel rejected and unwanted, when their performances, or lack of inclusion in the first team, are publicly acknowledged such that they suffer a loss of self-esteem and experience a diminished sense of self.

## Subjective careers

The discussion which is the focus of this chapter deals with the events connected with changes to, or the re-evaluation of, the social identities of professional footballers and of their changing conceptions of work; in other words, players' feelings about, rather than their formal positions within, the profession of football and its 'career structure' (although this phrase is slightly ambiguous since there exists in professional football no traditionally defined 'career structural path'). To be more concrete, the focus of the examination concerns the meanings the players interviewed impute to their experiences – and those they witness of other players – in the context of injury and transfers, and what changes these kinds of experiences bring about in terms of their attitudes towards their worlds of work. The blocks of time in which players experience injury or poor form, i.e. periods when they could be absent from the starting eleven, can be conceptualized as 'passages of vulnerability'. Such passages are times when the players' idealized versions of their careers 'collide' with the realities of internal competition for places and, according to Faulkner (1974), they consequently begin to construct new outlooks and motivations. Stebbins (1970) suggests that the significance of career contingencies or turning points, such as long-term injuries, protracted contract negotiations or even outright rejection, is that they heighten an individual's consciousness of what has happened to them in that particular identity and what may happen in the future. Similarly, for Strauss (1962), turning points in one's developing career occur when one has to take stock, to re-evaluate, revise and re-judge. For Strauss, turning points are conceptualized as incidents that may be examined in 'objective' terms but which lead individuals to revise or transform their identities.

It is arguable that the way in which footballers experience the particular career contingencies alluded to above may bring them to develop the view, as expressed by Les Ferdinand in the introduction to this chapter, that to their clubs, players are 'just a commodity' (Conn 1997: 226). Further to this view, Conn interviews Chris Armstrong, a former playing colleague of Ferdinand at Tottenham Hotspur, who expresses the common opinion that professional football is 'a dream job' (Conn 1997: 229). Even so, Armstrong continues his statement suggesting that:

Some players ... become cynical about the game, looking only for what they can get. With me, if I ever get tired of any aspect of being a footballer, I just think back to working in a factory, and realize that I'm in the best job in the world.

(Conn 1997: 229)

The notion that someone can consider themselves to be a 'commodity' to be bought and sold in a market economy, and the related idea that in this context a worker is 'looking only for what they can get' – one might recall Conn's suggestion about the importance of the 'crisp, dry matter of contract' – indicate the possibility of a working environment which produces the conditions of alienation for employees. Thus, while players like Chris Armstrong express a certain degree of satisfaction with their job, other footballers, not unlike other people who wish to earn a living from their creative activities, may regard their capabilities as commodities that are subject to the laws of a commodity economy: in other words, at times football players 'instrumentally' (Cotgrove 1972) attempt to work the market in which they are bound up in order that they secure employment and achieve 'success' in their own terms.

Marx wrote about the alienation of an individual when he becomes a commodity (Giddens 1977). For Marx, the alienation of workers in capitalism stems from the commodity-like status of their labour – see *Capital*, his *magnum opus* (1974). Marx's analysis in this regard relates to unavoidable objective states in which all workers who sell their labour power find themselves. Alienation therefore is not necessarily reflected in job dissatisfaction or in frustration (Watson 1995). It is clear that the work undertaken by footballers has complex and dynamic meanings for them, a 'fact' to which the comments of Ferdinand and Armstrong attest. It is argued here that the subjective feelings of players about their work experiences are patterned. For most players, achieving success at various career stages in part fulfils dreams and ambitions. Even so, they can develop a sense of 'alien'-ness in relation to their ego or sense of 'self' when they experience dissatisfaction with their situation. That is, *they* fail as professional footballers to live up to their intentions, expectations and the idealized images they have for themselves.

## Players' feelings at work

Professional football as a career is short-term and the labour market for players is highly competitive. Positions of employment are scarce. In the course of their careers players may experience what might be described as repeated lay-offs, work searches – albeit with the assistance of agents – and, if successful, a string of employers. In other occupations, particularly since the 1970s (Sennett 1998), these 'flexible' conditions of work have resulted in a lack of loyalty and the generation of fear and cynicism among workers (Flam 2002). The interview data collected for this study suggest that, when absent from training and matches for long periods of time, football players develop a *cynicism* in terms of the way in which they feel they are treated by significant others, particularly the manager. A Division One (i) club doctor indicates one likely source of the dissatisfaction and cynicism expressed by players when discussing the precarious nature of their monetary value. This doctor described the transfer system as 'a bit like a slave market', particularly when referring to players who sustained or who, wittingly or otherwise, played on with long-term injuries.[3]

An established Division Two (i) goalkeeper expressed his feelings towards 'his club' when he experienced problems dealing with medical staff in the course of attempting to find a specialized supportive strapping for his hand; one that was not possible for him to buy, in his words, 'off the peg'. The injury to his hand did not prevent him from playing but, after consulting club medical staff over an extended period, he sought advice from a specialist with whom he made contact on a chance meeting. When asked whether the club were happy for him to seek 'outside' advice in this way, he responded as follows:

> I don't really know, but at the end of the day I do what's best for me and not necessarily what they want me to do. You've got to look after yourself because at the end of the day they don't really look after you. You're just another number within the club.

The idea that it is necessary for players to 'look after themselves' is a common theme in this study and is expressed well in relation to injured players who seek second opinions.

In addition to this idea, a number of the players interviewed also expressed their feelings about their sense of self-worth, particularly at vulnerable times in their careers. A former Division Two player, who subsequently retired from the professional game because of a long-term knee problem, said that 'football is a totally different world to everything else and it's quite a fickle world as well'. When asked to elaborate on this point again, the player said that whilst rehabilitating from his first long-term injury as a professional, he had been left on his own, day after day, with little supervision. He said, 'I just realized then what professional football was all about. Because you just weren't worth anything. I felt like I didn't matter to the club.' An experienced former Premier League player expressed this point in more forceful terms. In the course of his interview he described the expectations on players to give 100 per cent at all times, even when carrying injuries, and was in little doubt about his position relative to others in the club. He said:

> People talk about loyalty, but I don't think there's any loyalty in football. Because at the end of the day a club will use you and use you and use you until you're no good to them, and then they'll get someone else. And I'm a

believer that a player to a certain extent has got to be the same. He's got to use the club as much as they use him.[4]

This point is confirmed, in part, by an experienced Division One (i) player who claimed to have been treated 'just like a piece of meat',[5] following periods of time in his career when he had been absent from the first team because of poor form or a disabling injury. He emphasized his dissatisfaction by adding that 'you get punished sometimes if you're not in the first team'. This player distances himself as a cause of his non-selection by suggesting implicitly that it was not necessarily his fault he wasn't in the starting line-up; but from his perspective, if it wasn't his fault then *why* was he being punished? When this player was asked to elaborate on the thought that he is treated like *a piece of meat* he made the following lengthy, but pertinent comment:

> You are being used to the best of your ability as part of the team but knowing full well that somewhere along the line they're hoping that somebody who has just come out of an apprenticeship or just signed a young pro contract will be ready for a game. They'll just keep him here and make sure he develops along the right lines and if they get an offer for me they'll sell me or let my contract expire and pay the younger player half my wages. That to me is how a lot of people think in the game ... Yeah, I want to be in the team, of course, but I'm being used by the management for whatever reason in a different position and against my better judgement. But at least I'm in the team. It's not what you want but, again, *you are treated as a piece of meat.*

This quote is interesting sociologically for the player makes reference to the 'market' realities for players who are 'ageing' – in an athletic-related biological sense – or not producing performances of a desired standard. In essence he talks in terms of the way in which players are vulnerable to others who may be younger, potentially more talented and cheaper. The majority of players interviewed, but particularly older players from all the professional divisions, referred to themselves in similar ways.

A highly pertinent description of the way in which players view their self-images at work was offered by an experienced former Premier League player, who was asked about the advice he received from club medical personnel during a period in which he was playing with an injury to his foot. When asked about the use of painkilling injections and whether or not players were able to refuse them, he made the following point:

> I think every player should have the opportunity to say, 'Well, to be honest with you, I appreciate what you're saying but it's not good enough', and [the medical staff and management] should respect that as well. It's fair for them to say to you that this is the only way you're going to get fit, 'we need

to dissolve the bit of tissue that's giving you problems'. But I think players tend to get treated as just a commodity. You're just part of the club.

When asked whether this was a common thought among players he replied:

Oh, I think every footballer's a commodity. I'm not saying we all feel like it in the sense of you're player A, you're player B, but I still think when push comes to shove you're a commodity and basically the club want as much as they can out of that commodity.

To summarize, the players interviewed referred to themselves as 'commodities', 'pieces of meat' and as 'just another number'. Wacquant (2001) refers to 'the language of exploitation' in order to describe boxers' consciousness of the way they are undervalued and manipulated. But how do football players come to develop this view of themselves, of other players and of their own sense of self-worth? Can a player who considers himself to be a *commodity*, or who thinks he is treated like a *piece of meat* by his employers, really be satisfied with or fulfilled by his work? Why would someone wish to pursue a career feeling that they are being used, in a profession for which they originally possess aspirations of 'achieved celebrity', financial reward and public acclaim? The following discussion may help to shed light on these questions.

## Orientations to work in professional football

It will be argued here that footballers begin their professional lives with idealistic dreams of success which, sooner or later, are replaced by more realistic outlooks. Many of the players interviewed for this study spoke of the way in which their status changed within the club, and from club to club, as they became more established and experienced. The fate of idealism has been well documented sociologically (Becker and Geer 1958), yet evidence of such adjustments to the realities of work for professional footballers, that is, the divesting of certain preconceived attitudes and expectations, has only recently started coming to light (see Parker 1996a). In the case of football, the process for players of coming to terms with the realities of day-to-day work life should not be confined to studies of apprenticeships and occupational socialization. Understood as an important career contingency, injury provides regular periods of time throughout the playing career when players are constrained to 'step out of the firing line', to watch and to reflect on their present and future circumstances.

A Division One (i) club captain provides a good example of a player enforced to reflect upon his status in work. This experienced player said that he was referred to a hospital by his club doctor with an infection which had resulted from a bad gash to his leg, sustained whilst playing. Having gone into hospital thinking initially that he would need a tetanus jab or some antibiotics, he was unexpectedly admitted for two weeks with a serious case of blood poisoning. Throughout his stay in hospital he received only one visit from the club physio-therapist; his only other visitors were his wife and children. Neither the club doctor nor manager nor other team members attempted to make contact with him through this time. He was, in his terms, justifiably 'pissed off' and it was this period in which he claims to have realized his status within the club, his value to the manager and, in simple terms, who cared about him. This player resented the way he was treated by the club's physiotherapist. As club captain he expected to receive some personal attention, if only, one suspects, in order to reduce his feel-ings of isolation; he assumed that a player of his status would be missed. In the following quote the player describes vividly the circumstances of and his feelings about his hospitalization. He said:

> I had my illness. I'm in hospital right, on antibiotics every four hours. Massive dosages. It took [the physiotherapist] two weeks to find out that I was nearly dead. He never rang me. A week went by and I'm thinking he hadn't been in to see me. No, actually, he'd been in once because it's on his way home. He wasn't there purposefully to check how I was. One of the other lads had just had an operation so he popped in at the same time. He never came purpose-fully to see me. It really pissed me off. And then I never saw him again. I was in hospital nearly two weeks and on the Friday they allowed me to come out for a couple of hours, so I rang him up and said, 'Look, I'm going home for a couple of hours. I didn't want you to have any wasted journeys.' So he said, 'I was planning to come across to see you.' But I didn't believe him. He didn't come to see me. It was a case of out of sight out of mind. That's how a lot of us have felt with him. A week later I said to the club doctor, 'Have you told the manager how serious this is?', and he had to go and tell him. He said to [the manager], 'Look, you had better realize that [the player] will not play for another three months, he is seriously ill.' Still, to this day, I would like to know if the manager knew exactly what happened.

It is not unusual for players to be sidelined for an extended period. It is clear how-ever that during his stay in hospital and subsequent convalescence, this player reflects on the treatment he receives from the club physiotherapist, and the degree to which the club manager misses his playing services. The player expresses the concern that someone should know that he is 'nearly dead'; for someone to express this concern is an acknowledgement that he is missed and that significant people – most importantly, for him, the team manager – have concerns about his state of health. Even though he cannot be *where the action is* (Goffman 1967), he still wants to feel needed. He is managing undesired feelings of isolation about his situation for he cannot contribute in a meaningful way to his sense of self as a player, to his employers, or to the wider community associ-ated with the club. For the player this need to feel wanted is expressed most clearly in the desire for others to display concern about his condition. The quote is significant because the player expresses dissatisfaction at an aspect of his work related to a particular period in time in which he experiences heightened vulnerability. It is typical of an experience that may be considered a 'triggering event' (Flam 2002). In other words, it is the type of experience which may trigger in a player a change of orientation to his work and, consequently, a changing view of himself at work.

The player quoted is clearly unsatisfied with the physiotherapist, yet one could not make the same assumption about the way this player feels about other members of the club, for instance, the team manager or his playing colleagues, or about his level of satisfaction as a professional footballer. The degree of satisfaction expressed by workers in relation to the part they play in terms of 'production', and their need to be considered by others to be an important part of these processes, has been given some attention by sociologists (see Blauner 1964; Dubin *et al.* 1976; Scase and Goffee 1989). To consider oneself an important part of a team, albeit a team of workers who bake bread, build houses or drill for oil, is one of many sources of meaning for employees: professional footballers are no exception. In many of the early studies concerning 'satisfaction at work' (Blauner 1964) it is acknowledged that the choices that people make about their occupation presuppose at least a minimal understanding on the part of the employee of likely sources of satisfaction as well as possible deprivations. Footballers understand too that the satisfactions to be derived from the professional game can be enormous in relation to occupational prestige and financial reward; even so, their orientation to their job can change over the course of time as they experience work-related deprivations. The following interview extract concerns a former Premiership centre-back who was asked about whether or not he still worried about gaining a new contract in a fashion similar to inexperienced players. In his reply he focuses attention on what he describes as his changing 'outlook'. He said:

> Player: It's not the same. I think your outlook changes. I mean the way I look at things in general has changed a lot and I've learnt a lot from things that have happened to me ... I'd go home after games and I would worry too much about it, particularly at times when we were struggling. If it affected the club then it affected me, but I've sort of learnt to distance myself a little bit now. It's my job and I do it to the best of my abilities.
> MR: Do you consider football an enjoyable job?
> Player: I wouldn't swap it for the world, definitely. I think people view it as 'Oh, you're a footballer, it must be fantastic', and it is. But there are down sides to it as well. If you had to weigh up the whole thing, I don't think you'd talk to many footballers who would swap their lives.
> MR: Down sides such as?
> Player: Well obviously there are the constant injuries. And last season I was getting abuse and the crowd was hammering me. There's not a better feeling

than getting 30,000 people cheering you on, but there's not much of a worse feeling than when 30,000 people are booing you. You go home and think, 'Oh, what's going on here. Do I need this?' You start wondering whether you are doing the right thing. How you can change things? Then you worry too much. That's what I end up doing and it makes things worse rather than better.

This former Premier League player expresses the view that his orientation or 'outlook', to use his words, changed as he experienced turning points in his career – a turning point or *triggering event* such as the one described by the player above who felt abandoned in hospital. This view is consistent with research undertaken on careers in a vast range of occupations (see Collin and Young 2000; Sennett 1998). Over the course of his experiences the player learns to 'distance' himself such that he begins to perceive his work as a professional footballer more in terms of a 'job' rather than, for example, a *calling* or *vocation*. The player comes to the understanding that he is playing and therefore living 'off' football. While he claims to be satisfied with his career choice, as indicated by his comment that few footballers would 'swap their lives', he goes on to provide contrasting examples of work satisfaction and deprivation. He learns how to 'distance' or detach his feelings in the course of experiencing the 'down sides' to which he makes mention. Thus, one can argue that the attitudes of players to their work are more complex than a crude satisfaction–dissatisfaction dichotomy suggests.

A Division Three (i) player also responds to a question in a way such that the complexities of workplace orientations are highlighted. When asked about the joking culture within the club and how this affects players who are injured long-term, he replied as follows: 'Players who are out injured tend to be quite cynical in their approach. I suppose deep down I enjoy my football so much that I'm not that cynical about the game myself.' The player was then reminded that, notwithstanding his remarks, he had described himself at an earlier point in the interview as 'a piece of meat'. In response to this point he made the following comment:

Yes, you are, but I think I've accepted that to a certain extent. I mean very much for the last year and a half I've been in and out of the first team, playing Saturday, not playing Tuesday but in the reserves Wednesday. And to a certain extent everything that goes on in my life outside of football at the moment is brilliant really. I'm in an area where I want to be living, the children are settled, my wife's settled. I'm doing all the things I want to do. If [my club] played the style of football that I hoped they would, and I was banging in twenty goals a season, then the whole 100 per cent of my life would be hunky dory. Well at times I am a bit cynical about the situation here but I never turn round and say anything. I just carry on and think I am earning the sort of money I hoped I would earn when I was a kid.

Of great interest is the fact that the player suggests that to a certain extent he has come to accept that he is, and will be treated as, 'a piece of meat'. He would 'never turn round and say anything', for the cultural values of professional football require players to hide their resentments and anxieties behind a demeanour of enthusiasm for the job. In the social context of the club he needs to show to significant others that, even though he knows that the manager may treat him like *a piece of meat*, he still 'loves the job'. For the sake of his reputation as a player, it is incumbent on him to continue to display the characteristics of a 'good professional attitude', despite the levels of 'spiritually demanding play acting' (Terkel 1975) this behaviour may require.

To come to this type of view requires this player to 'distance' or detach himself from his experiences and to gain a clearer understanding of them. In the course of their careers players come to be *resigned* to the fact that they must behave in this manner. Rather than attempting to examine the levels of satisfaction or dissatisfaction experienced by players – a task to which sociological questions have been raised in terms of reliability and validity (see Fox 1980; Parker *et al.* 1977) – it is clear, based on data collected for this study, that the orientations of players change, sometimes considerably, during their careers. Reflecting many of the worker satisfaction studies (which report general levels of satisfaction allied with outbursts of resentment, hostility, apathy and an acceptance of working arrangements and colleagues) players display complex and dynamic orientations to their work; and from time to time they question their own belief in the part they play in the production processes in professional football in which they are, albeit temporarily, bound. Many players possess mixed feelings about their work: the evidence presented may be to some degree a consequence of their acquiescence or resignation, rather than dissatisfaction in response to workplace deprivation. The prevalence of hostility and resentment about the way in which they are treated on a personal level by certain individuals, as expressed in the statements offered by them in interview, testifies to the survival of some conception of what work could be like for them. In time, unrealistic aspirations are limited and players develop 'outlooks' in which they are resigned to accept, however grudgingly, their work-related experiences. It also requires on their part an acceptance that the occupational aspirations they may once have harboured are unlikely to be fulfilled and that it is necessary for them to readjust their sights: such psychological readjustments are central processes in terms of understanding the ways in which players manage their exit from the professional game. The social circumstances described by players and their attempts to sustain positive self-images as players may lead them to regard their jobs as little more than a source of income.

## Playing 'off' football

In probing the attitudes to work possessed by football players it is important to consider also the expectations which other people have of them. Player attitudes to their work cannot be treated in a narrow economically oriented manner. Exploitative relations at work extend beyond the workplace itself, and have implications for people other than the player. The orientations of footballers are not understandable simply in terms of structural factors within the professional game, such as the high levels of competition for places among club colleagues. The attitudes of players arise and change among interdependencies with people, many of whom are not employed in a direct capacity within a football club. Many of the players interviewed for this study referred to circumstances *external* to the football club as being of central importance in terms of influencing their approach to work. For example, the wives and partners of players, as well as other family members, may have a strong bearing on the perspective a player adopts at any given time. An experienced Division Three (i) player who, at an earlier point in his interview, had discussed his initial career aspirations and dreams, provides an indication of such 'outside' issues. When asked to comment further about whether he felt the lives of footballers are glamorous he replied as follows:

> I would say that if you play at the very, very top it is glamorous. I have played at two clubs where it has been quite glamorous ... those dreams I had of having a nice car, walking down the street and being recognized only happened at two clubs ... so I think I've seen both sides of the coin. I won't deny that at times it has been glamorous, but the be-all and end-all for me is that I can pay the mortgage, drive a nice car, live in a nice house, and there's food on the table for the two kids. Those are the simple facts.

It is argued here that the orientation to his work developed by this player over the course of his career is indicative of an 'instrumental' approach (Watson 1995), for the player recognizes that he is undertaking his work in order to meet on balance the needs of his dependants rather than to experience the intrinsic fulfilment which may be gained from this type of employment. The 'simple facts' equate therefore to economic necessities.

Ideas of instrumentality were initially given credibility in the work of Goldthorpe *et al.* (1968)[6] who focused on the motives, interests and outside work 'backgrounds' of the manual workers in their study of social class in Britain. For Goldthorpe and his colleagues a Weberian ideal instrumental orientation to work is characterized by workers who are calculative in terms of their 'involvement', who view their work as a means of earning income, and for whom work is not a source of self-realization. These characteristics are present to some degree in a number of the statements given by professional footballers. Unlike the workers examined by Goldthorpe *et al.* (1968),[7] however, the players interviewed for this study cannot be said to have chosen professional football as a career for mostly 'extrinsic' rather than 'intrinsic' reasons. That is, the car workers who were the research focus in Goldthorpe *et al.* (1968) brought extrinsic orientations with them to the workplace, whereas footballers begin their working life 'chasing

the big time' (Parker 1996a): players are unlikely to have considered employment as a footballer as a means to an end and as a way to seek fulfilment *outside*
work. Whatever motives players may harbour for seeking a career as a footballer
– creative fulfilment, fame and celebrity status and conspicuous consumption –
they nevertheless make important accommodations and adjustments to their orientations once in work, as their experiences are influenced by structural factors
such as employer–employee power relations, internal competition for places,
constant injuries, their vulnerability to rejection and the inescapable threat of
ageing.

A good example of the way the personal 'outlook' of a footballer may come to
be transformed is provided by an experienced Division Three (i) player who had
played in all of the football divisions during his career. In the following extracts
the player, who at the time of his interview was injured, discusses whether or not
he would play in future matches carrying this injury. He pointed out that when
he initially sustained the injury he knew that he could have carried on playing:
'But I've learnt from *that time* that, if I don't feel 100 per cent then I don't play in
a game. It is a simple as that. If I've got a slight niggle then I say no.' In the following quote this player refers to 'that time' by way of explaining his thought
processes in such situations and, consequently, reveals something of his orientation to his work. So, when asked why he is taking a risk by exaggerating the full
extent of the discomfort he is feeling (by not playing with a soft tissue injury
which is the expected convention) he said:

> Yes, but I think that is a referral to what I went through when I had to play
> two weeks with a broken toe basically. And I think that is one of the things
> about growing up in football; you realize sooner or later that you are only a
> piece of meat, certainly at the levels I play at. They ask you to do specific
> jobs, and say, 'Oh look, I know you've been struggling all week, but can you
> do this for us and can you do that', and when you are young and naïve you do
> it, and when you get a bit older and a bit wiser you think, 'Hold on, I'm
> putting myself on the line here. No, I'm not going to risk the last five years
> of my career for the sake of one game.'

When asked whether it is a regular occurrence for players to be asked to play
either out of position or when they may be 'struggling' with an injury, he made
the following point:

> I think it is a regular occurrence for younger players. As I've got older and
> wiser I've been able to say, 'no, I'm not risking it', just for the sake of one
> game. If I rest myself for this weekend, then by the beginning of next week
> I'll be as right as rain for the next one. One game, that's all. One game dur-
> ing a career of 400 league games isn't a lot, is it! But I think people are put
> under certain pressure when they are younger, but when they get older I

don't think it happens so much. You've learnt to make up your own mind and make your own decisions.

Like other players whose views have been presented in this chapter, this player recognizes that exploitation is an inescapable fact of his career. As such, working under the relational pressures imposed by structural constraints, each player must *make do* as best he can. Wacquant makes a similar point in his highly relevant work on boxers. In a piece on the way boxers think and feel about their trade he remarks that boxing as a career

> is shot through with ambivalence and disquietude, even resentment in some quarters. For it is laced with the barely repressed, yet also embodied, knowledge of the dark side of pugilism, what one Chicago pug ... calls the 'barbaricness' of the sport: the 'daily grind' and 'torture' that one has to go through in preparation for a fight; the physical abuse that can 'make scrambled eggs outa your brains' ... the ruthless exploitation that spontaneously brings forth vituperative analogies with slavery and prostitution ... and threatens to reduce you to a 'piece of meat'.
>
> (Wacquant 1995b: 520)

In similar vein to the boxers examined by Wacquant (1995b and 2001), professional footballers come to varying degrees to acquiesce in the exploitative arrangements in which they are bound. On the one hand the football player quoted above recognizes that he will be treated like a piece of meat; on the other he is able to consider what in *his* terms is the most rational and appropriate way he can resolve the injury-related dilemma with which he is faced. He resolves his problem by taking a risk in not playing with a soft tissue injury and vacating his position in the starting eleven, although he must do this by appearing to his 'critical audience' (Kotarba 1983) to be unable to play because of pain. He is caught between his ambivalence of the necessity to identify with an occupational culture, in which he does not completely believe, which espouses loyalty to, and (bodily) sacrifice for the greater good of, the team, and a perception of the fact that he must *instrumentally* pursue his own ends if he is to be successful.

Resembling the workers examined in Kunda's (1992) study, who saw themselves as 'playing a game' in terms of their appearance and behaviour in the context of work, the players have few choices other than to appear devoted to the team and to the 'goals' of their management, or at least they must conform to the norms of the work culture, in order to avoid punishment, discrediting or outright rejection. The upshot of the continual need for players to manipulate their feelings and actions in order to 'play the game' of being a loyal team member, is the production over time of an instrumental individualism (Ezzy 2001) towards their work.[8] Thus, a club manager's (or director's) pursuit of 'success' requires the sacrifice of self-respect of their players, as the players imply in their comments;

still they require team members to devote themselves to the pursuit of their – that is the manager's – formulation of what constitutes 'success'. The occupational culture of players, central to which is what is known as a 'good attitude', is a normative form of social control that is and has been 'engineered' (Ezzy 2001) by managers (and directors) in order to reduce the ability of players to choose anything other than dedication to the team, even if this requires 'deep acting' (Goffman 1959) as players mature and gain playing experience. Players who display a 'good attitude' are led to believe that they will be rewarded, even if this is only an image of trust and community which, in time, they begin to see through – and become *cynical* towards. In response, players develop an instrumentalism in which they are constrained to 'play the game' of a simulated togetherness to further their own interests (Grey 1994; Casey 1995). For some players their 'interests' relate directly to maximizing their earnings and building their reputations among their developing social networks as good professionals, while for others it may be securing a future contract and avoiding unemployment.[9]

The way in which a player may demonstrate, albeit implicitly, an instrumental orientation to his work is most often via his actions in relation to injury and rejection from the team, as a number of players have explained. Their behaviour is understandable in terms of an acute appreciation of their position as professional footballers in the labour market (although aspects of their understanding are also acquired when viewing other playing colleagues experience key or fateful moments). In other words, players develop, usually at times of crisis in their lives, an understanding of their position relative to other players in terms of their reputations and also the 'simple facts' concerning economic necessities. Unlike other studies concerning attitudes to work that have focused and laid emphasis on the links between developing technologies and instrumental attitudes (Goldthorpe *et al.* 1968), this study confirms that the changes to which players become alerted are 'subjective' in nature. Players recognize that they are vulnerable to career contingencies and that they are in fact economically dispensable. The competitive nature of the labour market is an important feature of the occupation that underpins the instrumental individualist orientations adopted by professional footballers over the course of their careers.

A former Division One (i) defender who was then playing in Division Three (i) articulated an example of the way players express their feelings about the vulnerability of their market position. In the course of discussing the way players negotiate with managers and directors about the terms of their contracts, even though now many may negotiate through an agent, he made the following remarks:

> You become a bit more hardened to discussing contract terms and things like that. But in the early stages I just wanted to play football, I wasn't bothered about the money really. A couple of years later when you've played a lot of football, money becomes a lot more important because, you know, you are

buying a house and you've got a girlfriend or wife. So it's income you want really rather than just any sort of playing experience.

This player was then asked to expand on the suggestion that he changed his view knowingly to a position in which playing football wasn't the be-all and end-all, and that money had become, to use his terms, 'a lot more important'. At this moment the interviewer took the value-laden position of someone who *naturally* assumed – in a manner similar to that of journalist David Conn – that players play for the *love of the game*. The following lengthy interview extract concerns the responses of this player to this suggestion:

Player: I think in football you have to be single-minded. Nobody else looks after you, and you know you hear ... stories about players being, well it happened to me at [a former club] actually. There was this player there who'd been there seven years, played 350 games for the club, a new manager took over, who had previously been the coach and, I think the week before transfer deadline date, he gave him two weeks' wages. He'd been on non-contract for about two years because he couldn't agree a contract and in that time the club had gone from the fourth division into the new first division. But he was still on the same money as he was when the team was in the fourth division. I think they gave him two weeks' wages a week before deadline day and told him that was it, when he'd, you know, he'd been a regular for seven years and that was it, 'on yer bike'. So you've got to look after number one. There comes a point when you are a bit younger obviously when you just want to be a footballer, but when you've been a footballer for a while you realize that it is a job and you've got to maximize your earnings as much as you can. It probably comes with growing up as well when you start making commitments and you have to start thinking about mortgages and wives and children and things.
MR: Are such stories common in your opinion?
Player: Yes, I think every player has probably, well, as I said before, every player probably has gone through it or seen somebody go through it. I think you realize that, you know, it could be you in that situation ... I think players can get cynical and bitter, I think a lot of players are very cynical and bitter especially as they get older. I mean they know that the younger players come in a bit starry eyed, probably like I was, and then you start to realize that it is not about England caps and Wembley appearances and that it is a job and you've got to pay the mortgage like anyone else.
MR: So, is the need to pay the mortgage, and presumably the need to meet other *living* costs, the root of the pressure for players?
Player: Yes definitely. I think football must be a wonderful job if you are earning 10,000 pounds a week like a lot of these Premiership players are, but as you drop down the leagues ... once you've signed a contract there's a sort

> of honeymoon period really where everything is nice and you've got two years ahead of you, guaranteed money. But then six months into that you think, well this time next year I'm starting to panic about another contract, particularly if you are not in the team. I mean if you are in the first year of your contract and you don't play well or if you are not in the team you start to think well, I've got this season. But if I'm not in the team at the start of the next season, you know, it's ... so that's where the pressure comes, you know, its just constantly thinking about what's your next contract or if not where's the next club coming from.

This player makes a number of interesting points including his awareness of the lack of loyalty shown to players and the need for players to look after themselves. He refers also to the belief that players become cynical about their status; in particular they recognize their vulnerability in terms of securing future playing contracts.[10] In effect, this player articulates a fear of job loss. But whilst he isolates his explanations of his *instrumental* actions in relation to economic necessities such as paying the mortgage, his single-mindedness cannot be understood purely in terms of rational economic thinking on his part. Sociologically his work perspective must be understood as embedded in wider networks of social relations. Even if players feel confident about securing their next contract, they can still worry about the prospect of losing it as a result of injury or other contingencies such as a change in management; the loss of self associated with redundancy is particularly hard for players to sustain. Thus, the work perceptions of players are shaped by both the potential threat and the actual consequences of job loss. All players generate insecurities during passages of vulnerability in their careers. Their insecurities relate directly to, but can also be independent of, the workplace and are associated with personal circumstances (or risk factors) including ageing, the lack of transferable or alternative employment skills and responsibility for dependants.

A player, now retired, who played for clubs in all divisions except the Premiership, spoke in his interview of a developing realization concerning his initial career aspirations. In the course of detailing the events that concerned the re-negotiation of an existing contract and the anxieties that result from protracted contract negotiations, he makes the following comments:

> I really had nothing left to play for to be honest and so I thought, well maybe this was the time, you know, to go off in a different direction. I've been playing professional football for about ... the last fifteen years and you get to thirty-two and you realize that you are never going to be a millionaire or play for Manchester United and all that. But I've got the brains to go on and do something else.

He was asked to comment further about whether or not he still clung to the 'self-serving notion' (Wacquant 2001: 189) that he will be the ageing footballer who beats the odds by getting spotted and making a 'big move': the type of idealized thoughts he may have harboured as a young player. In response he said:

> I think every player playing in the lower divisions, you know, secretly yearns for the big move, but it doesn't come to many. That's the thing. But the older you get the less likely it is, if it's going to happen at all. Plus the loyalty shown to players at smaller clubs is non-existent really, so you can play 200 games in four years and the club will say, 'thanks a lot'. From the point of view of the club it's just an opportunity to get somebody off the wage bill and, you know, you are on the dole. I wasn't prepared to get myself in that situation where I could get pushed out at any time. I'd rather sort of jump before I was pushed basically.

Experiences such as these, and others which have been referred to in the course of this study, lead players to develop a heightened sense of self-worth and a more reality-congruent understanding of their status among colleagues. It is clear that career contingencies such as injuries, especially long-term injuries, changes in management and transferring to other teams, can be significant turning points in the careers of players in which, earlier or later, emerging realism and cynicism develop. Players learn during times absent from training and playing that *time* is paramount and internal colleague competition is intense.

To summarize: players develop instrumental attitudes towards their work such that they enable themselves either to achieve 'success' in terms of playing reputation or to satisfy their personal interests in relation to the future economic security of dependants. Attending to their 'interests', whichever way this term may be defined, may constrain players to think (and very occasionally to act) in a way that is at odds with the image of a 'good professional'. Players feel *morally* justified in adopting such work perspectives for they become cynical towards their employers who they come in time to believe will not reward their efforts with genuine displays of loyalty. Whilst 'the management' within a professional football club may attempt to foster an image of community among their employees – the players – the occupational culture in which all players work constrains their choices of action and leads to the development of a sense of individualism that results in an increasing neglect for any other people outside the players' immediate sphere of concern; in other words, genuine respect players may have for colleagues is devalued.

## Cynicism as resistance?

In this chapter a social pattern has been identified concerning how players develop a degree of cynicism towards professional football and come to adopt instrumental attitudes towards managing the social relations in which they are bound up at work. Apart from direct references to cynicism, perhaps the most obvious indication of this pattern is that players refer to themselves as 'pieces of meat' and 'commodities'. As the data presented in this chapter suggest, player cynicism results from circumstances in which they feel let down either because initially they believed and were committed to the idea that they were involved in a career that would lead to personal wealth and glory; or they develop a lack of trust in relation to the motives of people for whom they are expected to labour using their greatest efforts by virtue of their occupational position and from whom they expect a commensurate reward; or they lose their belief in, or develop a contempt for, the part they are asked to play in the *production* process. The way in which professional footballers come to think cynically about their work is no different in kind from the way many people generate contempt for, or how they begin to 'see through', a set of beliefs – for example an occupational culture – to which formerly they have been willingly committed.

At first glance, the idea that footballers can be disenchanted by and cynically detached from their profession is somewhat surprising, for the occupation of professional football provides a context – an opportunity – for certain males 'blessed' with special talents to construct a publicly recognized heroic or 'glorified self' (Adler and Adler 1989), and escape a common humdrum working life, the like of which bears down on the majority of 'ordinary' people. Sociologists interested in employees and their work have typically focused on manual and factory workers because, it seems, they are the people who might well consider their work to be unrewarding in terms of emotional gratification and are less likely to think of it as a 'central life interest' (Dubin *et al.* 1976). In contrast, it is a widely held assumption that a career as a professional footballer is infused with a sense of value, excitement and accomplishment – remember David Conn who describes a career as a footballer as 'a dream come true'. Professional football is a highly skilled (manual) activity to which a highly distinctive value is attached. The lives of players are imbued with a great deal of symbolic capital (Bourdieu and Wacquant 1992) and like singing and dancing and similar 'body-centred performance trades that occupy a pivotal place in working class culture' (Wacquant 1995b: 509), football talent is considered by many fans to be a sacred gift whose possession carries with it moral obligation to nurture and use it well; in short, a narrative typical of this moral obligation might suggest that in light of the fact that *anyone* can pick up a job in a factory, players should not waste the opportunity bestowed 'on them' by failing to realize their talent.

Despite these very general and for the most part mythical, yet well understood statements,[11] expressions of cynicism were regularly articulated in the narratives of players interviewed for this study. One might conclude from these data that players are cynically enlightened about the *realities* of football culture but they act or feel constrained to act as if they are not. There is a body of sociological literature that evaluates various interpretations of employee cynicism (see Anderson 1996; Casey 1995; Collinson 1992; du Gay and Salaman 1992; Fleming and Sewell 2002; Kunda 1992; Willmott 1993). Despite the fact that 'cynicism' has been discussed sociologically for some time – Simmel, for example, suggested that cynicism is an emotional screen or 'psychic response' to modernity (Shilling 2002) and Berger and Luckmann (1967) refer to the notion of 'cool alternation' by way of explaining the response where individuals subjectively 'distance' themselves from the roles they play – this recent literature, which mostly focuses on the subjectivities of workers, highlights examples of cynicism in 'modern' workplaces and draws attention to employee orientations to work that, in a number of respects, resemble those identified in this chapter. The literature on employee cynicism can be categorized, perhaps over-simplistically, into three broad groups. The first category, which will not be considered analytically here, contains 'managerialist' work that views cynicism as a psychological defect that needs to be 'corrected' (Fleming and Spicer 2003). However, the two remaining categories of research that are pertinent for the purposes of understanding player cynicism differ fundamentally on how this cynicism is interpreted.

The first argument identifies the cynicism characteristic of employees as a practice of dissent and a subtle way of resisting control by *dis-identifying* with contemporary occupational culture whilst concurrently complying with it. Fleming and Spicer (2003: 157), who advocate this view, suggest that in the new age of post-Fordist corporate culture employees are 'working at a cynical distance'. In addition to approaches that view employee cynicism as a defence mechanism that attempts to block the 'colonisation' (Casey 1995) of the identities of workers – that is, mechanisms that protect their 'back stage' selves – Fleming and Spicer (2003: 167) argue that

> when the dis-identification process is enacted it can establish an alluring 'breathing space' where people feel untrammelled by the subjective demands of the organization, but which ironically permits them to behave as an efficient and meticulous member of the team nevertheless.

In other words, it would be their likely suggestion that the footballers interviewed for this book come to 'see through', and dis-identify with, the rhetoric of a 'good professional attitude' as an occupational cultural ideology; even so, they still engage in behaviour through which it is supported and reproduced. Fleming and Spicer (2003) argue that a process of *cynical* dis-identification is a more subtle form of resistance that raises sociological questions about 'power' and 'subjectivity' in the workplace.

The second and dominant (Fleming and Spicer 2003) argument is characterized by an alternative perspective on this ambiguous point of debate. Sociologists Willmott (1993) and du Gay and Salaman (1992) suggest that even though workers may negatively distance themselves from the dictates of the occupational cultures in which they are embedded and work hard to dis-identify mentally with their prescribed social roles, their (contradictory) behaviour can be understood as *simple conformity*. This line of argument purports that cynicism as an unplanned awakening for players unobtrusively reproduces relations of power because cynical employees allow themselves to think (falsely) that they operate as autonomous agents, but they still practise the 'cultural' rituals regardless. As an audience viewing 'front stage' performances (Goffman 1959), sociologists such as Willmott and du Gay and Salaman would argue that the behaviour of professional footballers would appear to reproduce the very occupational culture – the 'good attitude' – that is and has been impressed upon them in part by club managers and coaches whose motives in their eyes are questionable and with whom some have lost faith.[12] Thus, cynical detachment as a tactic of transgression does not appear to alter or challenge existing power structures, for players become 'trapped' over the course of their careers in a 'vicious circle of cynicism and dependence' (Willmott 1993: 518).

The interpretations of employee cynicism put forward discuss the same general trend: that in contemporary working life managerial ideology targets the very 'selves' of employees (Fleming and Sewell 2002) who, in response, engage in an *active disengagement*. The footballers interviewed could be identified on the one hand as complying with cultural norms without conforming to them, or on the other hand as developing a false sense of autonomy that embeds them more profoundly to existing relations of power. The data obtained for this study indicate that both interpretations offer explanatory purchase. The cynical perspectives that footballers come to adopt can be interpreted as recognition of the fact that they see through the rhetoric and motivations of managers, enabling them to act in a manner that they believe is for their own good; that is, they act 'instrumentally'. Furthermore, the development of a cynical frame of mind towards their employers is a form of self-serving 'power' since they can be sceptical about, rather than blind to, the motives of other people and, in their own minds, acquire a more realistic understanding – a 'knowledge' – of what the circumstances in which they are embedded 'really mean' for them. Invoking the work of W.I. Thomas (see Bottomore and Nisbet 1979), knowledge of their circumstances is meaningful since the subsequent *informed* actions of players have intended and unintended consequences for people involved directly and indirectly with football club business. In this sense, cynicism can be conceptualized as a form of resistance against both the authoritarian and normative forms of control which constrain, at least on the surface, their actions and presentation of self.

It can be argued that both interpretations presented here are relevant because they offer insight in terms of how the players in this study come to think and feel about their work. The cynicism of players remains incomprehensible however without an examination of the interdependencies in which they are tied. In an effort to be more concrete, there are numerous references in the chapters concerning injury in which, for example, players exaggerate the full extent, or conceal or deny the existence, of pain and discomfort to *critical audiences* such that they can either play or miss games in accordance solely with *their* career interests at that point in time. Moreover, the covert method in which players seek second opinions about and treatment of their injuries, such that they are not overtly critical of the physiotherapists at their club, is further conformation of the development of a degree of *cynical detachment*. Action of this nature is deemed not to concur with anticipated occupational cultural norms and is considered intolerable by club directors, managers and physiotherapists who would label those players who engage in this type of resistance as 'troublemakers'. For all that, by seeking second opinions covertly players do not defy football club culture, for on the surface they behave in accordance with occupational conventions. Even so, their cynicism towards employers enables them to recognize and understand the motivations of managers who, for instance, ask players to 'do a job' even though they may be unfit. The cynical detachment displayed by players enables them legitimately to resist the wishes of managers without compromising their professional attitudes and reputations among either management or teammates. Players engage in (transgressive) behaviour that results from their adoption of a cynical perspective but which reproduces the cultural prescriptions and relations of power in which they are embedded. Thus, when it comes to occupational cultural prescriptions, players have few alternatives other than to be active participants in their own self-discipline whether that leads to consent, (blind) compliance or resistance in the form of cynicism.

## Conclusion

These concluding remarks have examined the cynicism expressed by players as a means of identifying a style of resistance that is arguably less evident in many of the academic studies of professional footballers. Like all other forms of resistance, cynicism involves a degree of 'defence of the self', an attempt by players to maintain a sense of personal integrity. It is argued here that the studies of players have had difficulty in examining forms of resistance to managerial controls for the following two reasons. First, traditional conceptions of resistance that emphasize open and organized – collective – dissent do not have a long history when considered relative to labour and industrial disputes in other industries, for instance, the transport and energy industries. Second, most people writing about the game on all levels are to some degree blinded by their value commitment to 'sacred' aspects of the game which raise the life of players above the level of the 'profane'. Player cynicism is understood as a method of 'distancing' in relation to their everyday engagements which reproduce exploitative relations on the one hand and enable players to externalize the control of management on the other as they become realistic and, to some extent, dis-identify with ideals about their statuses to which they were formerly committed.

# Conclusion

This book is about the careers of footballers, but why, as sociologists, should we be concerned to analyse and understand the work of professional players, some of whom are highly paid, often idolized by supporters and overly 'protected' (Gearing 1999) by club officials? A question of this nature can be addressed using both sociological and moral reasoning. Careers of professional footballers are worthy of serious sociological study because football clubs offer up for scrutiny a good example of what Eakin and MacEachen (1998) consider to be 'small work-places'.[1] Close-knit work environments of this kind, they argue, present the possibility of examining, for instance, the notion of teamwork as a means by which employees are integrated into the 'interests' of work organizations. However, striking at the heart of notions of 'social bonding' and 'social solidarity' – ideas associated strongly with team sports – is that among professional football players there is a lack of discourse of 'the family': a narrative on which Eakin and MacEachen (1998) focus in their work on small craft-based enterprises and Wulff (2001) and Turner and Wainwright (2003) analyse in their examinations of *corps de ballet*. In other words, Wulff (2001) found that ballet dancers tend to think of themselves as members of a 'family' when discussing their working environments. Clear distinctions exist in professional football however between the workplace goals and interests of employees and employers for, as we have seen, 'we–they' identities (Eakin and MacEachen 1998) are characterized generally by high rather than low polarization.

Although this list is not exhaustive, the following points contribute also to the moral reasons why footballers should be targets of examination by social scientists. First, players are role models for thousands of young people globally; their behaviour on and, increasingly, off the field of play is scrutinized and judged. There exists, therefore, a moral obligation for Premiership players in particular – for they appear on television and in the print media most regularly – to conduct themselves 'appropriately' in public, ever mindful of the fact that their behaviour is copied by children. Second, there are myriad assumptions generated about players and the inner workings of clubs: principally that footballers are all paid astronomical wages, are controlled by agents and that their individual autonomy is constrained by club management such that they remain immature and bereft of social skills useful in the 'real world'. As an occupation, it is often considered in glamorous terms. Thus, there is a need to destroy myths surrounding the sport and for more reality-congruent analysis to be undertaken. Third, it seems only right that if, as spectators and football devotees, we demand from players-as-employees that they protect and do not waste their talents, produce high level performances consistently and achieve and maintain a peak physical state, that the conditions for their personal development and individual health and well-being should also be nurtured.

In their study of Scottish professional footballers, McGillivray *et al.* (2005) indicate that the professional game represents a 'comfort zone' for players. Football is an occupational world that they comprehend intimately insofar as they recognize what is required of them, the conditions of their work and the consequences of success and failure. In other words, there is 'comfort' of a kind in their workplace knowledge for, as McGillivray *et al.* (2005) substantiate, they have neither experience of, nor transferable skills to apply in, alternative occupational settings. Nevertheless, in the light of the testimony provided by interviewees for this study, the majority of footballers neither experience nor describe a 'comfortable', secure existence. The 'footballing *illusio*' to which McGillivray *et al.* (2005: 108) refer, in which the 'hearts and minds' of players become entwined in football culture such that they can only comprehend their daily lives through the lens of the culture of the game, is not as all-encompassing, as 'totalizing' (Goffman 1961) or as inescapable as they indicate. This is principally because, over time, players' attitudes towards the professional game transform in significant ways in combination with an increasing reflexivity (Swain 1991) towards their careers as a whole. So, among the players interviewed, I did not detect a lack of consideration with respect to their present and future situations, albeit that many did not know what their next employment move might be. I formulated the opinion that while most players do not have an appreciation of career possibilities post-football, they are conscious of their limitations in this respect. Thus, players whose careers have reached a plateau or are in decline are, in simple terms, unable to imagine – although they may still be fearful about – occupational life after football, for their world views have been shaped by people within the game, such as club directors, managers and coaches, for whom second careers post-football are not a central concern. The problem conceived in this way is different from McGillivray *et al.*'s (2005) portrayal of employees who develop an occupational blindness. Players come to appreciate their limitations, even if they do not know how to deal with them – a significant educational issue for the Professional Footballers' Association and the agents who claim to look after the career and welfare interests of their players-as-clients.

McGillivray *et al.* (2005) and Gearing (1999) argue that the majority of footballers are unprepared for retirement (or post-career), the final stage or status of a traditional career model. This statement is almost certainly accurate for most players: it is not my belief that the bulk of players experience a 'social death' (Rosenberg 1984) or trauma (Gearing 1999), which is so often thought to be the case. In a documentary entitled 'Life After Football' (BBC1, 25 May 2005), former Liverpool player and Scotland international Alan Hansen examines the thoughts and outlooks of a number of players who are close to or in retirement. While a number of the players present mixed feelings about the game, it is clear from the outset that the point of Hansen's documentary is to highlight the potency of football as a form of work and that, for players, nothing can replace 'the buzz' of match days and the feelings generated when 'pulling on' the shirt on a Saturday afternoon. One of the drawbacks of Hansen's documentary however is that he focuses, as so many journalists tend to, on elite players solely. For example, he interviews former England international Les Ferdinand alongside his helicopter and passes judgement on Rio Ferdinand – a Manchester United and England international reputed to be earning in the region of £100,000 a week – for not having considered sufficiently his future beyond the game. Both of these players are representatives of the *football millionaires* who have been so evident in quasi-serious journalistic and academic discussion. A Premiership 'megastar' such as Rio Ferdinand rarely needs to adjust his career sights, for he has experienced transfers to 'big' clubs, appeared in Cup Finals and represented his country. The majority of players interviewed for this study did not achieve these types of career heights. Most found it necessary to revise their initial occupational 'goals' and 'dreams' and referred almost exclusively to immediate and pressing concerns such as maintaining a first team place and securing future contracts, particularly if they had dependants.

For many players included in my sample, and, I propose, the majority of footballers in general, their first steps away from the professional game are unlikely to be traumatic events similar in kind to those *falls from grace* (e.g. George Best and Paul Gascoigne) given so much exposure in the literature. As they approach their final career statuses, players lower expectations to the point that their departures are not wholly unexpected and, for many, retirement provides a degree of relief from the employment conditions and the merciless physical demands of this sport. Similar patterns have been established in other sports (Allison and Meyer 1988; Swain 1991). So, while players may harbour genuine concerns about future employment and may be inappropriately equipped for a second career, a step away from professional football is not necessarily experienced negatively. The experience of retirement from football is one that requires much further research, although it should not be distanced from the orientations of players to their work as they reach their final career stages. For example, a number of players – interviewees as well as friends in the game – indicated that they did not like or enjoy the football world any more. Opinions such as these however are voiced rarely. This negative view is rather more complex than a simple love–hate dichotomy. All players 'love' playing to some degree – they do, as Harding (2003) indicates, 'live to play' – for there is a *ludic* element that develops in childhood and which remains central to their positive workplace experiences. As it stands, this view is anecdotal and, like the subject of managing retirement from the game, needs further scrutiny by social scientists. Even so, it does hint at a requirement to reformulate the commonplace and overstated notion of professional football as a *labour of love*.

## Football as a labour of love

Professional football is a form of contingent employment. The data collected for this book indicate that *uncertainty* is central to, and is a built-in characteristic of, the experiences of players, for whom career advancement and attainment are never secure. In a manner similar to the (former IBM) computer engineers examined by Sennett (1998: 130), who slowly gained an appreciation of the fact that 'aggravated vulnerability' is a pervasive feature of (post-)modern, flexible careers, the players analysed in this study similarly acquired an understanding of the precariousness of football as a profession. Unlike the workers in Sennett's study, however, footballers do not embark on their careers anticipating lifelong, stable employment, for there is neither a professional nor public perception of job security in this industry. Even young players understand that injury may terminate the career prospects of a potential player, although such dangers may appear distant until feelings of vulnerability are experienced subjectively. In many studies undertaken in the sociology of work, the threat of unemployment constitutes, perhaps, the central risk factor (see Doogan 2001; Loÿttyniemi 2001; Sennett 1998). Job security, however, is only one of a number of uncertainties encountered by players throughout their careers.

In the world of professional football, injury and the threat of injury are routine. For all players, but particularly for those who are older and more established, pain is a more or less permanent feature of their careers (Roderick *et al.* 2000). However, it is not only that injuries for players are routine, but that other people expect them to play with pain and injury as an aspect of displaying a 'good professional attitude' to their work. Failure to display the right 'attitude' may lead players to be stigmatized as having 'no heart' or labelled as malingerers. Consequently, it is extraordinarily difficult for players not to play with an injured body. At times they exhibit stoical tolerance of pain; even so their behaviour and orientation towards their bodies are disciplined by the medical arrangements within football clubs. Fatigue and accidents during matches and training expose all players to the risk of injury, and because their identities are invested in the professional game, an injury that terminates that career abruptly and irrevocably is a major hazard to their identities. The problem of the social relations of managing injury, therefore, is particularly serious, given the fact that playing careers, even under ideal conditions, are relatively short. For the majority of players, the conjunction of ageing and injury, in a situation where discomfort and pain are accepted features of football life, finally brings about an end to their careers.

Implicit throughout each chapter has been an awareness of the changefulness of the frame of mind of players as they mature and age during their careers. Although the process of ageing is a universal biological fact, and one that ultimately has dire consequences for all footballers, those who are thought of as aged or old is a matter of social definition.[2] A number of empirical studies (Faulkner 1974; Gearing 1997; Weinberg and Arond 1970) confirm the notion that there is a 'social clock' in professional sport. For example, in his book, *Left foot forward*, former Charlton Athletic footballer Garry Nelson (1996) makes constant reference to his age and status among his contemporaries. Against a backcloth of the short-term nature of football careers, Nelson provides numerous telling examples of an older player's awareness of age grading and prejudice. In his playing life, therefore, a player's age can be viewed as a fundamental career contingency, a determinant upon which promotion or rejection may depend. The interview data collected for this study suggest that within professional football clubs, in which there exists youth-intensive recruitment and high levels of internal colleague competition, one's age may facilitate or impede access to opportunities and valued positions. That is to say, older players, like Nelson, may be stigmatized by others by virtue of their age, and not necessarily because of their cognitive or physical deterioration.

In a highly competitive labour market such as professional football, it is important for 'older' players to remain visible. This may require them to move clubs or, at least, to ensure they gather information from trusted individuals about potential connections to other teams. However, remaining visible presents a problem for them, as there is an oversupply of aspirants 'chasing the big-time' (Parker 1996a). In professional football, enormous rewards are concentrated in the hands of a minority of players, whereas, by contrast, the majority fare *relatively* poorly. Such contexts entail a high degree of uncertainty. The excess supply of football talent leads older players in particular to live in a climate of fear: fear that someone younger, cheaper, fitter and who is perceived to be hungrier for success, may replace them. In addition to the high numbers of aspiring British players, there is – particularly since the Bosman ruling in 1995 – a further fear of the increasing employment of non-British players. All players are now tied to the global flow of labour in the professional game: that is to say, footballers are now caught up in the flux of the global labour market. There is a general, albeit passive, fear of the internationalization of the professional game.

So, how do players cope with the pervasive insecurities which are a permanent feature of their working lives? This specific sociological question has been central to this book. All the chapters herein examine, in a modest way, the ways in which players come to deal with the realities of pursuing a career as a professional footballer. This task has been addressed, in part, by analysing crucial turning points in their lives, although none of the interviewees confined their thoughts solely (by reference) to single markers of change. The stories told by players about their developing orientations to work situations overwhelmingly depicted passages of transition as a slow, rather than sudden, process. Sociologically, then, focusing on crucial turning points enabled a clearer understanding of processes that are, in reality, rather chaotic and blind. For example, players slowly came to understand the normality of their exploitation. They gradually came to realize that their hopes and dreams, their pride, and their pain and discomfort are of little meaning or bearing to managers and club directors, who have their own desires to attend to. In a manner similar to Weber's protestant businessmen, who found in the performance of 'good works' the 'technical means, not of purchasing salvation, but of getting rid of the fear of damnation' (Wacquant 1995a: 87), footballers overcome their anxieties of the risk of rejection and unemployment by playing and training with wholehearted dedication. But this is, of course, exactly what their managers desire of them. For younger players, their 'love' of the game, provides the impetus to keep going when, as it were, 'luck' appears to be running counter to them. For the older players interviewed for this study, their cynicism towards the game in general is a form of *self*-protection and a way for them to maintain their personal integrity. In other words, it is a means by which players may detach or distance their 'selves' from the constraints of occupational prescriptions and controlling, authoritarian football managers, whilst continuing to appear to comply with them.

Roth (1963) argues that people will not accept uncertainty. They will make an effort, he suggests, to structure it. In his view one way to structure uncertainty is to structure the period of time through which uncertain events occur. The evidence collected for this book strongly suggests that players attempt to make some sense of the uncertainty of what future events might happen and the consequences of certain types of behaviour, by drawing, where possible, on the experiences of others. As a result of such comparisons, players develop benchmarks in relation to time and age to gauge whether their careers are going well or badly. Long periods of time out of the team due to an injury, for example, might be made more psychologically manageable by being broken down into smaller stages. Even so, while the players interviewed for this study were able to discuss their progress lucidly and create coherent narratives about events retrospectively, most, but particularly the older and former, players considered it impossible to create narratives about what will be. One way in which all employees, including footballers, may adopt a more structural approach to addressing the problem of uncertainty is by networking. Players draw on a fund of social capital to assist their occupational mobility and to take advantage of opportunities perhaps unforeseen by others. Among people within professional football there is a constant 'buzz', a ceaseless current of rumour flowing from one day to the next about who is unsettled and which managers *fancy* which players. Over time, the interviewees developed informal networks of people 'inside the game' to whom they turned when, for example, their position in the first team was under threat, or when they realized that they were no longer in their manager's plans.

But why, then, do players appear willing to persevere in a profession in which they collude in their own commercialization and in which they are reduced to the level of a commodity? The rationale of players for their occupational choice can be examined to some extent in relation to monetary rewards, although the skewed distribution of incomes in this sport, particularly since the end of the maximum wage in 1961, is well documented (see Szymanski and Kuypers 1999). Many players, however, continue to work because their training in professional football has resulted in them possessing few transferable skills (McGillivray *et al.* 2005). In this connection, former Republic of Ireland international Tony Cascarino states: 'I play football because I have to play football. I play football because I know nothing else' (Kimmage 2000: 6). Professional footballers provide, arguably, classic examples of 'trained incapacity' (Merton 1957). A question such as this cannot be tackled without reference to the *symbolic* structure of professional football. The work of footballers may appear highly attractive to young aspirants in relation to a number of dimensions of job satisfaction, including the opportunity to feel self-actualized at work, to live an idiosyncratic way of life, to feel a strong sense of community, and to establish publicly their character, ability and strength among the broader population of fans. Although he is referring to professional boxers, Wacquant (1995b: 514), whose point could apply equally to professional footballers, argues that 'eliciting the roar and appreciation of the crowd is a prized objective and ample gratification in itself'. Such 'psychic incomes' (Menger 1999) must be regarded as an essential dimension of their work. Yet, whether they win or lose, or whether they feel they have achieved all they set out to, players leave bits and pieces of themselves on every pitch. Every match, every tackle, every strained ligament and twisted joint, chips away at the prospect of a healthy future. The attachment of players to the professional game, then, may be understood as a distorted *labour of love*, ever tainted by their rising suspicion that they may be paying too steep a price for the opportunity for social recognition.

# Notes

## Introduction

1 Parker (1996a) makes connections between the occupational socialization of young apprentice-professional players and Goffman's (1961) notion of 'total institutions'.

2 All players interviewed were male and were experiencing (or had experienced) playing careers in English professional football clubs. This point is made at this juncture for there are now female professional players in England.

3 Seven doctors were at clubs in the Premier League, two were doctors at clubs in Division One (i), two with clubs in Division Two (i) and one doctor was employed by a Division Three (i) club. Three physiotherapists worked in Premier League clubs, two in Division One (i) clubs, two in Division Two (i) clubs and two in Division Three (i) clubs; in addition, one physiotherapist had formerly worked in two football clubs (one Division Three (i) club, one Premier League club) but now worked as a club physiotherapist in another sport.

4 The original intention of this proposal was to interview past and present club doctors, physiotherapists and players about the social constraints surrounding the management of injuries, the pressure to play while injured, the ways in which issues of confidentiality are handled and the way in which the interests of the club and the player are balanced. See Waddington *et al.* (1999).

5 See Dunphy (1987) *Only a Game* and Nelson (1996) *Left Foot Forward*. These two examples are notable because the players in question are *journeymen* players rather than well known Premier League stars.

6 Attitudes to football are examined closely in Chapter 2, although at this point it is enough to indicate that the whole notion of a professional attitude to the game remains largely undefined.

## Chapter 1

1 Sennett's (2003) argument is a historical one. Over time, the way in which talent has been rewarded has changed. Careers were not open to talent in pre-modern social life in the way that they are in post-industrial capitalist society.

2 Szymanski and Kuypers (1999) suggest that players' careers average around five years, with even the best players seldom lasting more than ten.

3 In 1963, George Eastham, Newcastle and England international, wanted to move south for personal reasons, but the club refused to agree and put him on the 'retained' list. Challenging the retain and transfer system, Eastham took the club to court and the judge, Mr Justice Wilberforce, declared that the club was acting unlawfully 'in restraint of trade'. Effectively, the judgement meant that a player had the right to play for any club, subject to respecting standard contractual terms (Szymanski and Kuypers 1999).

4 Players may also be signed on a week-by-week non-contract basis. Accurate figures for players who are attached to clubs on this basis are not available.

5 Economic rent is an important concept in economics. A short definition of this concept is as follows: any excess that a factor earns over the minimum amount needed to keep it at its present use. The term is often applied to 'superstars' who earn controversially large salaries in highly specialized types of labour. In short, many high profile football players have a style or a talent that cannot be duplicated, whatever the training. The earnings they receive are mostly economic rent from the viewpoint of the occupation. For example, Manchester United star Ryan Giggs would choose football over other alternatives even at a much lower salary than he was earning even as far back as 1994. However, because of Giggs's skill as a football player, most teams would pay handsomely to have him, and he is able to command a high salary from the team he does play for. From the perspective of the firm, Manchester United, most of Giggs's salary is required to keep him from switching to another team and, hence, is not economic rent. From the viewpoint of the football industry, however, much of his salary is economic rent.

6 In this respect one can think of Gary Lineker (footballer) and Andrew Castle (tennis player) who have developed second careers as television presenters, and footballers such as Alan Hansen and Ally McCoist who are football commentators and pundits.

7 In December 1995, Jean-Marc Bosman, a Belgian player who wished to transfer from RC Liege in Belgium to US Dunkerque in France, brought a case before the European Court. Liege were allowed to fix a fee for the player without negotiation and, as a result, the transfer fell through because Dunkerque could not afford the fee. The decision of the European Court found in favour of Bosman, deciding that the transfer system restricted the freedom of movement of employees (footballers) in the European Union in contravention of Article 48 of the Treaty of Rome. Thus, the court ruled that a club could not demand a transfer fee for a player who had completed his contract. The Bosman ruling referred to players moving between member states of the European Union, but the implication of the judgement is that transfer fees for any player out of contract could not be legally enforceable. This ruling affected English clubs since they could no longer demand a transfer fee for any player out of contract.

8 Below the four professional leagues in England there is what is known as the non-league pyramid, involving semi-professional, 'non-league' football clubs. The league at the top of this pyramid is called the Conference and feeds directly into League Two. So, the club that wins the Conference is promoted to the Football League and will, therefore, be counted among the ninety-two professional football clubs. Whilst clubs in the Conference are labelled semi-professional, players may be both professional and amateur. That is, some players who play for clubs in this league may be paid as full-time professional players while others may play for no or little monetary reward.

9 Although some players are also club managers. They are known as 'player–managers'.

10 The Professional Footballers' Association has had a largely passive membership since its formation in 1907. Wagg (1984) offers a thorough examination of labour relations disputes between players and their employers.

## Chapter 2

1 'Football Dreams' was a television documentary that followed the fortunes of a number of apprentice professional footballers who were 'chasing the big time' at Chelsea Football Club.

2 The position of thirteenth man does not exist in football any more, although prior to increases in substitute numbers, clubs always took an extra player to away matches who

would not be named on the team sheet. Their presence was required on the off chance that a first team player or substitute became ill overnight or that a player picked up an injury whilst warming up for the match.

3 This chapter is an expansion of a number of ideas contained in the following report: 'Managing Injuries in Professional Football' (Waddington et al. 1999).

4 Parker (1996b) argues that in order to understand sporting practices, one must acknowledge the social construction of differing masculine identities. He argues that one must recognize the existence of a multiplicity of masculinities according to the diverse cultural values in place at any given time.

5 See also, in this connection, the work of Nash (1979), who examines the plight of workers in Bolivian tin mines.

6 This idea is similar in kind to the discussion developed by Wacquant (1995b). In the following quote Wacquant (1995b: 496) discusses the attitude to their profession developed by boxers:

> The fistic trade puts a high premium on physical toughness and the ability to with-stand – as well as dish out – pain and bodily harm. The specific honour of the pugilist, like that of the ancient gladiator, consists in refusing to concede and kneel down. One of the visible outward signs of the much-revered quality called 'heart' said to epitomize the authentic boxer is the capacity not to bow under pressure, to 'suck it up' and keep on fighting, no matter what the physical toll.

## Chapter 4

1 Data for this chapter come from some interviews conducted with club doctors and physiotherapists as part of the Managing Injuries in Professional Football project (Waddington et al. 1999).

## Chapter 5

1 For Gowling (1974) a big move related to the movement of a player to a club in a higher division. A number of players however referred to certain clubs that they considered 'big', some of which were in the same division as the club for which they were currently playing.

2 For a fuller, sociological discussion of the idea of failure and rejection in sport, see Ball (1976), Failure in Sport.

## Chapter 6

1 The term 'grapevine' is employed by Magee (1998) in his research on the global labour mobility of professional footballers.

2 See Chapter 3, section on 'Individual progress versus team success'.

3 Although this point was not substantiated in the interview data.

4 Likewise, players should not be overly self-congratulatory about their successes among teammates.

5 That is, 'illegal' in terms of FIFA regulations.

6 Please see the report on managing injuries in professional football prepared for the PFA (Waddington et al. 1999).

7 See Chapter 1 for an explanation of the 1995 Bosman ruling.

8 Some players indicated that when they first arrived at the club they thought they were considered to be the manager's favourite by the other players who may not have been purchased by that particular manager.

9 As discussed in Chapter 1, regional preference may reflect a process that Kanter (1977: 48) terms homosocial reproduction. Kanter argues that managers who work in situations where performance cannot be prescribed with any confidence are inclined to recruit employees who are socially similar. They do so because they believe they know how employees will behave. Such risk-averse behaviour fosters social homogeneity, as managers tend to reproduce themselves in their own image.

## Chapter 7

1 Magee's categories are applicable only after 1963 and, in particular, following the Bosman ruling in 1995. Players could not be exploiters prior to 1995 to the same degree as post-1995.
2 See Chapter 8 for a fuller discussion of the work of Max Weber.
3 Agents have had to register with, and be approved by, FIFA since 1994. To register, an agent must deposit a £110,000 bond in a Swiss bank account.
4 Not all club physiotherapists are qualified to a chartered status and are therefore not members of a professional body. For a fuller discussion of this issue, please refer to Waddington et al. (1999).
5 For a general discussion of the roles and responsibilities of club doctors and physiotherapists see Waddington et al. (1999).
6 No wives or partners of players were interviewed for this study. Many of the players mentioned their wives in one way or another when discussing household decision-making processes.
7 For ease of reading, I propose to use the term 'partner' as a generic concept to cover both the wives of players as well as those women or men with whom players cohabit.
8 This principle was reflected in British law in the concept that prevailed until 1973: the wife's legal domicile was that of her husband.
9 Despite the evidence which continues to indicate a clear segregation of women's work, full-time working women and students are found to hold less traditional attitudes, but husbands were repeatedly found to be more traditional than their wives with regard to gender roles at home and work (Newell 2000).

## Chapter 8

1 Although most players are not relieved of these pressures.
2 Cashmore and Parker (2003) talk of football training as predictable, mundane, and heavily prescribed.
3 Wacquant quotes former boxer Ralph Wiley who talks of boxing as 'assault and battery'. Wacquant agrees suggesting that

> this assault causes irreversible damage and leaves indelible marks on the body. Fighters know this but, like all entrepreneurs worthy of their name, they are willing to take risks and put their capital – i.e. their body – on the line in the pursuit of occupational success. It is one of the founding antinomies, one of the irresolvable paradoxes of boxing that pugilists worship and cultivate their bodies in order to destruct that of their opponent and, in the process, too often, their own.
>
> (Wacquant 1995a: 82)

4 England international goalkeeper David James has commented on the issue of loyalty in professional football. When asked about whether he would leave West Ham United, who had been relegated to Division One (i) in 2003, James made the following point:

Loyalty in football is a contradiction. What is loyalty? It doesn't exist between a player and a club. The club uses the player and vice versa. Once the clubs took all the money and it went to a few individuals. Now it goes to the players but it's spread around a bit more. If there is ever any loyalty, it can only exist between a player and the fans. If Mr Eriksson says playing in the First Division doesn't mean I am going to be chucked out, that gives me the opportunity to repay the loyalty West Ham's fans have shown to me. If the club decides to sell me for balance sheet reasons, then what does my loyalty mean?

(*Sunday Times*, 8 June 2003)

5 Roy Keane said that Jaap Stam was treated as 'a piece of meat' by Manchester United (*Daily Mirror*, 10 September 2001).

6 As well as other sociologists such as Dubin *et al.* (1976).

7 The sources of this instrumental orientation were in the class, community and family backgrounds of the employees, not in the workplace itself.

8 The arguments presented here go some way to highlighting a weakness in the work of Magee (1998), for it is clear that players may be concurrently 'exploited' and yet be 'exploiters' of the circumstances in which they are bound up. Players who are in demand, and financially secure, may also be aware of *their* exploitation by agents and club merchandising directors, as was demonstrated by the example of Alan Shearer who was described as 'smiling the smile' (see page 147).

9 It is worth noting again that, like players, football club managers are also attempting to 'build' their reputations as skilful managers of player squads. Managers, perhaps more than players, are rated in terms of performance results. In short, both player and manager 'build' career reputations interdependently.

10 On 2 June 2003, the Professional Footballers' Association (PFA) announced that, on that date, the number of professional footballers released by clubs and therefore technically out of work was 586. This figure, according to PFA deputy chief executive Mick Maguire, constitutes approximately twenty per cent of the football industry's player workforce. The figure is five per cent higher than at the close of the 2002 season. Interviewed for the official website of the PFA, Maguire states that the total 'highlights the fragile nature of the industry', a point emphasized in his additional remark that 'seventy-five per cent of our membership play in the Football League and a great many of those are playing with no longer security than a one, or at best, two year contract' (2 June 2003). Former Crystal Palace and Brighton player Simon Rodger found himself out of contract for the second time in two successive seasons. Reflecting on the news of his first release from Crystal Palace in the close season in 2002, Rodger said

I was in shock. I'd been with the club for 13 years and it was a real kick in the teeth. I'd had a good relationship with the fans and thought I'd had one of my best seasons. There's no sentiment in football and we're commodities.

(The *Guardian*, 3 June 2003)

Former England international Chris Powell, who was also out of contract in the close season of 2003, said:

It's a weird situation because everyone wants a career in football but you never really think you could end up like this. Of course, it will never stop people loving the game and wanting to go into it in the first place.

(The *Guardian* 3 June 2003)

At the time of their interviews it is likely that both players and their dependants are experiencing large doses of uncertainty in terms of their future career prospects.

11 Like other myths about the game which take their cues from media interpretations based on a minority of multi-million pound transfers and contract transactions.

12 As it has been explained in Chapter 2, working hard to display the characteristics of a good professional is no guarantee of reward in terms of managerial favour.

## Conclusion

1 While it is difficult to be accurate, there are few football clubs who employ more than fifty professional players. In fact, a number of lower league clubs employ substantially fewer players.

2 No one laughs when a person in his/her forties is described as a 'young politician', but a Premier League footballer in his forties, excluding goalkeepers, is, perhaps, unthinkable. It is important, however, to recognize that social definitions of old age vary historically and between different groups within society.

# Bibliography

Abbott, A. and Hrycak, A. (1990). Measuring resemblance in sequence data: An optimal matching analysis of musicians' careers. *American Journal of Sociology*, 96, 1: 144–85.

Adamson, C. (1997). Existential and clinical uncertainty in the medical encounter: An idiographic account of an illness trajectory defined by inflammatory bowel disease and avascular necrosis. *Sociology of Health and Illness*, 19: 133–59.

Adler, P.A. and Adler, P. (1989). The gloried self: The aggrandizement and the constriction of the self. *Social Psychology Quarterly*, 52, 4: 299–310.

Albert, E. (1999). Dealing with danger: The normalization of risk in cycling. *International Review for the Sociology of Sport*, 34: 157–71.

Allison, M.T. and Meyer, C. (1988). Career problems and retirement among elite athletes: The female tennis professional. *Sociology of Sport Journal*, 5: 212–22.

Anderson, L. (1996). Employee cynicism: An examination using a contract violation framework. *Human Relations*, 49: 395–418.

Annandale, E. (2003). *The sociology of health and medicine: A critical introduction*. Cambridge: Polity Press.

Arnold, J. and Jackson, C. (1997). The new career: Issues and challenges. *British Journal of Guidance and Counselling*, 25, 4: 427–33.

Arthur, M.B. and Rousseau, D.M. (Eds) (1996). *The boundaryless career: New employment principle for a new organisational era*. New York: Oxford University Press.

Atkinson, P. and Housley, W. (2003). *Interactionism: An essay in sociological amnesia*. Sage: London.

Auster, C.J. (1996). *The sociology of work: Concepts and cases*. Thousand Oaks, CA: Pine Forge Press.

Back, L., Crabbe, T. and Solomos, J. (2001). *The changing face of football: Racism, identity and multiculture in the English game*. Oxford: Berg.

Bain, A. (2005). Constructing an artistic identity. *Work, Employment and Society*, 19, 1: 25–46.

Ball, D.W. (1976). Failure in sport. *American Sociological Review*, 41, 4: 726–39.

Banton, X. (1964). *The policeman in the community*. London: Tavistock.

Becker, H.S. (1952). The career of the Chicago public school teacher. *American Journal of Sociology*, 57: 470–77.

Becker, H.S. (1963). *Outsiders: Studies in the sociology of deviance*. New York: The Free Press of Glencoe.

Becker, H.S. (1982). *Art worlds*. Berkley, CA: University of California Press.

Becker, H.S. (1998). *Tricks of the trade: How to think about your research while you're doing it*. Chicago: University of Chicago Press.

Becker, H.S. and Geer, B. (1958). The fate of idealism in medical school. *American Sociological Review*, 23, 1: 50–6.

Bellaby, P. (1990). What is genuine sickness? The relation between work discipline and the sick role in a pottery factory. *Sociology of Health and Illness*, 12, 1: 46–68.

Berger, P. and Luckmann, T. (1967). *The social construction of reality*. New York: Doubleday Anchor Books.

Blair, H. (2001). You're only as good as your last job: The labour process and labour market in the British film industry. *Work, Employment and Society*, 15, 1: 149–69.

Blair, H. (2003). Winning and losing in flexible labour markets: The formation and operation of networks of interdependence in the UK film industry. *Sociology*, 37, 4: 677–94.

Blauner, R. (1964). *Alienation and freedom*. Chicago: Chicago University Press.

Blumer, H. (1969). *Symbolic interactionism: Perspective and method*. Englewood Cliffs, NJ: Prentice Hall.

Blyton, P. and Noon, M. (1997). *The realities of work*. London: Palgrave Macmillan.

Bonney, N. and Love, J. (1991). Gender and migration: Geographical mobility and the wife's sacrifice. *The Sociological Review*, 39, 2: 335–48.

Bottomore, T. and Nisbet, R. (1979). (Eds) *A history of sociological analysis*. London: Heinemann.

Bourdieu, P. and Wacquant, L.J.D. (1992). *An invitation to reflexive sociology*. Cambridge: Polity Press.

Bower, T. (2003). *Broken dreams*. London: Pocket Books.

Braverman, H. (1974). *Labour and monopoly capital*. New York: Monthly Review Press.

Brohm, J.M. (1978). *Sport: A prison of measured time*. London: Pluto Press.

Bruegel, I. (1996). The trailing wife: a declining breed? Careers, geographical mobility and household conflict in Britain 1970–89. In R. Crompton, D. Gallie and K. Purcell (Eds), *Changing forms of employment: Organisations, skills and gender*. London: Routledge.

Calnan, M. (1984). Clinical uncertainty: Is it a problem in the doctor–patient relationship? *Sociology of Health and Illness*, 6: 74–85.

Cannon, S. (1992). Reflections on fieldwork in stressful situations. In R.G. Burgess (Ed.), *Studies in qualitative methodology. Vol. 3: Learning about fieldwork*. London: JAI Press.

Casey, C. (1995). *Work, self and society after industrialism*. London: Routledge.

Cashmore, E. (2002). *Beckham*. Cambridge: Polity Press.

Cashmore, E. and Parker, A. (2003). One David Beckham? Celebrity, masculinity and the Soccerati. *Sociology of Sport Journal*, 20, 3: 214–32.

Caulkin, G. (1999). Lee's number is up at Newcastle. *The Times*. 3 August.

Chaudhary, V. (2001). Football drags its feet on the magic roundabout. *Guardian*. 8 September.

Charmaz, K. (2003). Experiencing chronic illness. In G.L. Albrecht, R. Fitzpatrick and S.C. Scrimshaw (Eds), *Handbook of social studies in health and medicine*. London: Sage.

Coburn, D. and Willis, E. (2003). The medical profession: Knowledge, power, and autonomy. In G.L. Albrecht., R. Fitzpatrick. and S.C. Scrimshaw (Eds), *Handbook of social studies in health and medicine*. London: Sage.

Cockburn, C. (1983). *Brothers*. London: Pluto Press.

Collin, A. and Young, R.A. (2000). *The future of career*. Cambridge: Cambridge University Press.

Collinson, D.L. (1988). Engineering humour: Masculinity, joking and conflict in shopfloor relations. *Organization Studies*, 9, 2: 181–99.

Collinson, D.L. (1992). *Managing the shopfloor: Subjectivity, masculinity and the workplace culture*. Berlin: Walter de Gruyter.

Collinson, D.L. (2000). Strategies of resistance: Power, knowledge and subjectivity in the workplace. In K. Grint (Ed.), *Work and society: A reader*. Cambridge: Polity Press.

Collinson, D.L. and Hearn, J. (1994). Naming men as men – implications for work, organization and management. *Gender, Work and Organization*, 1, 1: 2–22.

Conn, D. (1997). *The football business: Fair game in the '90s*. Edinburgh: Mainstream Publishing.

Connell, R.W. (1995). *Masculinities*. Cambridge: Polity.

Conrad, P. (1987). The experience of illness: Recent and new directions. In J. Roth and P. Conrad (Eds), The experience and management of chronic illness. *Research in the Sociology of Health Care*, 6, 1–31. Greenwich: JAI Press.

Cotgrove, S. (1972). Alienation and automation. *British Journal of Sociology*, 23, 4: 437–51.

Crawford, S. (2002). The real footballer's wives. *Daily Mirror*. 3 January.

Critcher, C. (1979). Football since the war. In J. Clarke, C. Critcher and R. Johnson (Eds), *Working class culture: Studies in history and theory*. London: Hutchinson.

Curry, T.J. (1993). A little pain never hurt anyone: Athletic career socialization and the normalization of sports injury. *Symbolic Interactionism*, 16: 273–90.

Davies, H. (1996 [1972]). *The glory game*. Edinburgh: Mainstream Publishing.

Davies, H. (2000). After the fall. *Observer*. 12 February.

Davis, F. (1960). Uncertainty in medical diagnosis: Clinical and functional. *American Journal of Sociology*, 66: 41–7.

Denzin, N. (1989). *The research act: A theoretical introduction to sociological methods*. Englewood Cliffs, NJ: Prentice Hall.

Deutscher, I. (1962). Socialisation for postparental life. In A.M. Rose (Ed.), *Human behaviour and social processes: An interactionist approach*. Henley: Routledge.

Dickenson, M. (2005). Record fines will not cut off tap at source. *The Times*. 2 June.

Dobrow, S.R. (2004). Extreme subjective career success: a new integrated view of having a calling. *Academy of Management Conference best paper proceedings*.

Dobson, S. and Goddard, J. (2001). *The economics of football*. Cambridge: Cambridge University Press.

Dodier, N. (1985). Social uses of illness at the workplace: Sick leave and moral evaluation. *Social Science and Medicine*, 20, 2: 123–8.

Donaldson, M. (1991). *Time of our lives: Labour and love in the working class*. Sydney: Allen and Unwin.

Doogan, K. (2001). Insecurity and long-term employment. *Work, Employment and Society*, 15, 3: 419–41.

Drawer, S. (2000). *Risk evaluation in professional football*. University of Loughborough: Unpublished PhD thesis.

du Gay, P. and Salaman, G. (1992). The cult[ure] of the customer. *Journal of Management Studies*, 29, 5: 615–33.

Dubin, R., Hedley, A. and Taveggia, C. (1976). Attachment to work. In R. Dubin (Ed.), *Handbook of Work, Organization and Society*. Chicago: Rand McNally.

Dunphy, E. (1987). *Only a game: The diary of a professional footballer*. Harmondsworth: Penguin.

Durkheim, E. (2001). *The elementary forms of the religious life.* Oxford: Oxford University Press.

Eakin, J.M. and MacEachen, E. (1998). Health and the social relation of work: A study of the health-related experiences of employees in small workplaces. *Sociology of Health and Illness,* 20, 6: 896–914.

Elias, N. (1978). *What is sociology?* London: Hutchinson.

Elliot, L. and Atkinson, D. (1998). *The age of insecurity.* London: Verso.

Ezzy, D (1997). Subjectivity and the labour process: Conceptualising 'good work'. *Sociology,* 31: 427–44.

Ezzy, D. (2001). A simulacrum of workplace community: Individualism and engineered culture. *Sociology,* 35, 3: 631–50.

Faulkner, R.R. (1971). *Hollywood studio musicians: Their work and careers in the recording studio.* New York: University Press of America.

Faulkner, R.R. (1973). Career concerns and mobility motivations of orchestra musicians. *The Sociological Quarterly,* 14: 334–49.

Faulkner, R.R. (1974). Coming of age in organizations: A comparative study of career contingencies of musicians and hockey players. In D. Ball and J. Loy (Eds), *Sport and social order: Contributions to the sociology of sport.* Reading, MA: Addison-Wesley.

Faunce, W. (1968). *Problems of an industrial society.* New York: McGraw-Hill.

Finch, J. (1983). *Married to the job: Wives' incorporation in men's work.* London: Allen and Unwin.

Finch, J. (1993). 'It's great to have someone to talk to': Ethics and politics of interviewing women. In M. Hammersley (Ed.), *Social research: Philosophy, politics and practice.* London: Sage.

Fine, G.A. (1993). The sad demise, mysterious disappearance and glorious triumph of symbolic interactionism. *Annual Review of Sociology,* 19: 61–87.

Flam, H. (2002). Corporate emotions and emotions in corporations. In J. Barbalet (Ed.), *Emotions and sociology.* Oxford: Blackwell Publishing.

Fleming, P. and Sewell, G. (2002). Looking for the Good Soldier, Svejk: Alternative modalities of resistance in the contemporary workplace. *Sociology,* 36, 4: 857–73.

Fleming, P. and Spicer, A. (2003). Working at a cynical distance: Implications for power, subjectivity and resistance. *Organization,* 10, 1: 157–79.

Form, W.H. and Miller, D.C. (1949). Occupational career patterns as a sociological instrument. *American Journal of Sociology,* 54, 1: 317–29.

Foster, K. (2001). *Transfer fees: Still (il)legal after all these years?* Singer and Friedlander review 2000–2001 season. London: Singer and Friedlander.

Foucault, M. (1997). Technologies of the self. In P. Rabinow (Ed.), *Michel Foucault. Ethics. The essential works 1.* London: Allen Lane.

Fox, A. (1980). The meaning of work. In G. Esland and G. Salaman (Eds), *The politics of work and occupations.* Buckingham: The Open University Press.

Fox, R. (1988). Training for uncertainty. In R. Fox (Ed.), *Essays in medical sociology: Journeys into the field.* New Brunswick, NJ: Transaction Books.

Freidson, E. (1970). *Profession of medicine: A study of the sociology of applied knowledge.* New York: Dodd Mead.

Freidson, E. (1990). Labours of love: A prospectus. In K. Erikson and S.P. Vallas (Eds), *The nature of work: Sociological perspectives.* New Haven, CT: Yale University Press.

Friedman, N.L. (1990). The Hollywood actor: Occupational culture, career, and adaptation in a buyers' market industry. In C.J. Auster, *The sociology of work: Concepts and cases*. Thousand Oaks, CA: Pine Forge Press.

Gardiner, S., James, M., O'Leary, J., Welsh, R., Blackshaw, I., Boyes, S. and Caiger, A. (1998). *Sports law*. London: Cavendish Publishing.

Gardner, H. (1993). *Frames of mind: The theory of multiple intelligences*. London: Fontana.

Gearing, B. (1997). More then a game: The experience of being a professional footballer in Britain. *Oral History*, 25, 1: 63–70.

Gearing, B. (1999). Narratives of identity among former professional footballers in the United Kingdom. *Journal of Ageing Studies*, 13: 43–58.

Gerstel, N. and Gross, H. (1984). Commuter marriage: Deciding to commute. In C.J. Auster, *The sociology of work: Concepts and cases*. Thousand Oaks, CA: Pine Forge Press.

Giddens, A. (1977). *Capitalism and modern social theory: An analysis of the writings of Marx, Durkheim and Max Weber*. Cambridge: Cambridge University Press.

Giddens, A. (1991). *Modernity and self-identity: Self and society in late modern age*. Cambridge: Polity Press.

Giulianotti, R. (1999). *Football: A sociology of the global game*. Cambridge: Polity Press.

Giulianotti, R. and Gerrard, M. (2001). Evil genie or pure genius?: The (im)moral football and public career of Paul 'Gazza' Gascoigne. In D.L. Andrews and S.J. Jackson (Eds), *Sports stars: The cultural politics of sporting celebrity*. London: Routledge.

Glaeser, A. (2000). *Divided in unity: Identity, Germany and the Berlin Police*. Chicago: University of Chicago Press.

Goffman, E. (1952). Cooling out the mark: Some adaptations to failure. In A.M. Rose (Ed.), *Human behaviour and social processes: An interactionist approach*. Henley: Routledge.

Goffman, E. (1959). *The presentation of self in everyday life*. New York: Doubleday Anchor Books.

Goffman, E. (1961). *Encounters: Two studies in the sociology of interaction*. Indianapolis, IN: Bobbs-Merrill Company.

Goffman, E. (1963). *Stigma: Notes on the management of spoiled identity*. Harmondsworth: Penguin.

Goffman, E. (1967). Where the action is. In E. Goffman, *Interaction ritual: Essays on face-to-face behavior*. New York: Pantheon Books.

Goffman, E. (1968). *Asylums*. Harmondsworth: Penguin.

Gold, M. and Fraser, J. (2002). Managing self-management: Successful transitions to portfolio careers. *Work, Employment and Society*, 16, 4: 579–97.

Goldthorpe, J.H., Lockwood, D., Bechhofer, F. and Platt, J. (1968). *The affluent worker: Industrial attitudes and behaviour*. Cambridge: Cambridge University Press.

Goodwin, J. and O'Conner, H. (2002). 'They had horrible wallpaper': Representations of respondents and the interview process in interviewer notes. CLMS Working Paper No. 39: University of Leicester.

Gouldner, A.W. (1964). *Patterns of industrial bureaucracy*. New York: Free Press.

Gowling, A. (1973). The place of luck in the professional footballer's life. In D. Weir (Ed.), *Men and work in modern Britain: An introductory reader*. Glasgow: Fontana/Collins.

Gowling, A. (1974). *The occupation of the professional footballer*. University of Manchester: Unpublished MA thesis.

Greenfield, S. and Osborn, G. (Eds) (2000). *Law and sport in contemporary society*. London: Frank Cass.

Grey, C. (1994). Career as a project of the self and labour process discipline. *Sociology*, 28, 2: 479–97.

Grint, K. (2005). *The sociology of work, 3rd edition*. Cambridge: Polity.

Foucalt, M. (1977). Technologies of the self. In P. Rabinow (Ed.), *Ethics: The essential works 1*. London: Allen Lane.

Hall, D.T. and Chandler, D.E. (2005). Psychological success: When the career is a calling. *Journal of Organizational Behaviour*, 26: 155–76.

Hall, O. (1948). The stages of a medical career. *American Journal of Sociology*, 53, 5: 327–36.

Handy, C. (1990). *The age of unreason*. London: Arrow Books.

Hanson, S. and Pratt, G. (1995). *Gender, work and space*. London: Routledge.

Harding, J. (2003). *Living to play: From soccer slaves to socceratti – a social history of the professionals*. London: Robson Books.

Hayward, P. (2001). Player power threatens football to the core. *Daily Telegraph*. 11 November.

Hochschild, A.R. (1983). *The managed heart: Commercialization of human feelings*. Berkeley: University of California Press.

Hughes, E.C. (1958). *Men and their work*. Glencoe, IL: The Free Press.

Ingham, A.G. (1975). Occupational subcultures in the work world of sport. In D. Ball and J. Loy (Eds), *Sport and social order: Contributions to the sociology of sport*. Reading, MA: Addison-Wesley.

Ingham, A.G., Blissmer, B.J. and Davidson, K.W. (1999). The expendable prolympic self: Going beyond the boundaries of the sociology and psychology of sport. *Sociology of Sport*, 16, 3: 236–68.

Jarvis, H. (1999). The tangled webs we weave: Household strategies to co-ordinate home and work. *Work, Employment and Society*, 13, 2: 225–47.

Johnson, W. and Peters, K. (1998). Gillespie deal off after medical. *Daily Telegraph*. 3 August.

Johnston, T.J. (1972). *Professions and power*. London: Palgrave Macmillan.

Jones, D. (2005). *Deloitte Annual Review of Football Finance 2005, 14th edition*. London: Deloitte and Touche LLP.

Jones, R.L. and Chappell, R. (1997). The continued rise of the global sport–media complex as reflected in elite soccer migration patterns. *Sport Education Journal*, 1: 1–9.

Kanter, R.M. (1977). *Men and women of the corporation*. New York: Basic Books.

Kimmage, P. (2000). *Full time: The secret life of Tony Cascarino as told to Paul Kimmage*. London: Simon and Schuster.

King, A. (1999). *The end of the terraces. The transformations of English football in the 1990s*. Leicester: Leicester University Press.

King, C. (2004). *Offside racism: Playing the white man*. London: Berg.

Kotarba, J.A. (1983). *Chronic pain: Its social dimensions*. Newbury Park, CA: Sage.

Kunda, G. (1992). *Engineering culture*. Philadelphia: Temple University Press.

Lanfranchi, P. and Taylor, M. (2001). *Moving with the ball: The migration of professional football*. Oxford: Berg.

Lawton, M. (2001). Campbell looks to the future with Tottenham. *Daily Telegraph.* 26 March.

Lee, R.M. (1992). Nobody said it had to be easy: Postgraduate field research in Northern Ireland. In R.G. Burgess (Ed.), *Studies in qualitative methodology. Vol. 3: Learning about fieldwork.* London: JAI Press.

Littleton, S.M., Arthur, M.B. and Rousseau, D.M. (2000). The future of boundaryless careers. In A. Collin and R.A. Young (Eds), *The future of career.* Cambridge: Cambridge University Press.

Lovejoy, J. (1998). Houllier's task hots up. *Sunday Times.* 6 December.

Lovejoy, J. (2000). Pointing the way. *The Times.* 4 February.

Loÿttyniemi, V. (2001). Doctors drifting: Autonomy and career uncertainty in young physicians' stories. *Social Science and Medicine,* 52: 227–37.

Luo, L. and Cooper, C.L. (1990). Stress of job relocation: progress and prospect. *Work and Stress,* 4, 2: 121–8.

Lupton, D. (1996). Your life in their hands: Trust in the medical encounter. In V. James and J. Gabe (Eds), *Health and the sociology of emotions.* Oxford: Blackwell.

Lupton, T. (1963). *On the shop floor.* Oxford: Pergamon.

Magee, J.D. (1998). *International labour migration in English league football.* University of Brighton: Unpublished PhD thesis.

Maguire, J. and Stead, D. (1998). Border crossings: Soccer labour migration and the European Union. *International Review for the Sociology of Sport,* 33: 59–73.

Martin, R. (1996). A longitudinal study examining the psychological reactions of job relocation. *Journal of Applied Social Psychology,* 26, 3: 265–82.

Martin, R. (1999). Adjusting to job relocation: Relocation preparation can reduce relocation stress. *Journal of Occupational and Organizational Psychology,* 72: 231–5.

Marx, K. (1974). *Capital, Vol. 1–3.* London: Lawrence and Wishart.

McDonnell, D. (2001). Sir Alex accused. *The Mirror.* 13 September.

McGill, C. (2001). *Football inc.* London: Vision Paperbacks.

McGillivray, D., Fearn, R. and McIntosh, A. (2005). Caught up in the beautiful game: A case of Scottish professional footballers. *Journal of Sport and Social Issues,* 29, 1: 102–23.

McGovern, P. (2000). The Irish brawn drain: English league clubs and Irish footballers, 1946–95. *British Journal of Sociology,* 51, 3: 401–15.

McGovern, P. (2002). Globalization or internationalization? Foreign footballers in the English league, 1946–95. *Sociology,* 36, 1: 23–42.

McKensie, B. (1999). Retiring from the sideline: becoming more than 'hockey's daughter' and 'football's wife'. In J.J. Coakley and P. Donnelly (Eds), *Inside sports.* London: Routledge.

Menger, P-M. (1999). Artistic labour markets and careers. *Annual Review of Sociology,* 25: 541–74.

Merton, R.K. (1957). *Social theory and social structure.* New York: The Free Press of Glencoe.

Merton, R.K. (1972). Insiders and outsiders: A chapter in the sociology of knowledge. *American Journal of Sociology,* 78, 1: 9–47.

Messner, M. (1990). When bodies are weapons: Masculinity and violence in sport. *International Review for the Sociology of Sport,* 25, 3: 203–19.

Messner, M. (1992). *Power at play: Sports and the problem of masculinity.* Boston, MA: Beacon Press.

Monk, D. (2000). Modern football apprenticeships in football: success and failure. *Industrial and Commercial Training*, 32, 2: 52–60.

Morgan, D.H.J. (1992). *Discovering men*. London: Routledge.

Morrow, S. (1999). *The new business of football: Accountability and finance in football*. Basingstoke: Macmillan.

Munton, A.G. (1990). Job relocation, stress and the family. *Journal of Organisational Behaviour*, 11: 401–6.

Munton, A.G. and West, M.A. (1995). Innovations and personal change: Patterns of adjustment to relocation. *Journal of Organisational Behavior*, 16: 363–75.

Nash, J. (1979). *We eat the mines and the mines eat us: Dependency and exploitation in Bolivian tin mines*. New York: Columbia University Press.

Nelson, G. (1996). *Left foot forward: A year in the life of a journeyman footballer*. London: Headline.

Nevin, P. and Sik, G. (1998). *In ma head, son: The footballer's mind revealed*. London: Headline.

Newell, S. (2000). The superwoman syndrome: Gender differences in attitudes towards equal opportunities at work and towards domestic responsibilities at home. In K. Grint (Ed.), *Work and society: A reader*. Cambridge: Polity Press.

Nixon, H.L. II (1992). A social network analysis of influences on athletes to play with pain and injuries. *Journal of Sport and Social Issues*, 16: 127–35.

Nixon, H.L. II (1993). Accepting the risks of pain and injury in sport: Medicated cultural influences on playing hurt. *Sociology of Sport Journal*, 10: 183–96.

Noon, M. and Blyton, P. (1997). *The realities of work*. Basingstoke: Macmillan.

O'Conner, A. (2005). Rich get richer thanks to Abramovich effect. *The Times*. 8 June.

Oakley, A. (1980). *Women confined: Towards a sociology of childbirth*. Oxford: Martin Robertson.

Oakley, A. (1990). *Housewife*. London: Penguin.

Offe, C. (1985). *Disorganized capitalism*. Cambridge: Polity Press.

Ortiz, S.M. (1997). Traveling with the ball club: A code of conduct for wives only. *Symbolic Interaction*, 20, 3: 225–49.

Padavic, I. (2005). Laboring under uncertainty: Identity renegotiation among contingent workers. *Symbolic Interactionism*, 28, 1: 111–34.

Parker, A. (1996a). *Chasing the Big-Time: Football apprenticeship in the 1990s*. University of Warwick: Unpublished PhD thesis.

Parker, A. (1996b). Sporting masculinities: Gender relations and the body. In Máirtin Mac an Ghaill (Ed.), *Understanding masculinities: Social relations and cultural arenas*. Buckingham: Open University Press.

Parker, A. (1998). Staying on-side on the inside: Problems and dilemmas in ethnography. *Sociology Review*, 7, 3: 10–13.

Parker, S.R., Brown, R.K., Child, J. and Smith, M.A. (1977). *The sociology of industry*. London: Allen and Unwin.

Parkinson, N. (2001). Stam was treated like a piece of meat. *Daily Mirror*. 10 September.

Prus, R. (1984). Career contingencies: examining patterns of involvement. In N. Theberge and P. Donnelly (Eds), *Refereed proceedings of the 3rd annual conference of the North American Society for the Sociology of Sport*. Fort Worth, TX: Texas Christian University Press.

Ramsey, K. (1996). Emotional labour and qualitative research: How I learned not to laugh or cry in the field. In J. Busfield and E. Stina Lyon (Eds), *Methodological imaginations (Explorations in sociology)*. London: Palgrave Macmillan.

Reid, J., Ewan, C. and Lowy, E. (1991). Pilgrimage of pain: The illness experiences of women with repetition strain injury and the search for credibility. *Social Science and Medicine*, 32, 5: 601–12.

Richardson, M.S. (2000). A new perspective for counsellors: From career ideologies to empowerment through work and relationship practices. In A. Collin and R.A. Young (Eds), *The future of career*. Cambridge: Cambridge University Press.

Rigauer, B. (1981). *Sport and work*. New York: Columbia University Press.

Rojek, C. (1993). *Ways of escape: Modern transformations in leisure and travel*. London: Macmillan.

Rojek, C. (2001). *Celebrity*. London: Reaktion Books.

Rosenberg, E. (1984). Athletic retirement as social death: Concepts and perspectives. In N. Theberge and P. Donnelly (Eds), *Sport and the sociological imagination*. Fort Worth, TX: Texas Christian University Press.

Roth, J.A. (1962). The treatment of tuberculosis as a bargaining process. In A.M. Rose (Ed.), *Human behaviour and social processes: An interactionist approach*. Henley: Routledge.

Roth, J.A. (1963). *Timetables: Structuring the passage of time in hospital treatment and other careers*. Indianapolis, IN: Bobbs-Merrill Company.

Rudd, A. (2000). The second half. In *The Times Football Handbook*.

Sabo, D.F. and Panepinto, J. (1990). Football ritual and the social reproduction of masculinity. In M.A. Messner and D.F. Sabo (Eds), *Sport, men and the gender order: Critical feminist perspectives*. Champaign, IL: Human Kinetics.

Salaman, G. (1981). *Class and the corporation*. Glasgow: Fontana.

Scase, R. and Goffee, R. (1989). *Reluctant managers: Their work and lifestyles*. London: Unwin Hyman.

Sennett, R. (1998). *The corrosion of character: The personal consequences of work in the new capitalism*. New York: W.W. Norton and Co.

Sennett, R. (2003). *Respect*. Harmondsworth: Penguin.

Shibutani, T. (1962). Reference groups and social control. In A.M. Rose (Ed.), *Human behaviour and social processes: An interactionist approach*. Henley: Routledge.

Shilling, C. (2002). The two traditions in the sociology of emotions. In J. Barbalet (Ed.), *Emotions and sociology*. Oxford: Blackwell.

Shilling, C. (2005). *The body in culture, technology and society*. London: Sage.

Silverman, D. (2001). *Interpreting qualitative data: Methods for analyzing talk, text and interaction*. London: Sage.

Simpson, C.R. (1981). *Soho: The artist in the city*. Chicago: University of Chicago Press.

Sloane, P.J. (1969). The labour market in professional football. *British Journal of Industrial Relations*, 7, 2: 181–99.

Smith, A. (1993 [1976]). *An inquiry into the nature and causes of the wealth of nations*. Oxford: Oxford University Press.

Spencer, N. (2000). Record deal in doubt. *Daily Telegraph*. 26 April.

Spilerman, S. (1983). Careers, labor market structure, and socioeconomic achievement. *American Journal of Sociology*, 83, 3: 551–93.

Stead, D. and Maguire, J. (2000). 'Rites de passage' or passage to riches: The motivation and objectives of Nordic/Scandinavian players in the English league soccer. *Journal of Sport and Social Issues*, 24, 1: 36–60.

Stebbins, R.A. (1970). Career: The subjective approach. *The Sociological Quarterly*, 11, 1: 32–49.

Strauss, A. (1962). Transformations of identity. In A.M. Rose (Ed.), *Human behaviour and social processes: An interactionist approach*. Henley: Routledge.

Swain, D.A. (1991). Withdrawal from sport and Schlossberg's model of transition. *Sociology of Sport Journal*, 8: 152–60.

Szymanski, S. and Kuypers, T. (1999). *Winners and losers: The business strategy of football*. London: Viking.

Taylor, I. (1970). Football mad: A speculative sociology of soccer hooliganism. In E.G. Dunning (Ed.), *The sociology of sport*. London: Frank Cass.

Taylor, L. (1998). Goodison Goliath. *Daily Telegraph*. 30 July

Taylor, M. (1999). No big deal. *When Saturday Comes*, 153: 28–9.

Taylor, R. and Ward, A. (1995). *Kicking and screaming: An oral history of football in England*. London: Robson Books.

Tebbutt, M. and Marchington, M. (1997). 'Look before you speak': Gossip and the insecure workplace. *Work, Employment and Society*, 11, 4: 713–35.

Terkel, S. (1975). *Working: People talk about what they do all day and how they feel about what they do*. New York: Avon Books.

Thomas, K. (1999). Introduction. In K. Thomas (Ed.), *The Oxford book of work*. Oxford: Oxford University Press.

Thompson, P. (1983). *The nature of work: An introduction to debates on the labour process*. London: Macmillan.

Thompson, W. (1999). Wives incorporated: Marital relationships in professional ice hockey. In J.J. Coakley and P. Donnelly (Eds), *Inside sports*. London: Routledge.

Tomlinson, A. (1983). Tuck up tight lads: Structures of control within football culture. In A. Tomlinson (Ed.), *Explorations in football culture*, no. 21. Eastbourne: Leisure Studies Association Publications.

Townsend, N. (1998). The real boss-man ruling. *Independent*. 8 November.

Turner, B.S. and Wainwright, S.P. (2003). Corps de ballet: The case of the injured ballet dancer. *Sociology of Health and Illness*, 25, 4: 269–88.

Vinnai, G. (1973). *Football mania*. London: Ocean Books.

Wacquant, L.J.D. (1992). The social logic of boxing in black Chicago: Towards a sociology of pugilism. *Sociology of Sport Journal*, 7, 3: 221–54.

Wacquant, L.J.D. (1995a). Pugs at work: Bodily capital and bodily labour among professional boxers. *Body and Society*, 1, 1: 65–93.

Wacquant, L.J.D. (1995b). The pugilistic point of view: How boxers think and feel about their trade. *Theory and Society*, 24, 4: 489–535.

Wacquant, L.J.D. (1998). A fleshpeddler at work: Power, pain, and profit in the prizefighting economy. *Theory and Society*, 27, 1: 1–42.

Wacquant, L.J.D. (2001). Whores, slaves and stallions: Language of exploitation and accommodation among boxers. *Body and Society*, 7, 2–3: 181–94.

Waddington, I. (1996). Professions. In A. Kuper and J. Kuper (Eds), *The social science encyclopedia, 2nd edition*. London: Routledge.

Waddington, I. and Roderick, M.J. (2002). The management of medical confidentiality in English professional football clubs: some ethical problems and issues. *British Journal of Sports Medicine*, 36: 118–23.

Waddington, I., Roderick, M. and Parker, G. (1999). Playing hurt: Managing injuries in professional football. *International Review of the Sociology of Sport*, 35: 165–80.

Waddington, I. and Walker, B. (1991). Aids and the doctor–patient relationship. *Social Studies Review*, March, 128–30.

Wagg, S. (1984). *The football world: A contemporary social history*. Brighton: Harvester.

Walker, C.R. and Guest, R.H. (1952). *Man on the assembly line*. Cambridge, MA: Harvard University Press.

Walker, I. (2003). Player lay-offs no cause for alarm. *Daily Mirror*. 3 June.

Wallace, S. (2001). Bayern dismiss Campbell bid. *Daily Telegraph*. 2 July.

Walsh, D. (2003). James saves best for last. *Sunday Times*. 8 June.

Watson, T.J. (1995). *Sociology, work and industry*. 3rd edn. London: Routledge.

Webb, S. (1998). *Footballers' wives tell their tales*. London: Yellow Jersey Press.

Weber, M. (1965). Politics as a vocation. In H.H. Gerth and C.W. Mills (Eds and trans.), *From Max Weber: Essays in sociology*. London: Routledge.

Weber, M. (2002). *Protestant ethic and the spirit of capitalism*. Harmondsworth: Penguin.

Weinberg, S.K. and Arond, H. (1970). The occupational culture of the boxer. In E.G. Dunning (Ed.), *The sociology of sport*. London: Frank Cass.

White, J. (2000). White's week. *Guardian*. 22 January.

Whyte, W.H. (1956). *The organization man*. Harmondsworth: Penguin.

Wilensky, H.L. (1961). Work, careers and social integration. In T. Burns (Ed.), *Industrial man*. Harmondsworth: Penguin.

Williams, J., Hopkins, S. and Long, K. (2001). *Passing rhythms: Liverpool FC and the transformation of football*. Oxford: Berg.

Willis, P. (1977). *Learning to labour*. Westmead: Gower.

Willmott, H. (1993). Strength is ignorance; slavery is freedom: Managing cultures in modern organizations. *Journal of Management Studies*, 30, 4: 515–52.

Wilson, P. (2001). The fall and fall of fast Eddie. *Observer*. 7 January.

Woods, R. and Dobson, R. (2002). In a league of their own. *Sunday Times*. 13 January.

Wright Mills, C. (1951). *White collar*. New York: Oxford University Press.

Wulff, H. (2001). *Ballet across borders: Careers and culture in the world of dancers*. Oxford: Berg.

Young, K., White, P. and McTeer, W. (1994). Body talk: Male athletes reflect on sport, pain and injury. *Sociology of Sport Journal*, 11: 175–94.

Young, R.A. and Collin, A. (2000). Introduction: Framing the future of career. In A. Collin and R.A. Young (Eds), *The future of career*. Cambridge: Cambridge University Press.

# Index